South Carolina Postcards
Volume V

Richland County

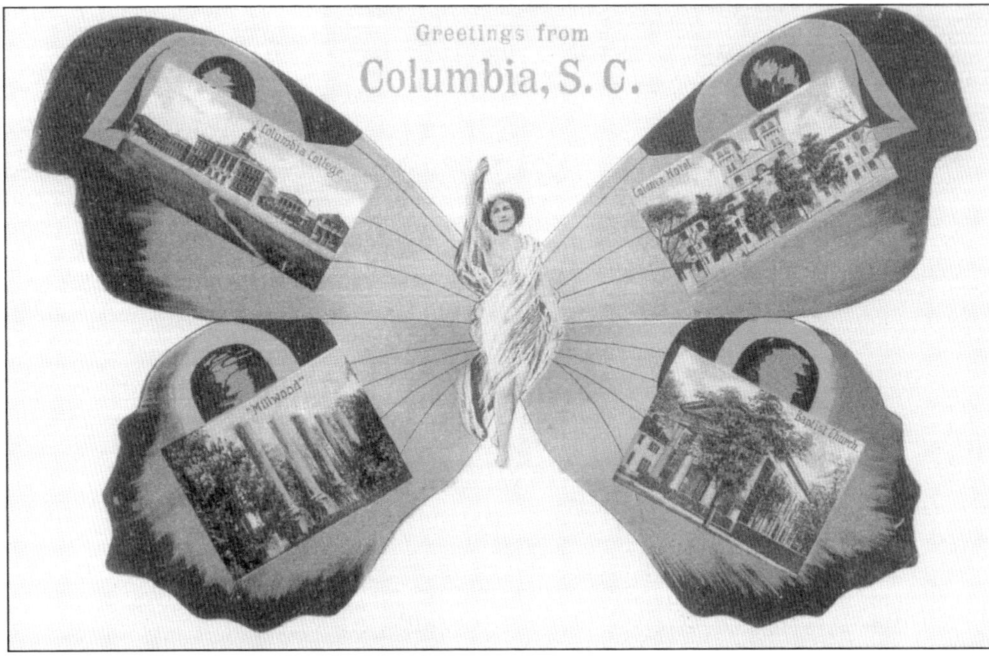

GREETINGS FROM COLUMBIA, SC, *c.* 1908. This generic novelty postcard was printed by the millions with blank spaces left for future city names and images of popular buildings or sites of that city. The pictures from upper left to right are Columbia College and the Colonia Hotel, with the lower ones being the "Millwood" ruins and the First Baptist Church.

ON THE FRONT COVER: [CONFEDERATE VETERANS, CAPITAL STEPS, 1915.] The April 23, 1915 reunion of the United Confederate Veterans met in Columbia and had their opening ceremonies in the Columbia Theatre with Gen. W.A. Clark calling the session to order and Gov. Richard Manning welcoming the veterans. The estimated 1,000 veterans assembled for a parade that began at the post office and moved down Main Street to the State House. The veterans were greeted by three UCV generals of the South Carolina Division: Gen. C. Irvin Walker, honorary commander-in-chief and the first commander of Camp Hampton; Maj. Gen. B.H. Teague, commander; and Brig. Gen. C.A. Reed, commander of first brigade. One thousand boys and girls dressed in red, white, and blue formed a living confederate flag on the steps of the north portico of the State House. At the conclusion of the reunion, the veterans were given an honorary payment in authentic Confederate money.

The United Confederate Veterans was organized in 1892 to support the aging confederate veterans. A 1908 South Carolina state bill was passed to care for "infirm and destitute Confederate soldiers and sailors." The home at 1417 Confederate Avenue opened on Memorial Day, May 10, 1908, with 21 veterans in residence. In 1925, wives and widows were permitted to live at the home.

ON THE BACK COVER: [TUESDAY AFTERNOON CLUB, *c.* 1911.] The African-American Tuesday Afternoon Club was made up of teachers who taught at Columbia's Howard School and wives of black professional men. Members were, from left to right, (front row) Ethelyn Thompson, Sarah Henderson, Shellie Gantt, and Fannie Thompson; (second row) Daisy Myers, Charlotte Seabrooks, Belle Vincent, Nell Simkins, and Corrine Carroll Frederick; (third row) Lydia Biggs, Maude Dillard, Jeanette Poinsette, Olive Shelton, Charlotte Garner, Belle Nix, Lottie Pinckney, Hattie Cornwell, and Mittie Pugh.

POSTCARD HISTORY SERIES

South Carolina Postcards
Volume V
Richland County

Howard Woody

ARCADIA
PUBLISHING

ISBN 978-0-7385-0672-2

Published by Arcadia Publishing
Charleston, South Carolina

Printed in the United States of America

Library of Congress Catalog Card Number: 98-087877

For all general information contact Arcadia Publishing at:
Telephone 843-853-2070
Fax 843-853-0044
E-Mail sales@arcadiapublishing.com
For customer service and orders:
Toll-Free 1-888-313-2665

Visit us on the Internet at www.arcadiapublishing.com

In memory of my grandparents, Omer and Alice Woody;
my father, Thomas W. Woody; and his brothers, Howard and Irvin;
and in honor of his brother Robert;
and his sisters, Estelle, Lucille, Pauline, and Virginia
for your thoughtful support. —H.W.

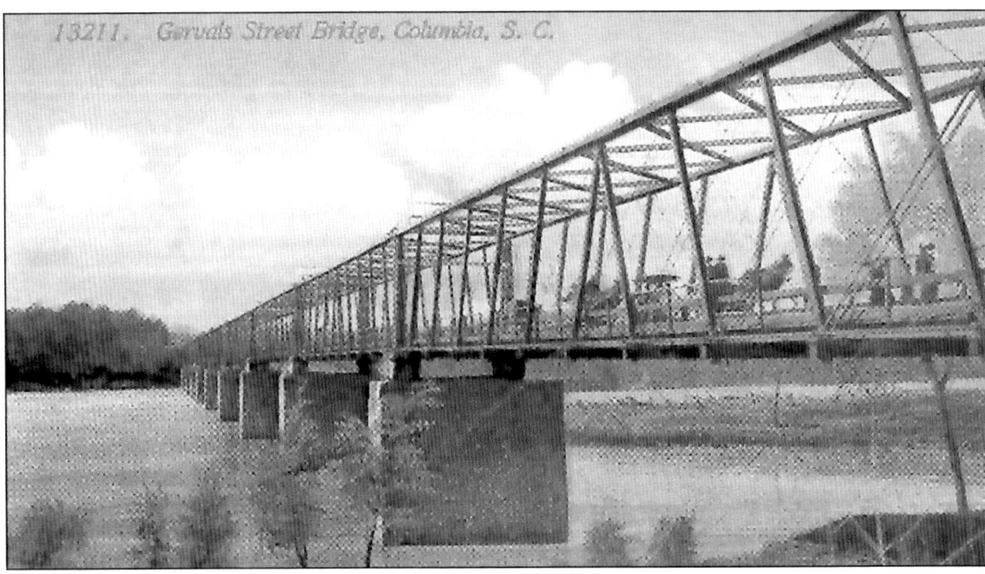

GERVAIS STREET BRIDGE, COLUMBIA, SC [*c.* 1907]. The Gervais Street bridge, constructed in 1827, was the first successful attempt to cross the Congaree River. The structure supported on granite pillars was a steel framed bridge with a plank floor. The upper structure of the toll bridge was destroyed in the fire of 1865. Rebuilt after the Civil War, it was bought by Richland County in 1903 and the bridge tolls were discontinued. Since the Duck Mill placed their village in New Brookland, their operatives had to use it to go to and from work.

Contents

Acknowledgments		6
Introduction		7
1.	Historic and City Views of Columbia	9
2.	Views of Columbia Canal and Mills	41
3.	Cultural Views of Columbia	51
4.	Views of Camp Jackson	97
5.	Views of Lower Richland	101
6.	Views of Upper Richland	113
Index		127

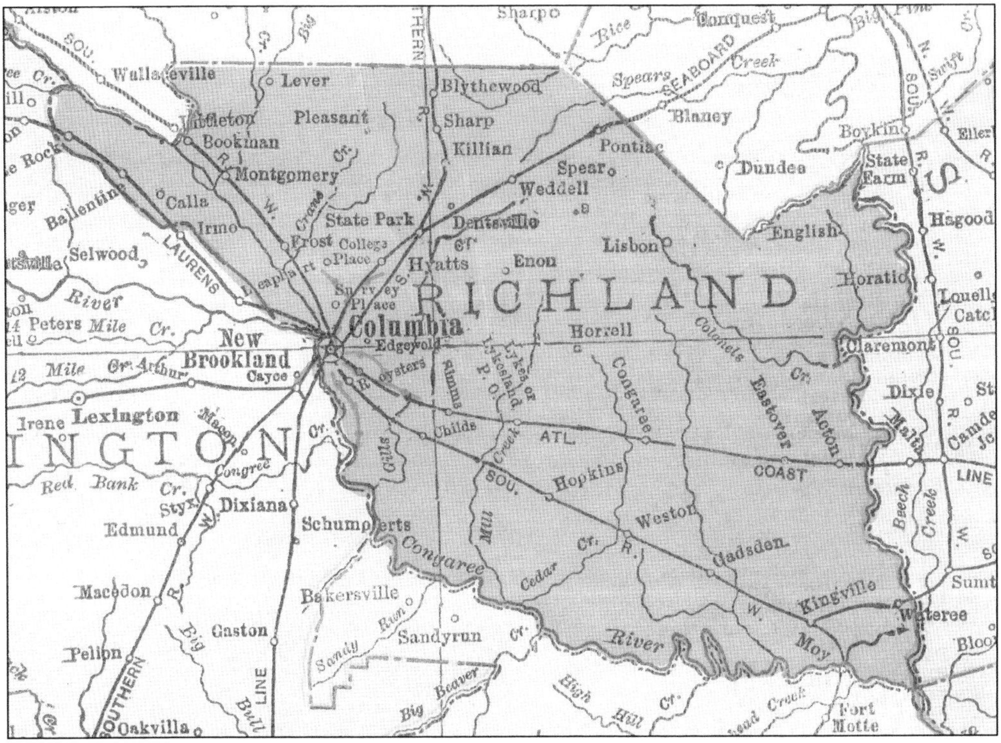

[Map of Richland County, c. 1913.] This map includes the annexation of both of the 1912 section of Lexington County and the 1913 portion of Fairfield County. It does not include the 1922 annexation from Lexington County.

ACKNOWLEDGMENTS

Many persons and institutions have contributed to the preparation of this book. I wish to express my gratitude to Allen Stokes, Thomas L. Johnson, Beth Bilderbeck, Robin Copp, and Thelma Hayes of the South Caroliniana Library, and Elizabeth West and Joe Long of the University of South Carolina archives. Other essential contributions were made by Fannie Adams and Mary McAfee, Benedict College; Lou Brooks; Callie K. Burnside; Robert L. Busbee; the Cayce Historical Museum; Columbia College; the Columbia Fire Department; the Columbia Police Department; Mattie Dixon; Sandra Dodd; Judy Galloway, Dunbar Funeral Home; Rebekah Bailey, Eau Claire Community Council; Ebenezer Lutheran Church; First Baptist Church; First Presbyterian Church; the Fort Jackson Museum; L.C. "Sonny" Hall; Monya Havekkost, Palmetto Richland Memorial Hospital; Ruth Hoover; Doyle Jaco; Paul Jeter; Dr. Lawrence Jowers; Kent Studios; Rose Kline; Horace Harmon, the Lexington County Museum; Main Street Methodist Church; Warren Montgomery; Olympia Lodge; the Richland County Public Library; Austin Sheheen; Steve Tuttle, the South Carolina Department of Archives & History; Richard Lee, the South Carolina Electric and Gas Company; the South Carolina State Museum; Melanie Stamper, St. John's Episcopal Church; the Town Theatre; A.P. Williams III; and Mr. and Mrs. Furman Younginer.

Introduction

For this fifth volume in Arcadia's special series of South Carolina postcard views, the journey continues from Lexington County eastward to Richland County and is seen through selective photographic imagery that shows glimpses from the late 1890s to 1935. This journey that began in Charleston, then shifted south to Beaufort and the Low Country (volume two), continued on to Aiken and the West Central Carolina section (volume three), before visiting Lexington County (volume four), now pauses in Richland County before continuing the documentation of each region and county of South Carolina. Lexington County's postcards concluded in West Columbia with a view of the Gervais Street bridge and Columbia. The visual record of volume five, *Richland County*, will follow the practice of reviewing the governmental structure by showing architecture and events, the major business district, social and cultural images, and then the rural areas of the county.

The evolution of Richland County's administrative placement began in 1682 when it became a small part of Craven County. By 1757, it shifted to St. Marks Parish, and in 1769, it moved to the Camden District. Finally, this area became Richland County in 1785. The first Richland County seat was in Horrell Hill until 1799 when the politicians shifted it to Columbia. Richland County, an agrarian area with limited commerce, initially planted indigo, wheat, corn, and rice as its major cash crops. That planting scheme was replaced when Wade Hampton I developed his cotton plantation in 1799. Other cotton planters followed his lead and expanded their acreage into large plantations, which made a number of lower Richland planters very wealthy. They needed slaves to cultivate the land so large numbers of African Americans came into the area. The isolation of the county partially changed when the first railroad service to Columbia was accomplished in 1842. The South Carolina Railroad crossed the Congaree River near McCord's Ferry; that path was later used by the Southern Railroad to connect Richland County to Charleston. In 1852 and 1853, rail connections to Charlotte and Greenville opened Richland County to additional commerce.

Columbia and Richland County both suffered greatly in 1865 with the destruction of every facet of the governmental, industrial, commercial, and transportation structures. During the next three decades, each of those structures evolved into an expanded level. The political organization became a populist structure. Engineering innovations in new cotton mills led Columbia's industrialization growth with electricity being used for manufacturing and lighting. Communication by telephone and telegraph assisted in the evolving economic structure. The fragmented small railroad lines merged and expanded into a regional system with Columbia turning into a major transportation center. Columbia became a hub with 500,000 potential customers and a central location suitable for federal agencies needing city, state, or regional offices. The county's wealth shifted from rural plantation sources to city bankers, merchants, and manufacturers.

The beginning of modern public schools and the growth of higher education developed the human resources into a more literate and efficient level. New municipal services, a larger population, and increased employment possibilities gave Main Street merchants and bankers a new measure of prosperity. The signs of a new century were everywhere:

completion of the State House, construction of skyscrapers, the new electrical street car service across the city, the paving of Main Street, the automobile becoming the vehicle of choice, the new opera house that attracted major national performances, and the enthusiastic community support of baseball and football that attracted people of all ages to the ball parks. The expansion of Columbia outward from 1900 to World War I showed a new confidence in the economy and in future opportunities. Finally, the appearance of Camp Jackson, and later the creation of the Lake Murray Dam, opened new windows of opportunity and expansion for the county. Columbia's population growth from 21,108 in 1900 to 51,000 in 1930 reflects those evolutionary trends.

Secular views of daily life reflected the most exciting elements in the visual imagery selected for this series. It should be understood that mass produced postcard pictures of the major sites and subjects became superfluous scenes. Merchants of that period chose from 10 to 20 postcard views of Columbia and ordered 500–1,000 issues per picture with reorders made annually. This volume created a total of over 200,000 commercial postcards bought and mailed in that era. When possible, these redundant views were avoided; however, examples showing significant buildings and scenes are included. Several concepts guided the selection of the images and the exclusion of others: often, the earliest views were chosen, along with examples of visual activities illustrating the life styles of the era and those showing structures that no longer exist. Historical, social, or cultural event images that reflect the interests and the passions of that time came to be singled out. The public educational evolution of the county was significant for the area's economical and cultural growth, so images and data on this subject have been given a prominent position in both the urban and rural sections.

What is a postcard image? Would the subject in the picture be of interest to others elsewhere? Would someone buy multiple copies of that view for mailing? These questions and their answers related to the intended or extended use of the subjects in the photograph. The image could be made full scale for postcards, enlarged for framing, or reduced for montage use. The commercial view cards came from pictures made by traveling postcard salesmen or others for retail sales. Yet another type, advertisement cards, had a commercial purpose. Probably the most interesting postcard images relate to the extended uses of the negatives. Photographers wanted to make the greatest income possible from each negative. For example, the 1908 flood of the Congaree River gave the photographer an opportunity to produce many images to be used in newspapers, reused as instantaneous (Kodak) postcards, and later placed in books. Another prototype is the group portrait taken for the sponsors' use in annuals or office display, and then often printed on postcards for each participant's individual use. Needless to say, pictures reprinted years later would be mailed to others for various reasons. The amateur candid snapshots also contained interesting images though sometimes found in poorly crafted conditions. Most of the views in this volume fit into the latter extended categories. The numerous sources included archives, collections, and private albums. The owners' generosity permitted a full review of their collections, which uncovered numerous images that had not been reviewed and documented before. All agreed that the significant imagery found in these pictures should be published so that everyone interested in South Carolina history can enjoy the insights found in these isolated fragments of visual history.

The objective of the previous books in this series has been two-fold. The first being edification and the second enjoyment. It is hoped that these experiences continue to be found in this volume.

—Howard Woody

Author's Note:The scale of pictures on the cover and in the book has been altered to relate to page layout and the length of captions.

One

Historic and City Views of Columbia

The previous South Carolina volumes in the Postcard History series have begun with images showing the prominent facilities of that county. This volume begins with Columbia and includes city, county, state, and federal edifices in addition to views of the state fair, parades, prisons, and municipal fire and police departments. Columbia grew from a rural site to the beginnings of a regional center for commerce. Then it was burned to the ground and under outside occupation that hindered its regrowth. With such a rich and troubled history, the community looked to past glories and held them close to their hearts. The images contained herein reflect the full spectrum of emotions and passions of the time and attempt to capture the activity that passed by or through a building, rather than simply a display of the facades.

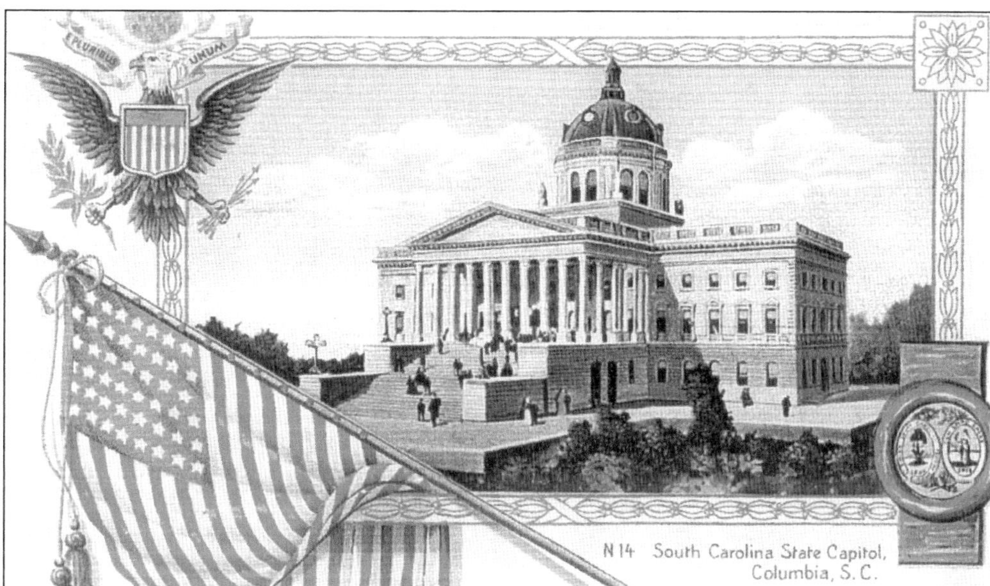

South Carolina State Capitol, Columbia [*c.* 1907]. This postcard image used the initial architectural drawing's details and differs from the final features of the building. The architects for the third State House and the dates of their revisions were John Rudolph Niernee, 1855; Frank Milburn, 1900; and Charles C. Wilson, 1904. After 56 years, the exterior was finished in 1907, at a cost of $3,450,000. The exterior dimensions are 264 feet east to west, 167 feet north to south, and 164 feet from ground to the top of the dome.

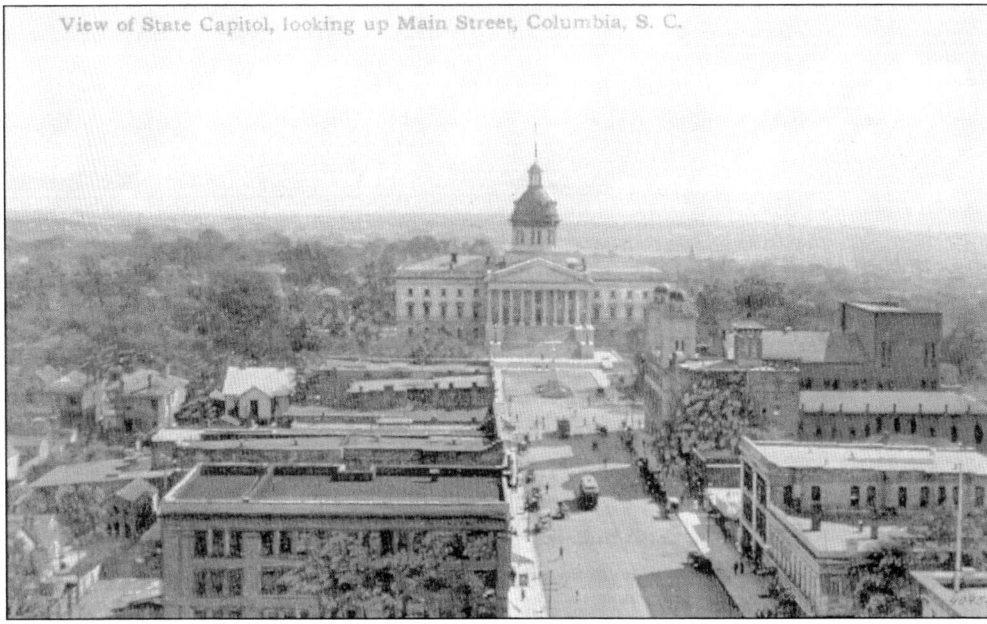

VIEW OF STATE CAPITOL LOOKING UP MAIN STREET, COLUMBIA, SC [1907]. This view of the Capitol building and grounds, photographed by Blanchard, became the standard view of this site and was mass produced in every series of Columbia postcard images made and sold. The photographic image on the negative was printed in various scales: near full scale for postcards, enlarged for framing, and reduced for montage imagery.

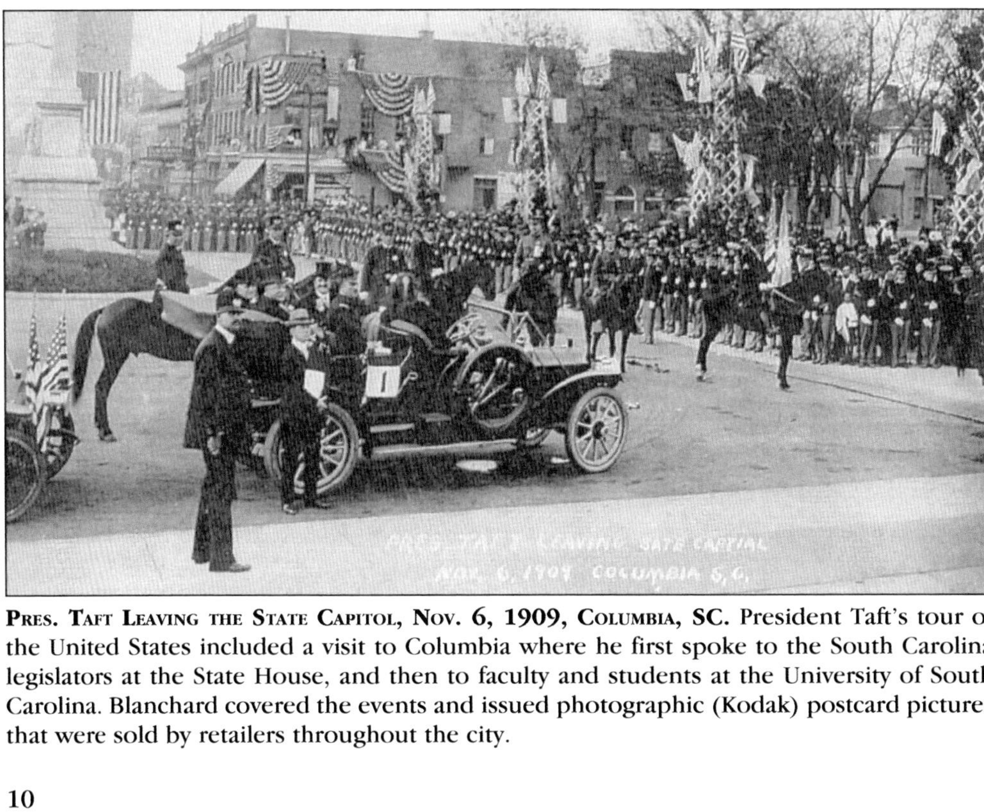

PRES. TAFT LEAVING THE STATE CAPITOL, NOV. 6, 1909, COLUMBIA, SC. President Taft's tour of the United States included a visit to Columbia where he first spoke to the South Carolina legislators at the State House, and then to faculty and students at the University of South Carolina. Blanchard covered the events and issued photographic (Kodak) postcard pictures that were sold by retailers throughout the city.

MEXICAN WAR MONUMENT, COLUMBIA, SC [c. 1908]. This iron Palmetto Tree Monument was purchased from Christopher Werner of Charleston for $5,000 and erected in 1858 on the State House grounds. The Palmetto Regiment, commanded by Col. Pierce M. Butler of Edgefield (governor from 1836 to 1838), served in the Mexican War of 1847. Butler was killed in the Battle of Churubusco.

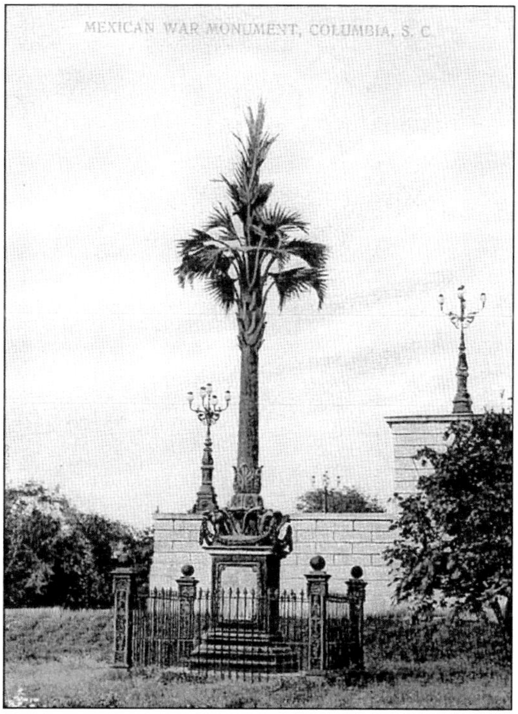

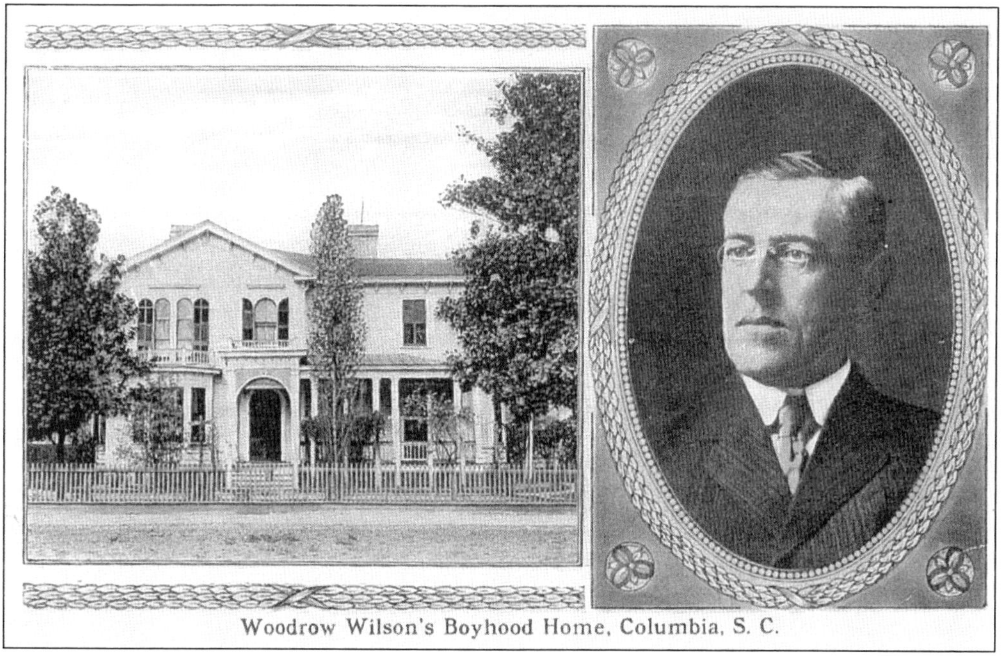

WOODROW WILSON'S BOYHOOD HOME, COLUMBIA, SC, c. 1910. This two-story "Cottage Style" frame house at 1705 Hampton Street was built in 1872 by the Reverend Joseph R. Wilson, professor at Columbia Theological Seminary from 1870 to 1874 and minister of the First Presbyterian Church from 1871 to 1873. He was the father of Thomas Woodrow Wilson, who became the 28th president. In 1875, the Wilsons moved from South Carolina.

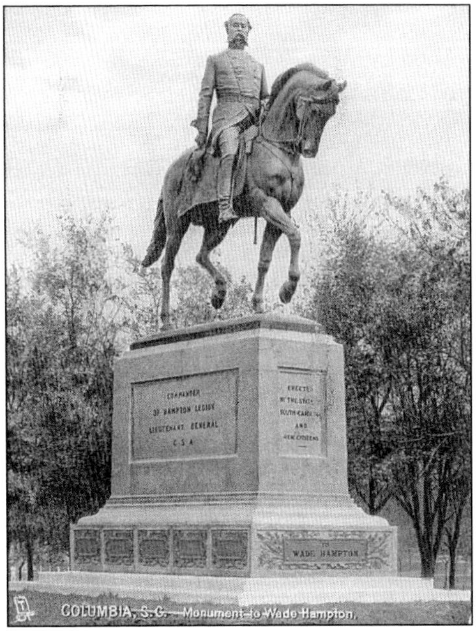

MONUMENT TO WADE HAMPTON COLUMBIA, SC [*c.* 1907]. Wade Hampton (1818–1902) raised and outfitted "Hampton's Legion" (infantry, calvary and field artillery) to serve in the Confederate States Army. His "Legion" saw action with Gen. Stonewall Jackson at Bull Run, Gen. J.E.B. Stuart, and Gen. Robert E. Lee at Petersburg. Lieutenant General Hampton assisted Gen. Joseph E. Johnston in the battles of the Carolinas and commanded the Confederate cavalry in Columbia under Gen. P.G.T. Beauregard, as they surrendered the city to protect property and save lives. His bronze equestrian statue, which is 15 feet high and 17 feet long and cost $30,000, was sculpted by Frederick W. Ruckstull and was dedicated in 1906 on the State House grounds in front of an audience of 10,000 citizens.

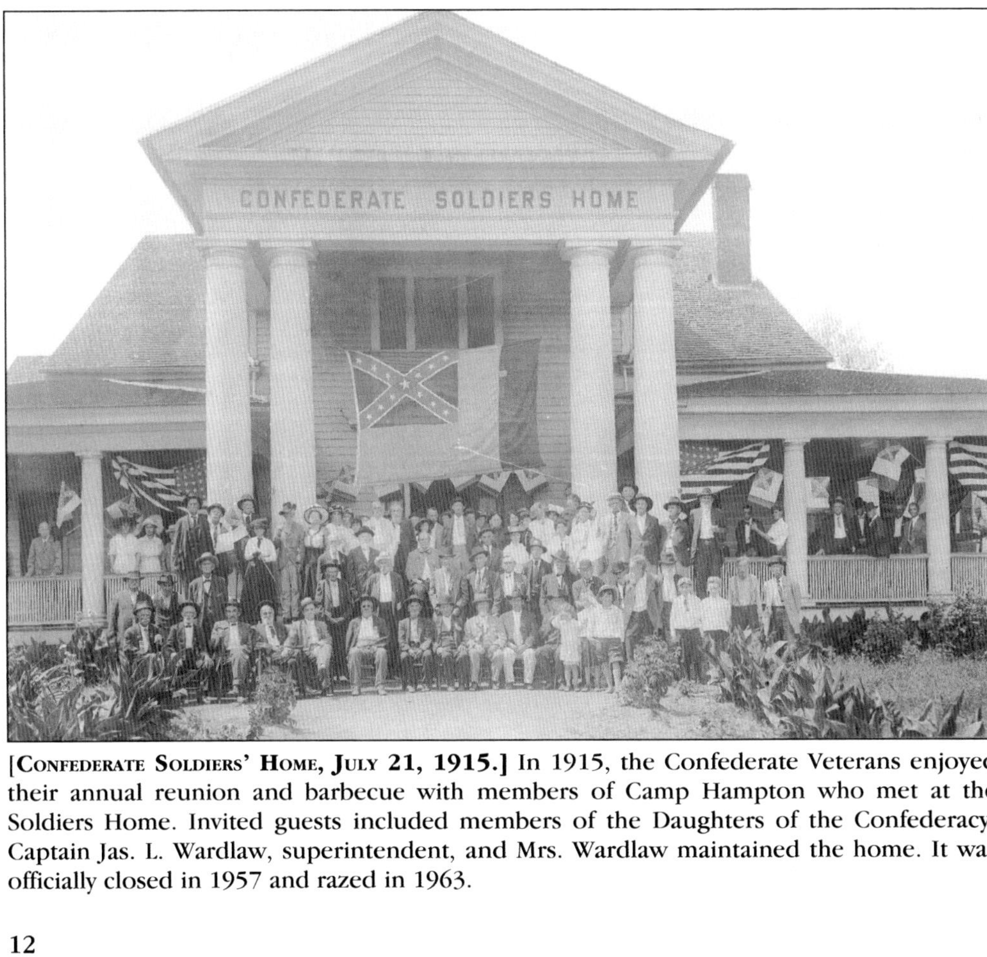

[CONFEDERATE SOLDIERS' HOME, JULY 21, 1915.] In 1915, the Confederate Veterans enjoyed their annual reunion and barbecue with members of Camp Hampton who met at the Soldiers Home. Invited guests included members of the Daughters of the Confederacy. Captain Jas. L. Wardlaw, superintendent, and Mrs. Wardlaw maintained the home. It was officially closed in 1957 and razed in 1963.

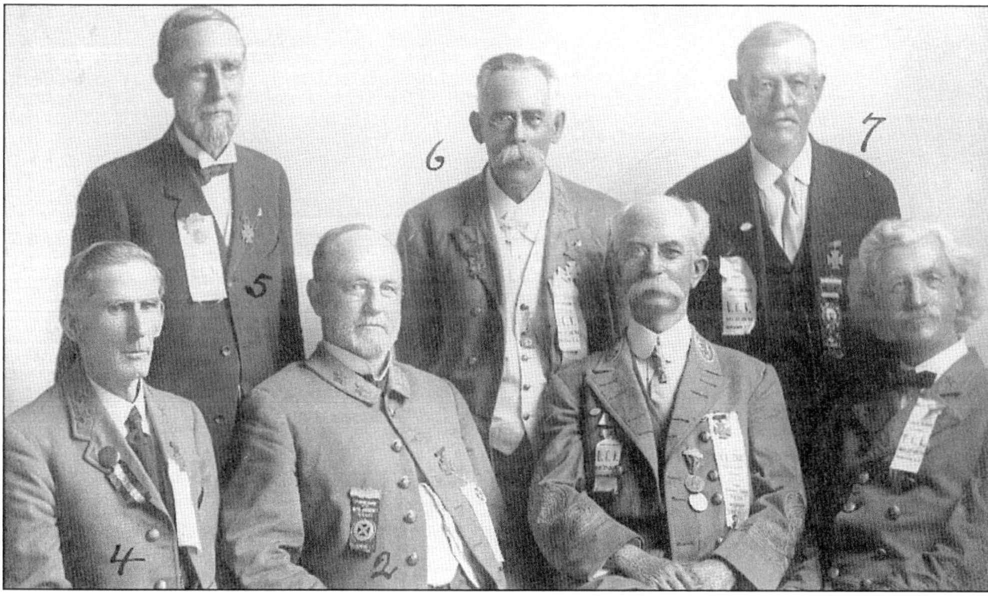

[**Portrait of Confederate Reunion Members, 1913.**] Officers of the SC Division of the United Confederate Veterans, from left to right, are: (seated) W.D. McLaurie; Maj. Gen. W.A. Clark, chief of Camp Hampton; Maj. Gen. B.H. Teague; and Maj. M. David; (standing) W.G. Hinson, Camp Sumter; Rev. Lt. Col. F.O.S. Curtis, Chapin; and Charley Reck, Camp Hampton. Each attended the July 1–4, 1913 reunion at Gettysburg, Pennsylvania.

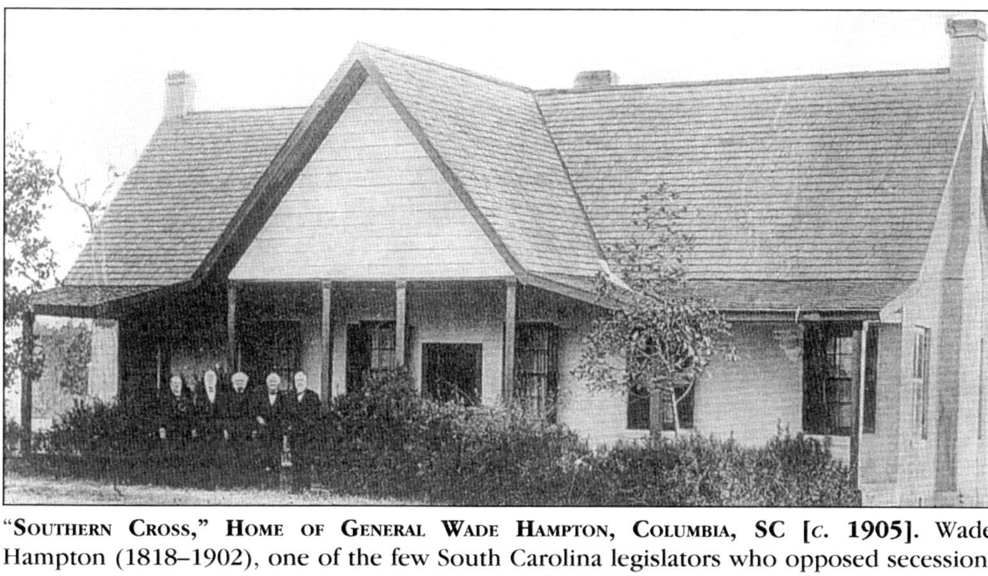

"Southern Cross," Home of General Wade Hampton, Columbia, SC [*c.* 1905]. Wade Hampton (1818–1902), one of the few South Carolina legislators who opposed secession, had a distinguished service record in the Confederate States Army. During the period of reconstruction, he worked for reconciliation and the restoration of home rule for South Carolina and was elected governor for the 1877–1879 term. Later, Hampton was elected to the United States Senate, serving from 1879 to 1891. With his plantation "Millwood" destroyed by Sherman's troops, he used the house "Southern Cross," located on Forest Drive near Forest Hills Nursing Home, as his residence. The image above shows Hampton in the center of a group of Columbia leaders. He died in Columbia in 1902.

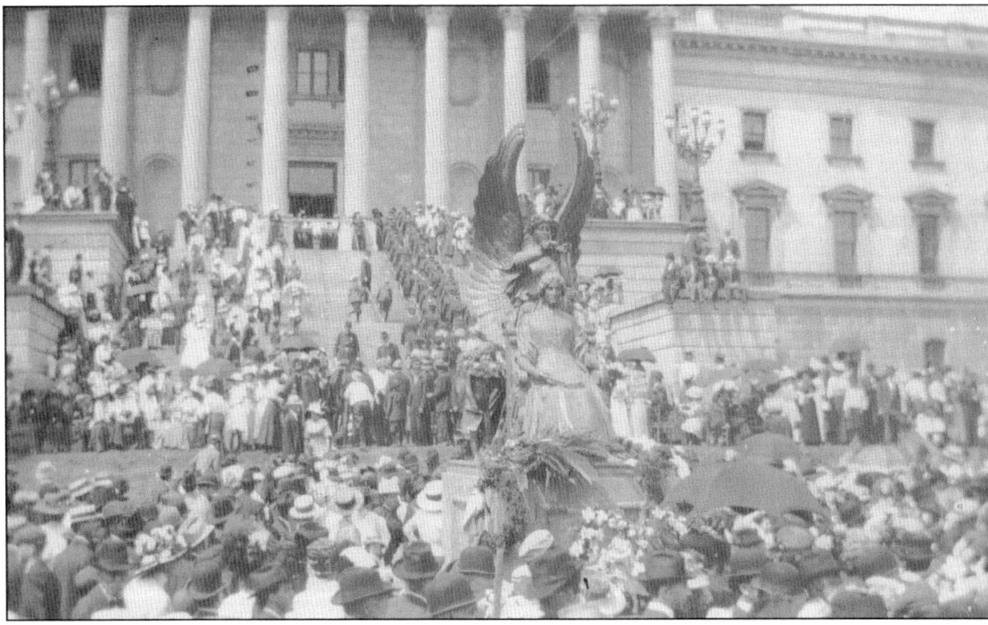

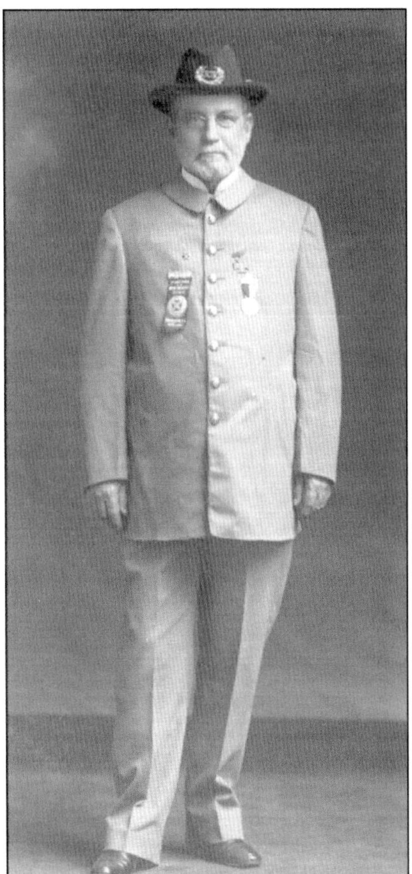

[THE DEDICATION OF THE MONUMENT TO THE WOMEN OF THE CONFEDERACY, **1912.]** In 1909, the General Assembly appropriated $7,500 with an additional $11,000 from public gifts to create this bronze monument to the Women of the Confederacy, sculpted by Frederick W. Ruckstull. The unveiling ceremonies on the south side of the Capitol grounds occurred on April 11, 1912. A crowd of over 10,000 people gathered to see the monument that they had contributed money to create and to listen to the music and speeches of the dignitaries assembled on the dais.

[PORTRAIT OF MAJOR GENERAL W.A. CLARK, **1912.]** This Blanchard portrait of Maj. Gen. Washington Augustus Clark (1842–1931), commander of the South Carolina Division, United Confederate Veterans, was taken after the semi-centennial reunion July 1–4, 1912, of the two armies at the battle of Gettysburg, Pennsylvania. The Confederate organization consisted of men who in their youth served as a military person, and in 1892 created an association that could honor and assist those veterans in need of help. The organization granted honorary military titles to their leaders.

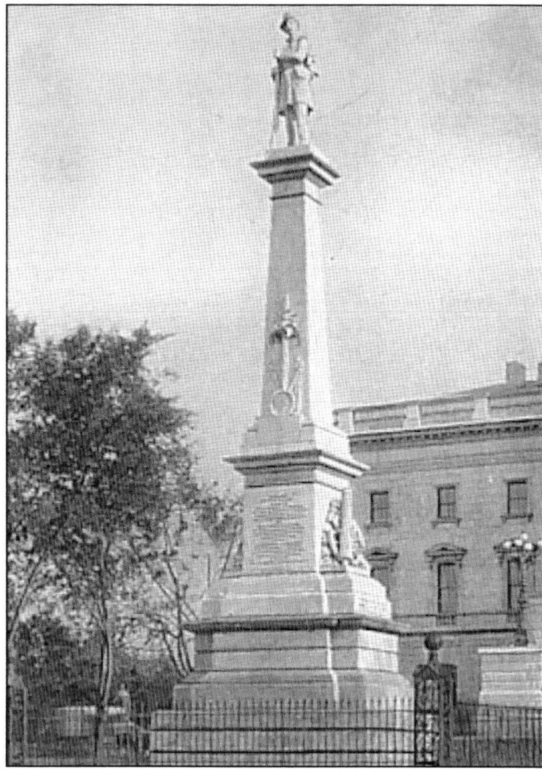

CONFEDERATE MONUMENT COLUMBIA, SC [1907]. The women of South Carolina sponsored this monument, dedicated to those who died in the Confederate War from 1861 to 1865. The South Carolina Memorial Association was formed in November 1869. The first statue, about seven feet high, costing $11,760, was carved in Italian carrara marble and placed on top of a 40-foot pedestal made from South Carolina granite. The May 1879 unveiling occurred on State House grounds; however, after being struck by lightning, a second monument was ordered and was unveiled with limited fanfare on May 9, 1882.

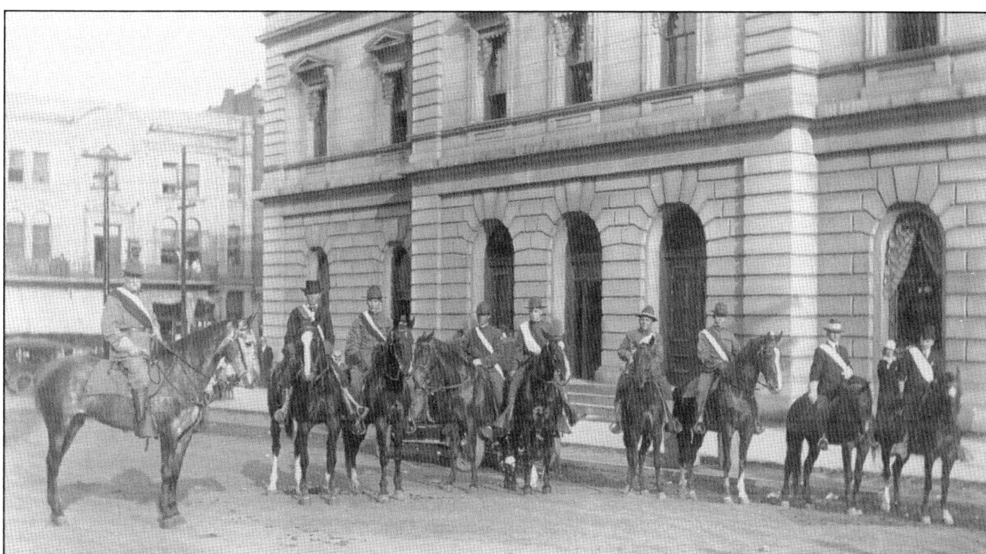

[HONOR GUARD, CONFEDERATE REUNION PARADE, 1915.] Maj. Gen. Wilie Jones, chief marshal, is shown here with his mounted staff in front of the Laurel Street post office—which became the fourth city hall in the late 1930s. Jones led the initial five companies of the National Guard including the Governor's Guard, Brookland Light Infantry, and the Columbia Light Infantry. The next unit consisted of 11 squads of Columbia police who were followed down Main Street to the Capitol by veterans walking or seated in cars.

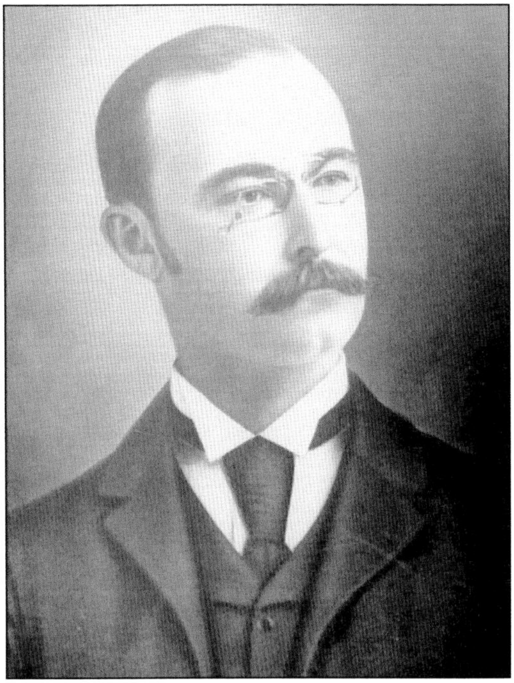

[Portrait of Narciso Gener Gonzales, *c.* 1890s.] N.G. Gonzales (1858–1903) was born on Edisto Island and later became a Columbia reporter for Charleston's *News and Courier*. He founded and was the first editor for Columbia's paper, *The State*. Gonzales' creed, published in 1891, was as follows: "No editor having strong convictions of public duty and expressing them without fear can hope to escape criticism; and the worse the men or politics he antagonizes, the more certain it is that this criticism will be violent, unscrupulous and vituperative. I must perform my public duties as I see them." "The measure of success is not what we get out of life, but what we leave after it."

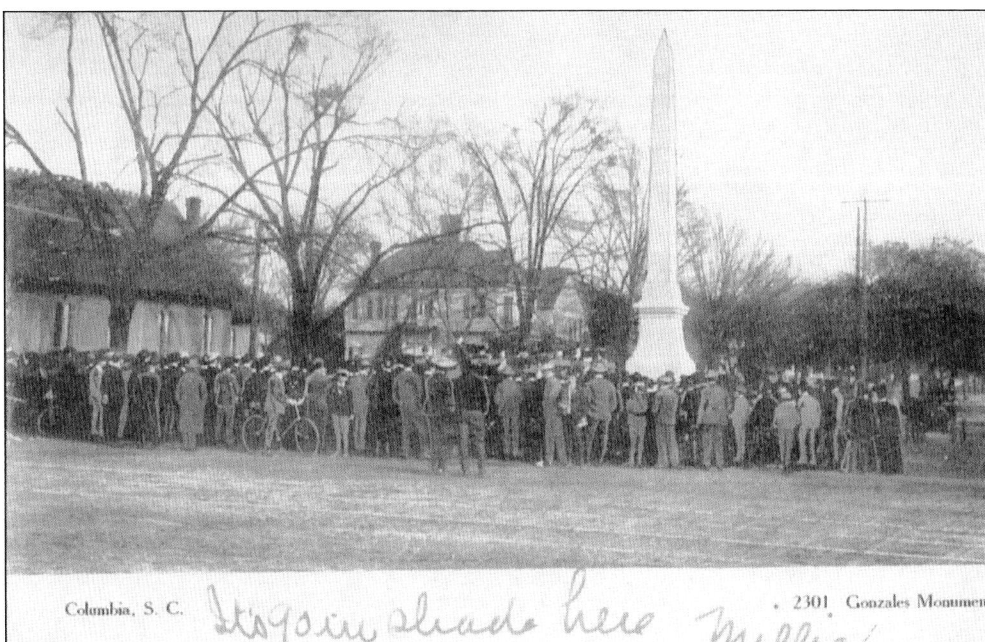

Gonzales Monument, Columbia, SC [1905]. On January 15, 1903, Lt. Gov. James H. Tillman, nephew of Sen. B.R. Tillman, mortally wounded the unarmed Gonzales, as the editor walked to the corner of Main and Gervais Streets, because he was angry about Gonzales' negative newspaper editorials. The murder trial was held in Lexington, and Tillman was found innocent. The monument was unveiled in 1905 before a gathering of 2,000 people at the Senate and Sumter Street site.

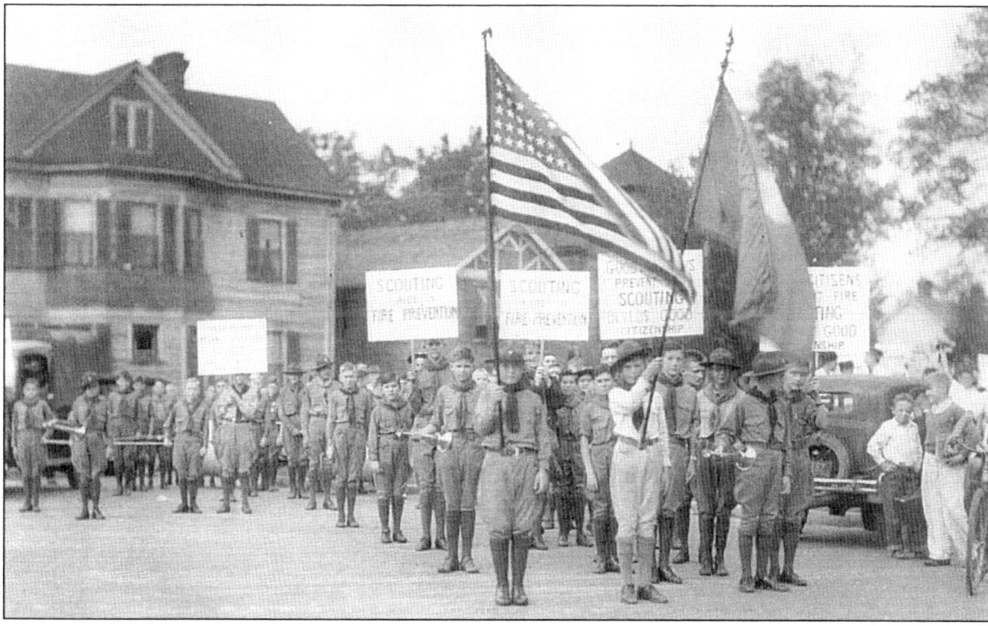

[Scouting for Fire Prevention, 1934.] The activity of Boy Scout troops marching in parades, supporting popular civic concerns, was popular in this era. This 1934 image was taken as they assembled on a side street waiting for their turn to join the parade that would march down Main Street to the State House.

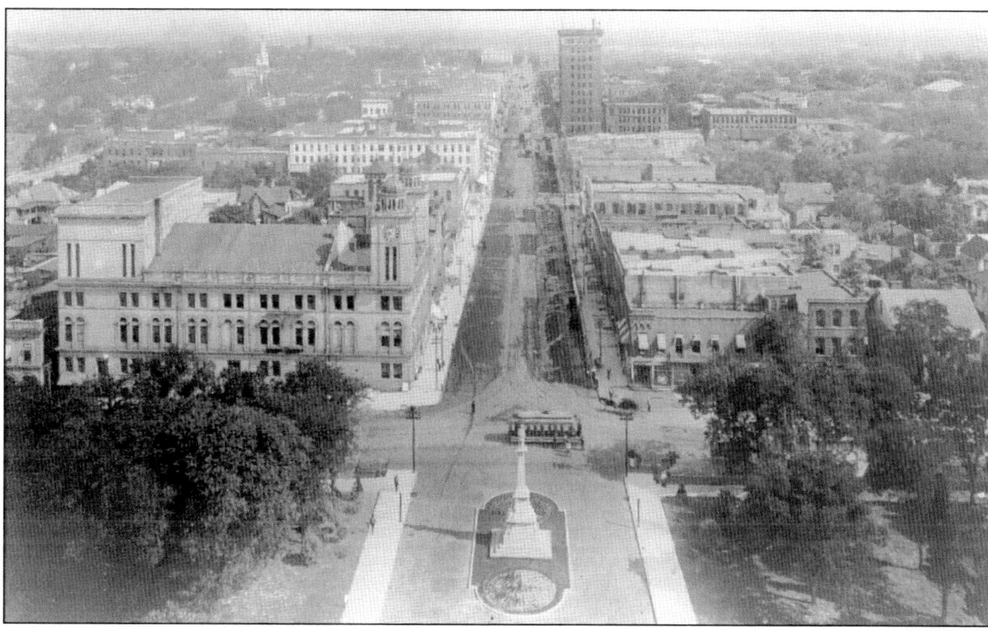

[Bird's-Eye View of Main Street Looking North from the Capitol, c. 1910.] This view, taken from the Capitol dome looking north, shows the junction of Gervais and Main Streets with city hall (1900) at left and the streetcar transfer station to the right. In the distance, the National Loan and Exchange Bank Building, Columbia's first skyscraper, stands on the corner of Main and Washington Streets.

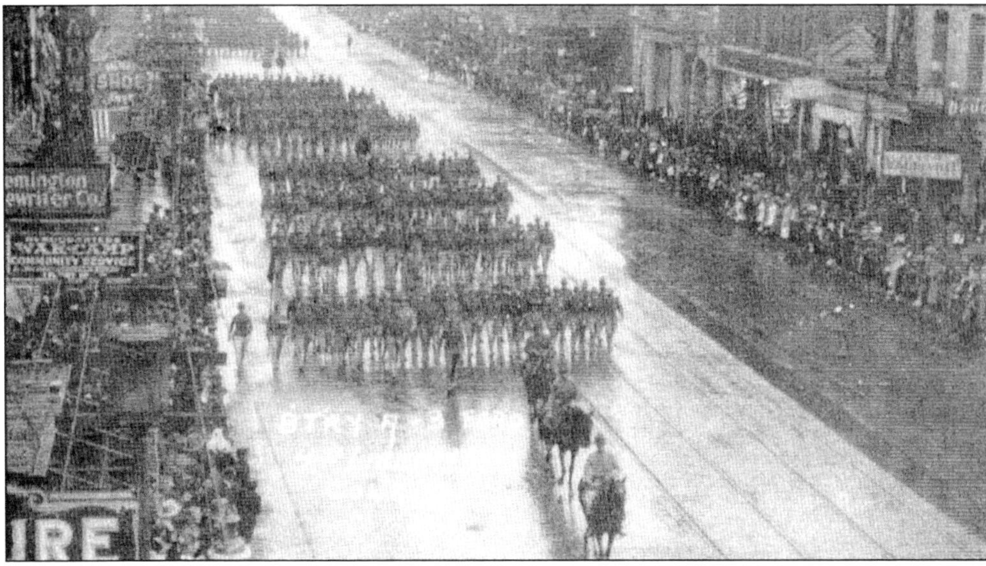

[The 4th Liberty Loan Bond Parade, 1918.] This postcard view of the September 28, 1918 parade in a steady rain shows Camp Jackson troops from the Third and Eighth Regiments marching up Main Street, passing thousands of solemn viewers who watched the massive display. Above, five air machines flew low over the crowds dropping bond literature with one crashing and killing Lt. L.E. Goodman near Assembly Street. The parade launched South Carolina's effort in a national sales drive to sell $6 billion in Liberty Bonds to support the American Expeditionary Forces in Europe.

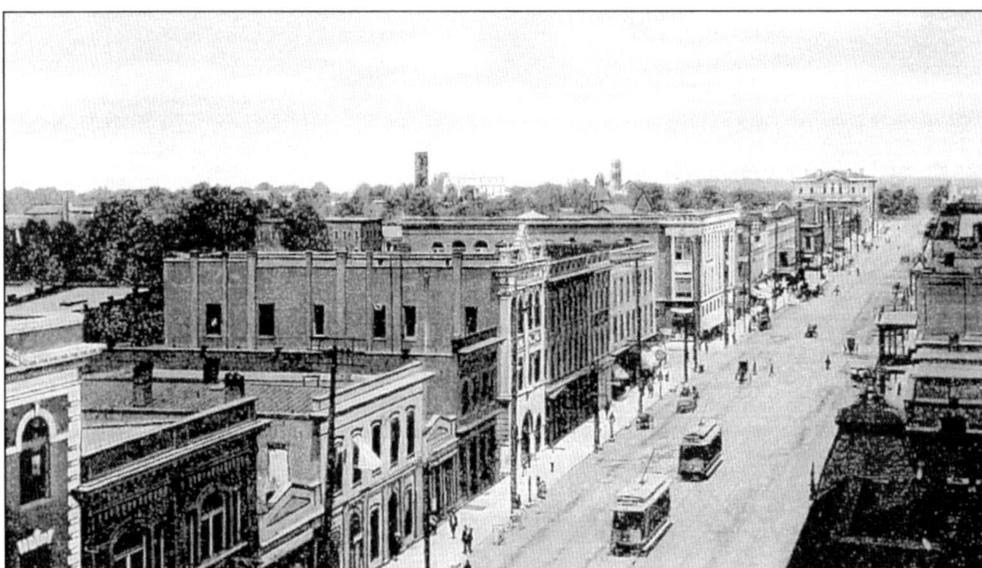

View from Skyscraper, Columbia, SC [*c.* 1907]. In January 1901, Edwin W. Robertson, banker and utility magnate, announced he would erect a 12-story skyscraper on the southeast corner of Main and Washington Streets. At a cost of $250,000, the new home for the National Loan and Exchange Bank was finished in April 1903. This view of the left side of Main Street looks north from Washington Street up to the post office on Laurel Street.

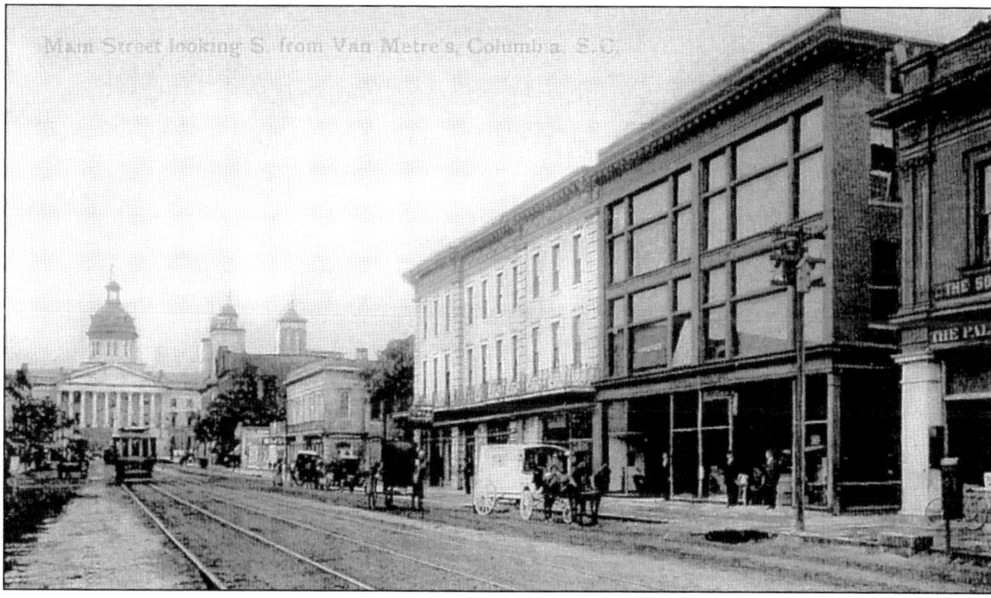

MAIN STREET LOOKING SOUTH FROM VAN METRE'S, COLUMBIA, SC [*c.* 1908.] This street level postcard view shows the retail section on the west side of Main Street, from Washington Street looking south toward city hall and the State Capital. The lightest brick building in the center was the Jerome Hotel, 1301–1307 Main Street.

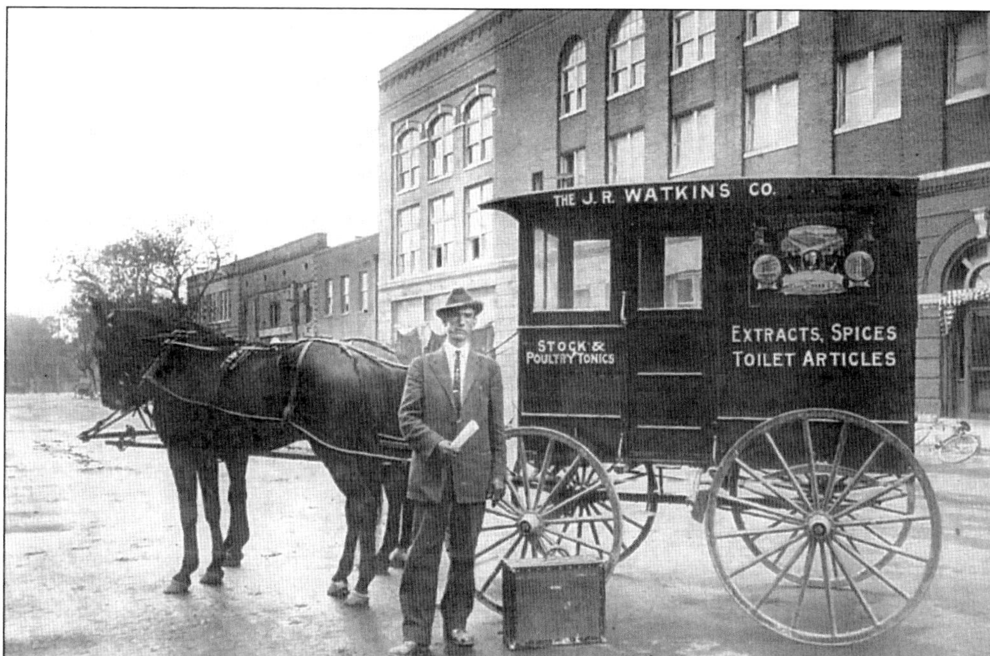

[J.R. WATKINS COMPANY'S WAGON, *c.* 1905.] The J.R. Watkins Company's agent and wagon paused on Hampton Street beside Mimnaugh's Department Store at 1501 Main Street. Watkins's salesmen went from town to town and door to door directly selling their kitchen spices, extracts, and toilet articles to housewives throughout the South.

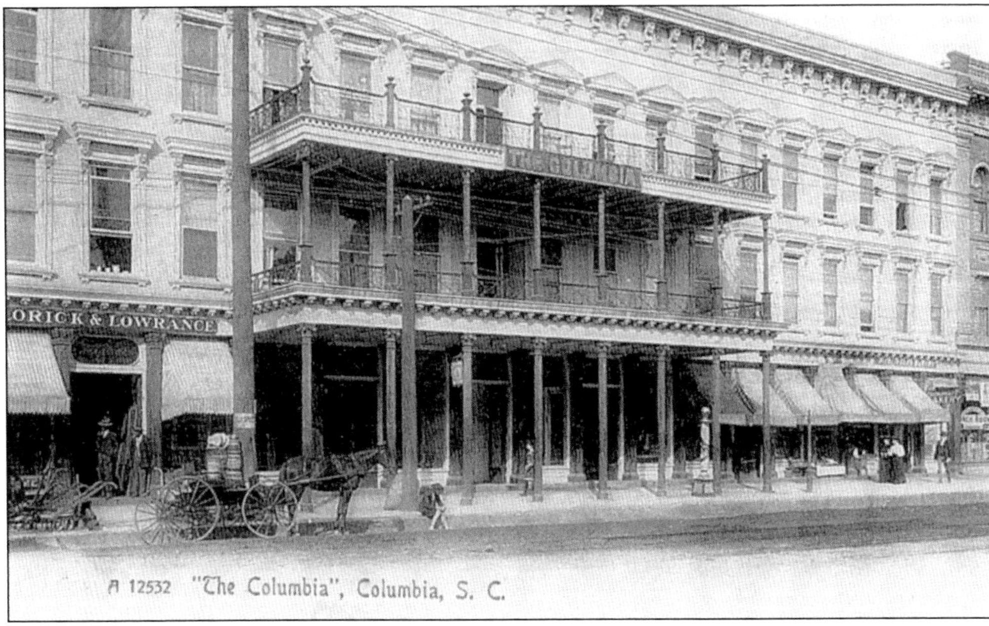

"THE COLUMBIA," COLUMBIA [*c.* 1906]. The three-story Columbia Hotel was located at 1531 Main Street between Kinards Clothing Store on the left side of an alley and the Bank of Columbia on the right corner of the block. Street level retail stores had Lorick and Lowrance Hardware Store on the left side of the hotel entrance with grocery stores on the right.

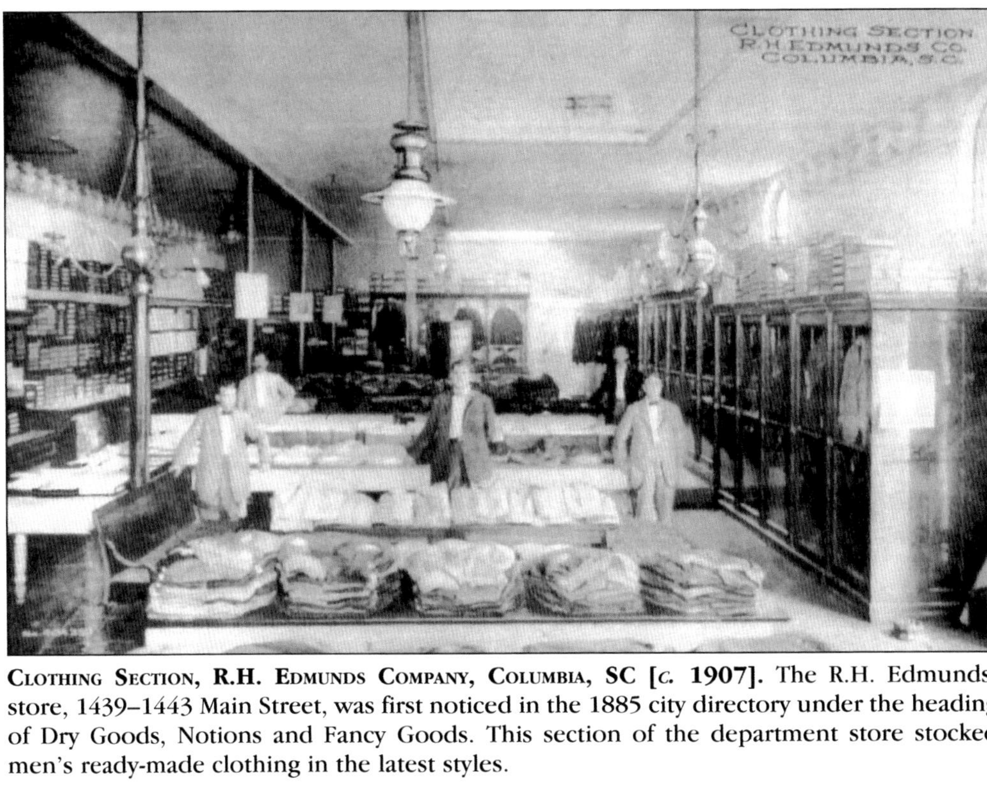

CLOTHING SECTION, R.H. EDMUNDS COMPANY, COLUMBIA, SC [*c.* 1907]. The R.H. Edmunds' store, 1439–1443 Main Street, was first noticed in the 1885 city directory under the heading of Dry Goods, Notions and Fancy Goods. This section of the department store stocked men's ready-made clothing in the latest styles.

Main Street, Columbia, SC [*c.* 1908]. The circus attracted local attention by scheduling a parade down Main Street with spectacular displays of decorated wagons, carnival music, clowns, and caged exotic animals before going to the fair grounds. This photographic postcard was probably commissioned by the local agent for the circus, who would require several hundred Kodak cards to be made over night for immediate mailing. This advertisement issue would invite the recipients to attend the shows.

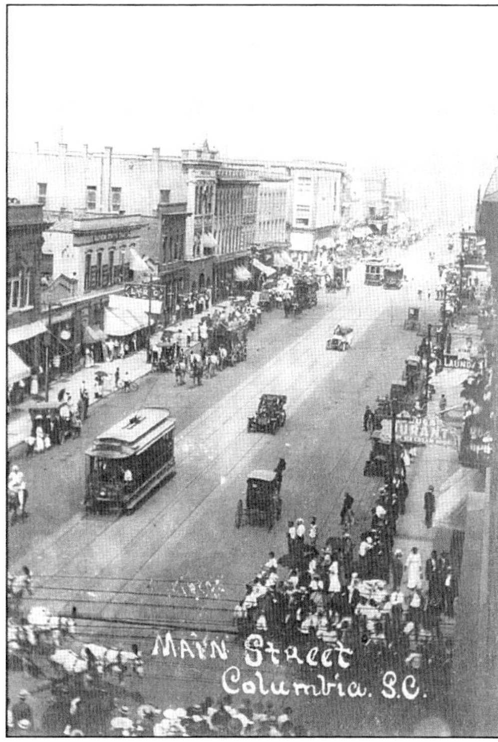

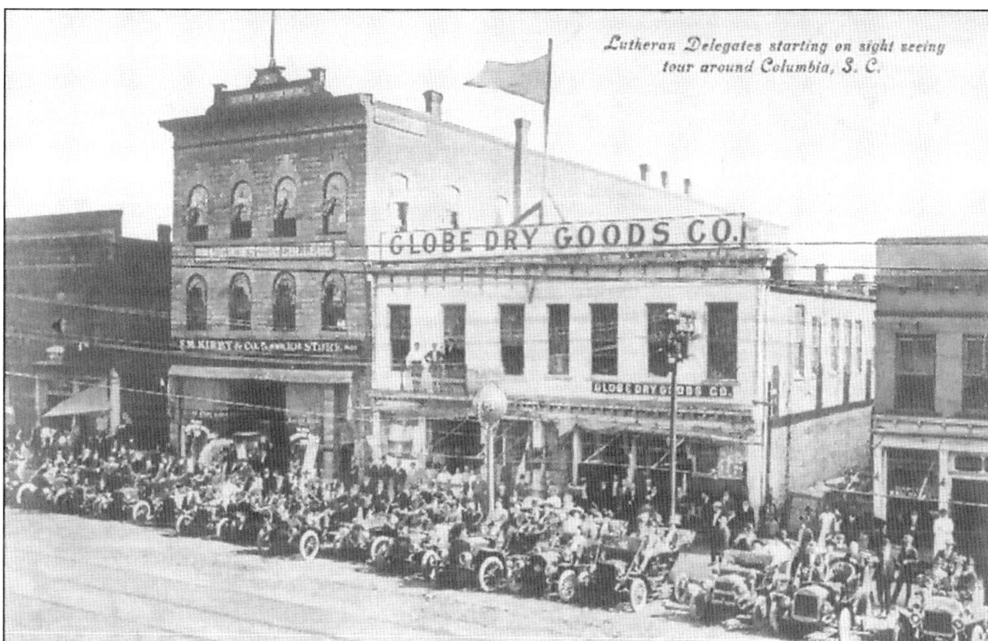

Lutheran Delegates Starting on Sight Seeing Tour Around Columbia, SC [*c.* 1910]. After transacting the business of the Lutheran conference, the delegates from around the district would take a sightseeing tour of the new sections of Columbia, using the latest automobiles for added excitement. This view is of the middle 1600 block of Main Street.

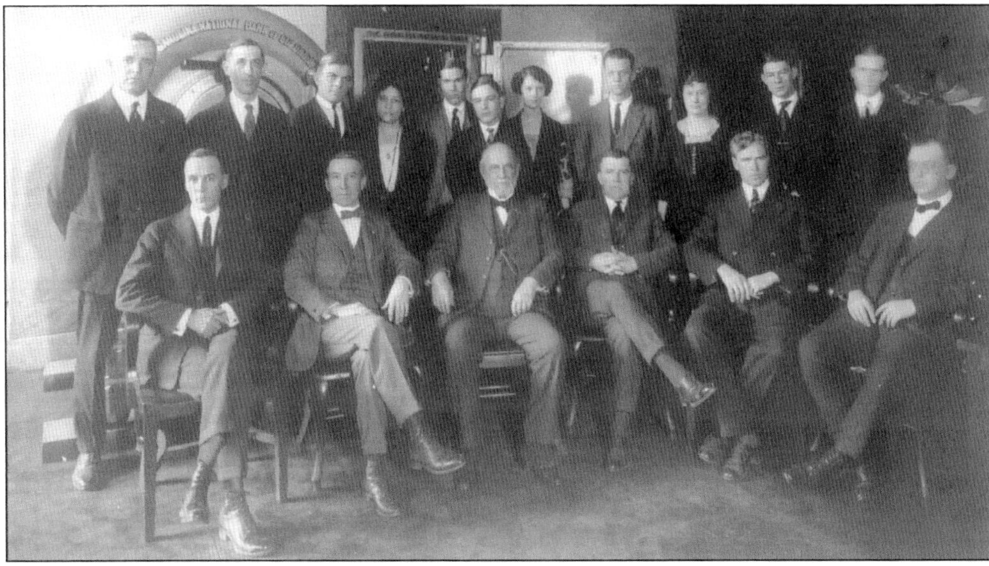

[Carolina National Bank Staff, c. 1914.] The officers and staff of the Carolina National Bank in 1914, from left to right, were (seated) J.J. Robb, J M. Bell, Gen. W.A. Clark, J.D. Bell, T.J. Fickling, and J. McIntosh; (standing) E.J. Brenner, J.B. DuBose, J.F. Sims, E. Holland, T.B. Rion, C.L. Duren, E. Wade, A.H. Harris, E. Brazell, A.P. Salley, and C.F. Young.

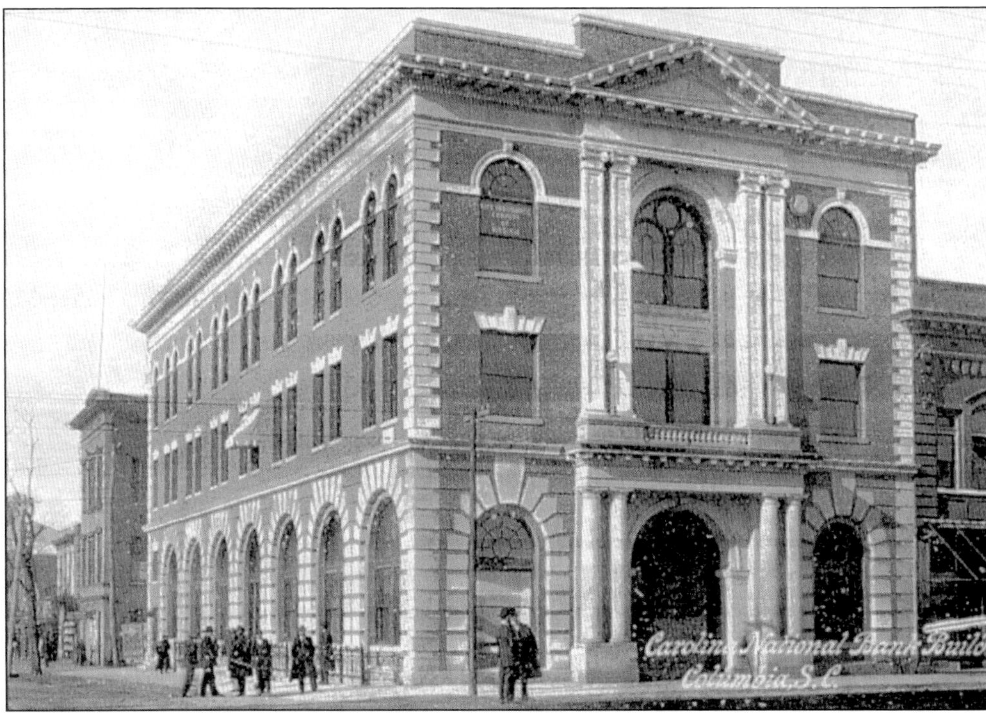

Carolina National Bank Building, Columbia, SC [c. 1908]. The northwest corner of Main and Washington Streets, where the earlier second city hall stood before being destroyed by fire in 1899, was the location of the Carolina National Bank that was designed by Shand & Lafaye architects and erected by the J.J. Cain Company. The building no longer stands.

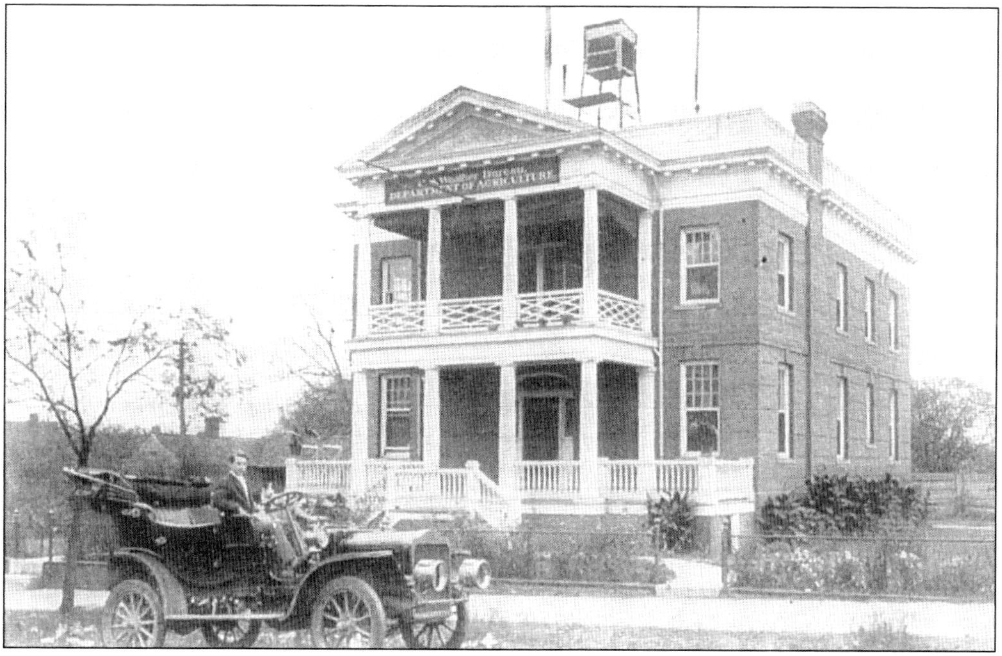

U.S. Weather Bureau Building, Columbia, SC [*c.* 1906]. The U.S. Weather Service's office moved from one building to another until 1905, when the meteorological station was built at 1004 Laurel Street by the corner of Laurel and Assembly Streets. J.W. Bauer was listed as the manager of the office from 1889 until at least 1905. Bauer released the U.S. Department of Agriculture's weather reports daily. The structure was razed in 1935 to make way for a new U.S. Courthouse that still stands in 2000.

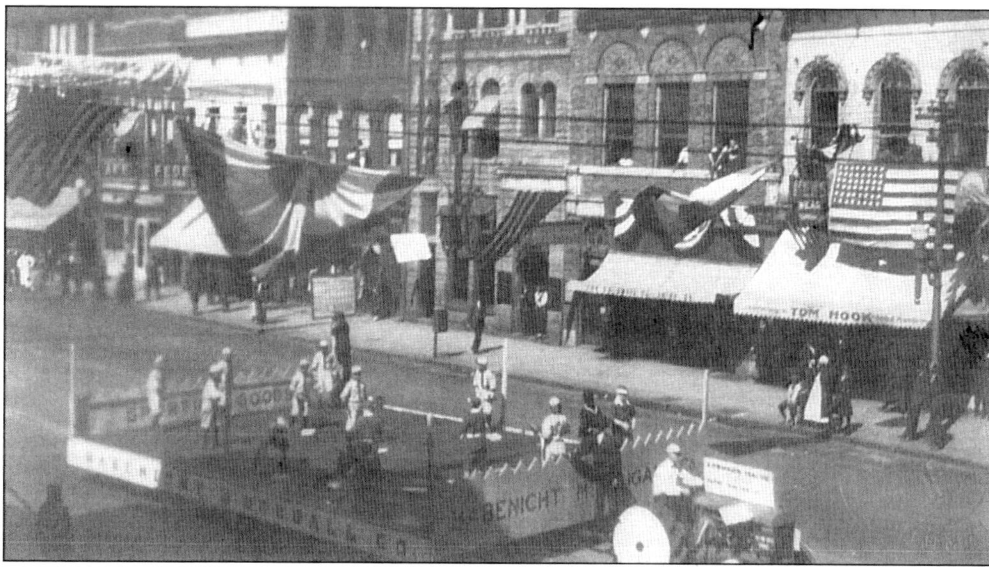

[Main Street, Baseball Parade Float *c.* 1910.] This postcard shows a float with men in baseball uniforms standing at each base and field position; it was sponsored by Habenicht and McDougall (1631 Main Street) who sold sporting goods and trophies. Possibly this spring parade celebrates both a holiday and the beginning of baseball season.

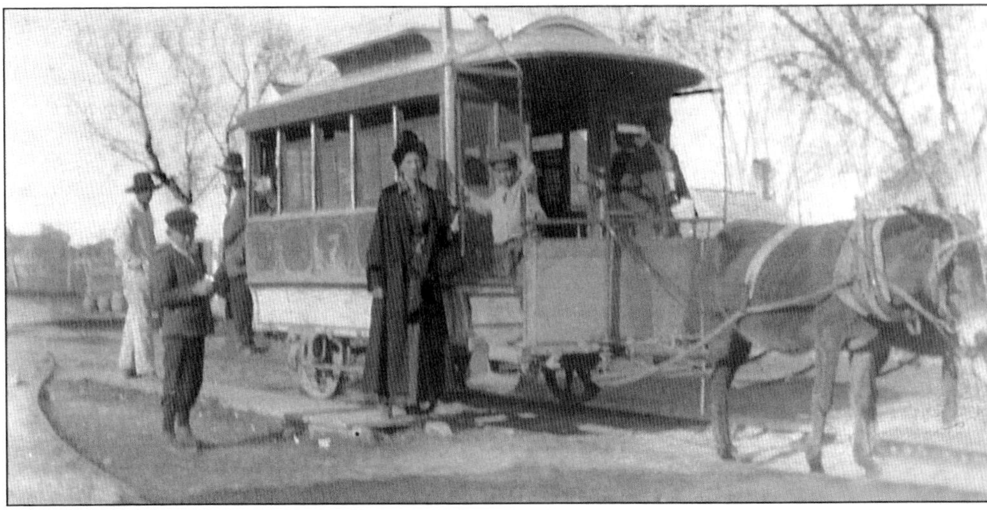

[MULE-DRIVEN STREET CAR, *c.* 1888, REPRINTED IN 1907.] The Columbia Street Railway System began in 1886 with 6 small cars, 20 mules, and 4 miles of track that carried passengers to the initial city limits from the Seaboard depot to the fairgrounds, the Charlotte depot, and the State Hospital, each for a 5¢ fare. Passenger averages were 800 riders a day with each car seating 16–24 passengers.

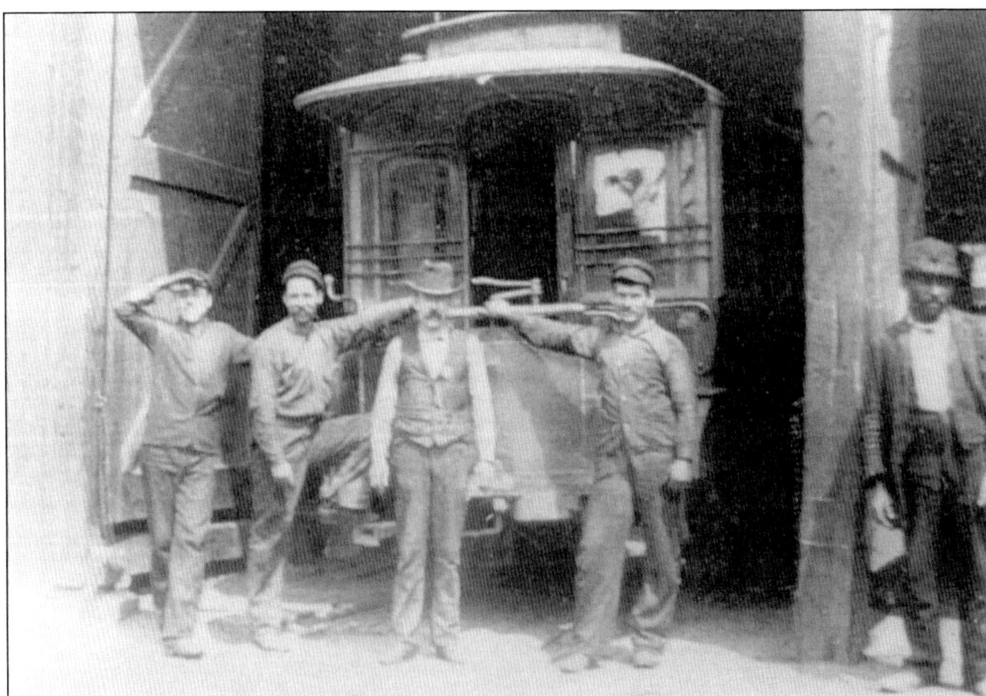

[TROLLEY BARN, 823 GERVAIS STREET, 1893.] In December 1890, the incorporation of the Columbia Electric Street, Suburban Railway, and Electric Power Company purchased the old street railway line. Electric trolleys appeared in May 1893. The entire streetcar system was electrified in 1894. By 1899, tracks running north to Eau Claire and the "Belt Line" circling east via the Shandon-Five Points area were added.

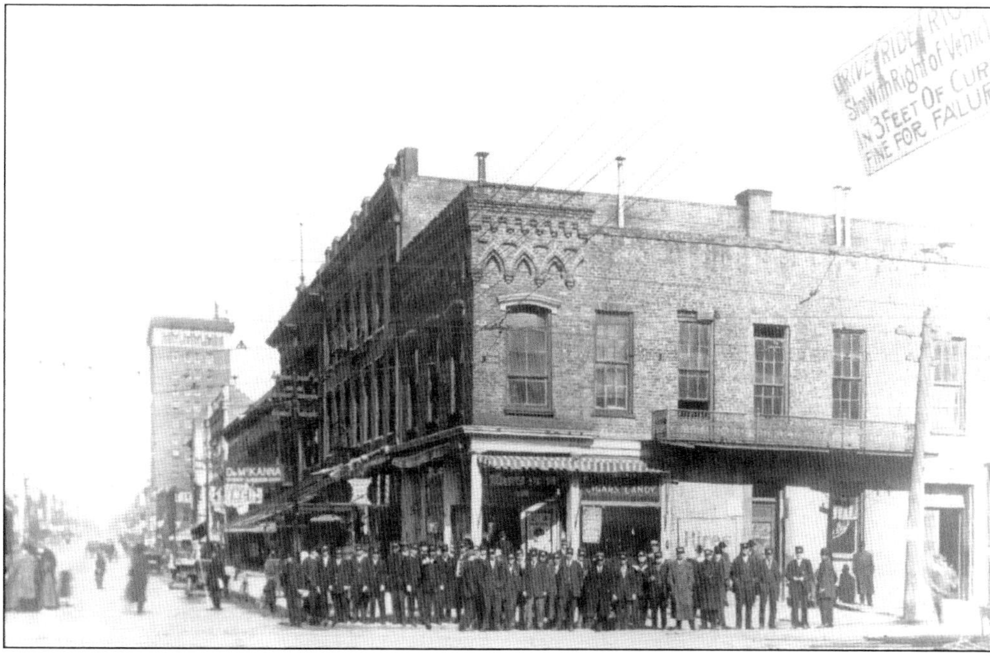

[Trolley Motormen and Conductors, 1905.] This image of the trolley workers was taken at the transfer station at the corner of Gervais and Main Streets. Most of the central business streets, the train depots, and commercial sites had trolley service. In 1900, service expanded south to the mill villages, further into the Shandon area.

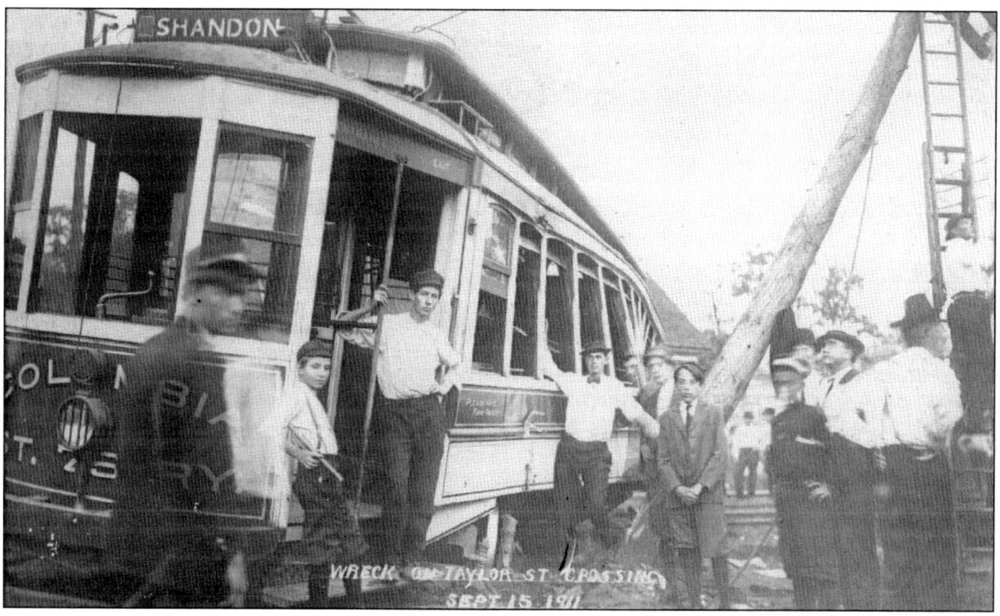

Wreck on Taylor Street, Columbia, SC, Sept. 15, 1911. This postcard view shows the street car wreck on Taylor Street after it was rammed by a locomotive engine at the train crossing in 1911. Rail extension ended with the Camp Jackson route in 1918, creating a rail system of 25 miles of track, 100 cars, and over 11 million passengers annually. Trolley service was reduced in the early 1920s with most routes shifting from trolleys to buses.

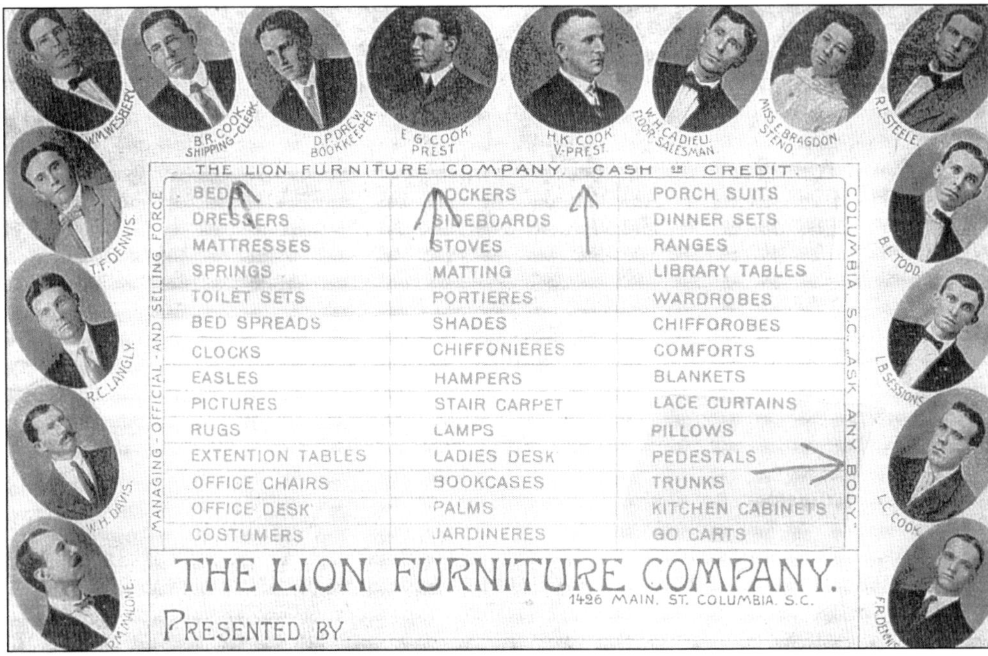

The Lion Furniture Company, Columbia, SC [*c.* 1910]. This advertising postcard has a montage of miniature portraits of the sales staff at the Lion Furniture Company, 1426 Main Street. An extended list of their sales stock is also included.

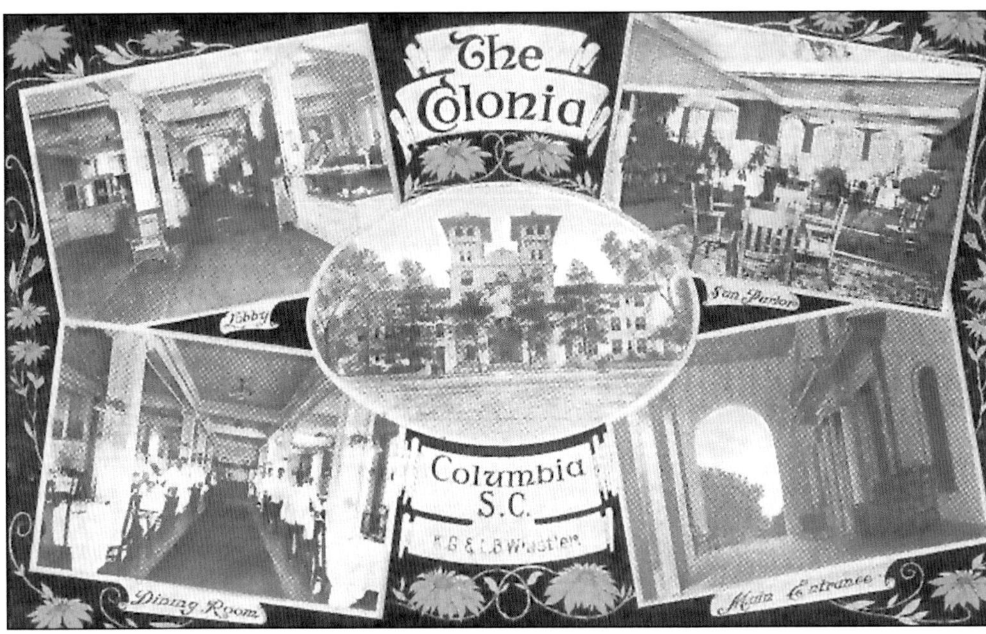

The Colonia, Columbia, SC [*c.* 1910]. The Columbia Female College (1859) first used this structure on 1614 Plain (Hampton) Street. In 1905, the school moved to its new Eau Claire campus. Then, Ambrose Gonzales purchased and remodeled the building into a hotel that he called "The Colonia." When a fire destroyed many of Columbia College's buildings, the students returned and "boarded out" for the remainder of the term.

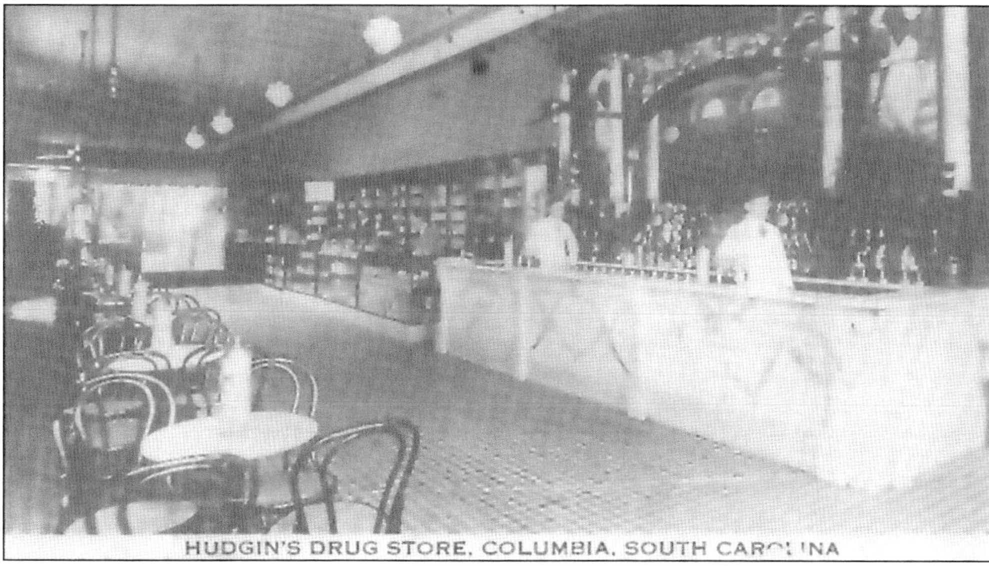

Hudgin's Drug Store, Columbia, SC [1917]. The well-appointed interior of Hudgin's Drug Store at 1738 Main Street depicts that era's art deco with its bold colors in the stained-glass panels and mirror behind the marble soda-fountain counter. The elegant furniture and fixtures invited customers to enjoy a snack, peruse gifts in the display cases, and select confectioneries or cosmetics while waiting for prescriptions. This postcard, along with other views of Columbia, were sold there.

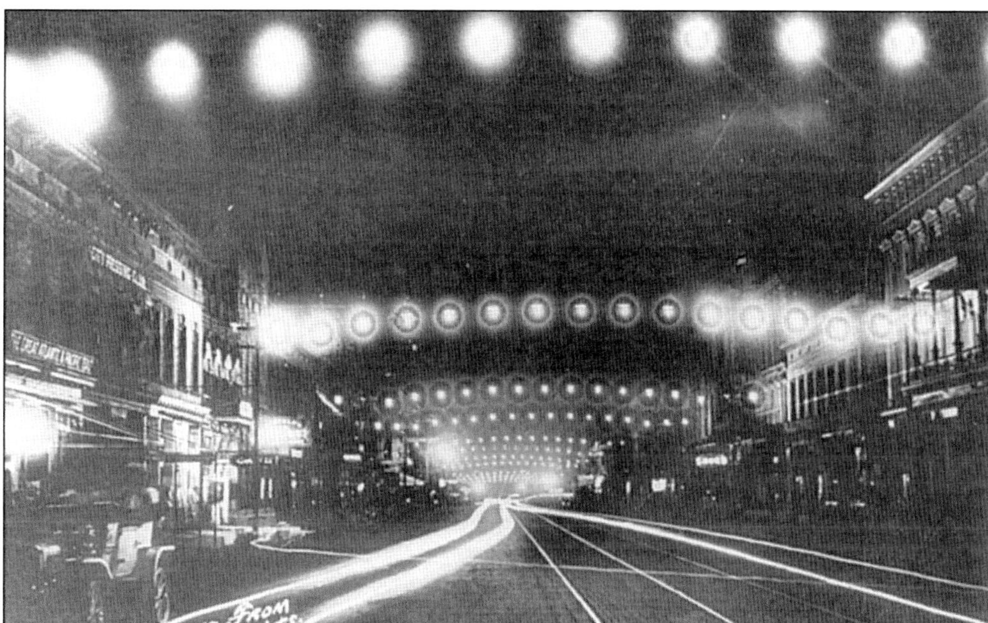

The Great White Way, Columbia, SC [*c.* 1910]. The Blanchard image above was a photographic (Kodak) postcard of Main Street. The open lens time exposure at night permitted the street lights, installed by the Perry Mann Elec. Co., to be recorded as round white spots, while the uneven white streaks came from automobile search lights.

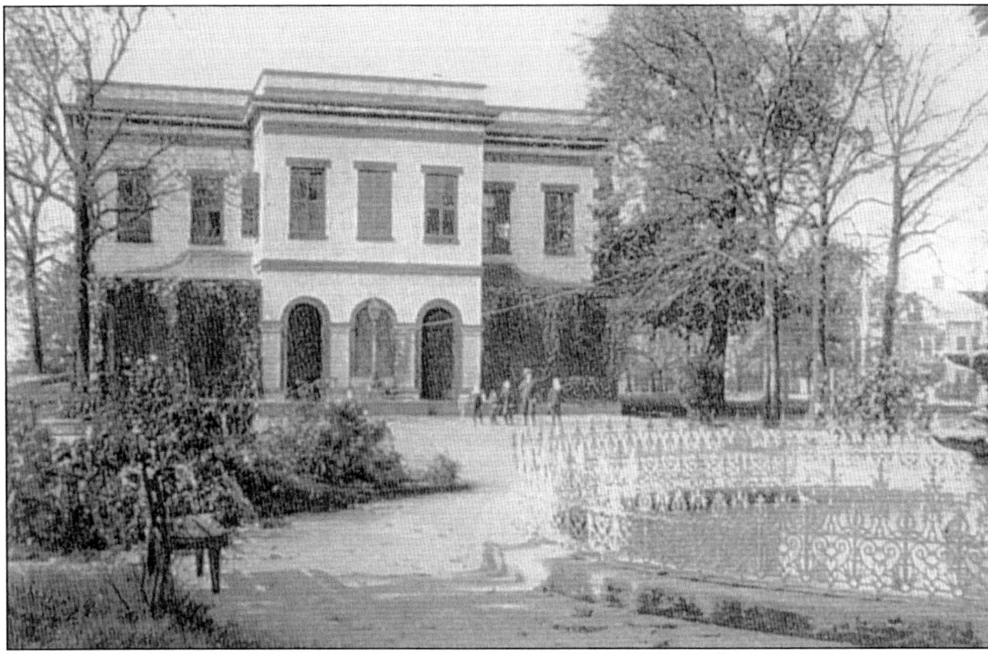

The Governor's Mansion, Columbia, SC [1903]. In 1842, the legislature created The Arsenal Academy. This structure was built in 1855 as quarters for two of the officers that taught at the nearby Arsenal Academy. The school burned in 1865. Located at 800 Richland Street, it has served over 30 governors.

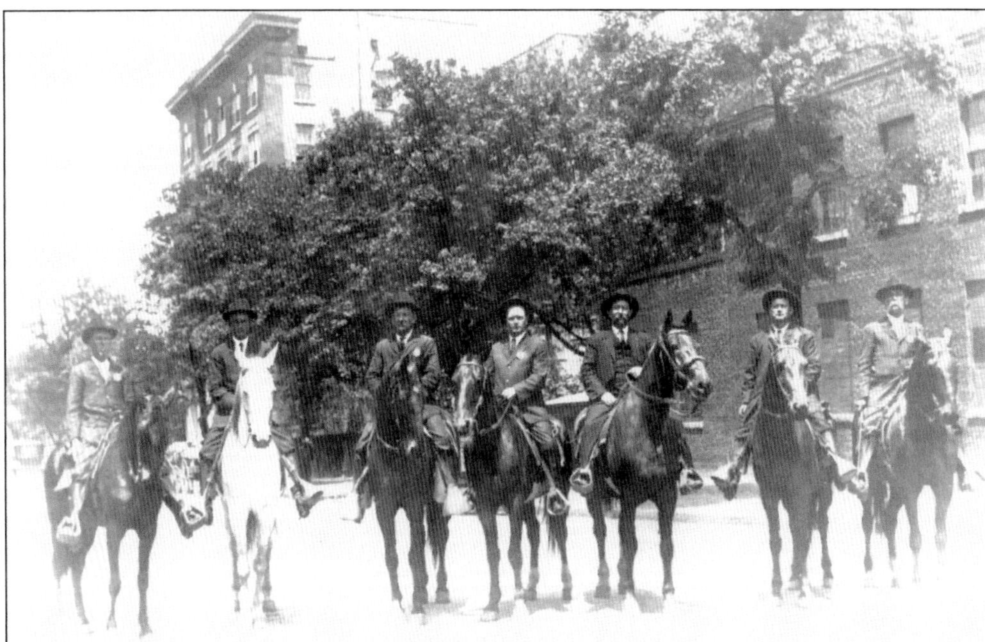

[Mounted Richland County Sheriff's Patrol, *c.* 1914.] The entire mounted Richland County Sheriff's Patrol was photographed in Columbia. Their daily duties usually had them traveling outside the city limits. This image is a reprint.

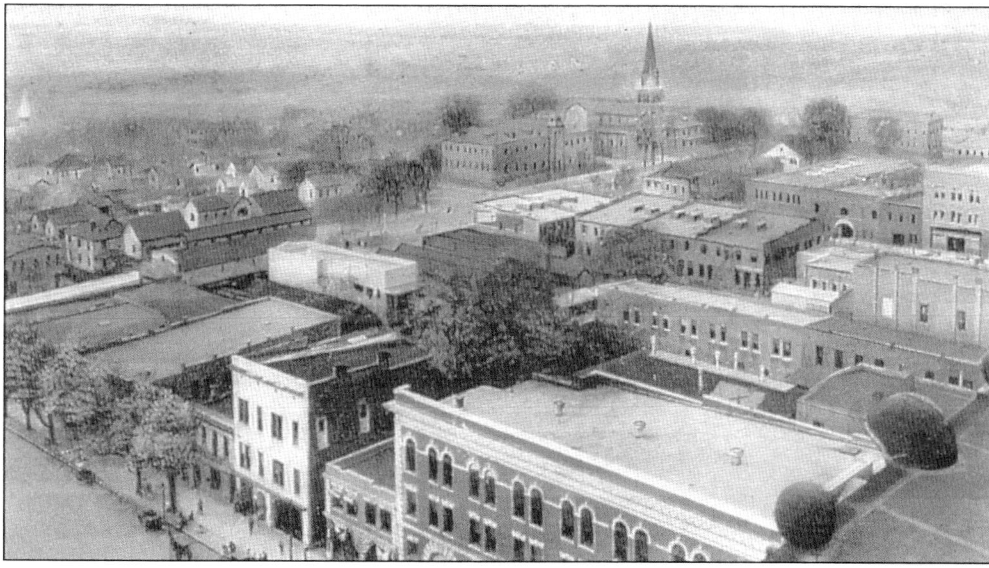

Bird's-Eye View, Columbia, SC, [*c.* 1909.] This picture was taken from the top of the National Loan and Exchange Bank Building on the corner of Main and Washington Streets. The view looks west showing a portion of the Carolina National Bank Building in the center foreground and the Ursuline Convent and St. Peter's Catholic Church in the right center background.

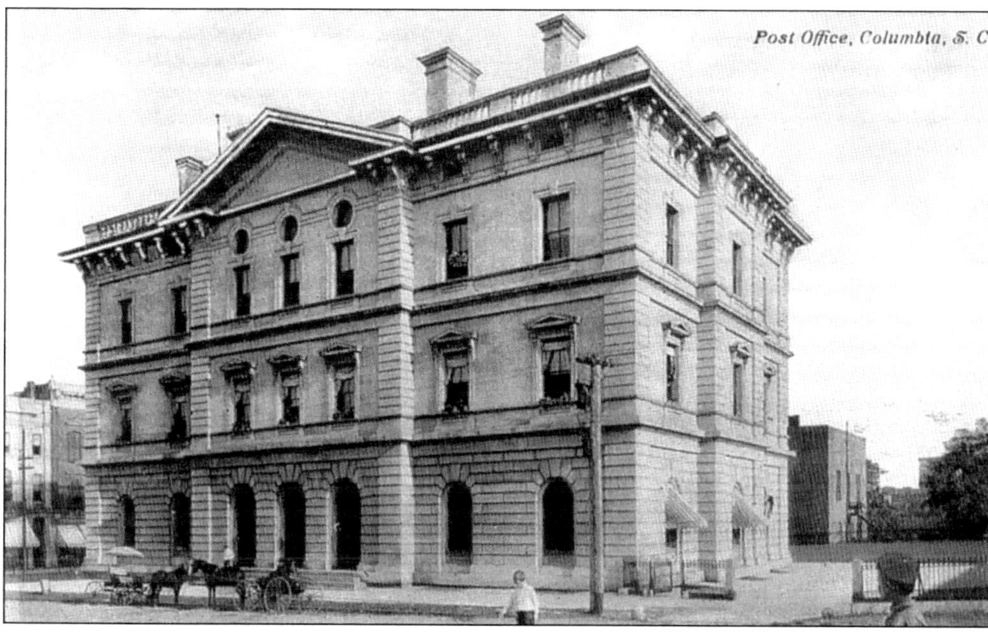

Post Office, Columbia, SC [*c.* 1908]. Architect Alfred Buit Mullet designed the post office (1874) in the European Second Empire style. The 1737 Main Street structure was built using gray Fairfield granite. In 1908, the post office received and dispatched 28 mail shipments daily and had a total income of $36,240 from stamps and box rents. The staff included 23 clerks, 19 carriers, 4 rural routes, and 3 special delivery messengers with an annual salary total of $25,171. The fourth town hall shifted here in 1936.

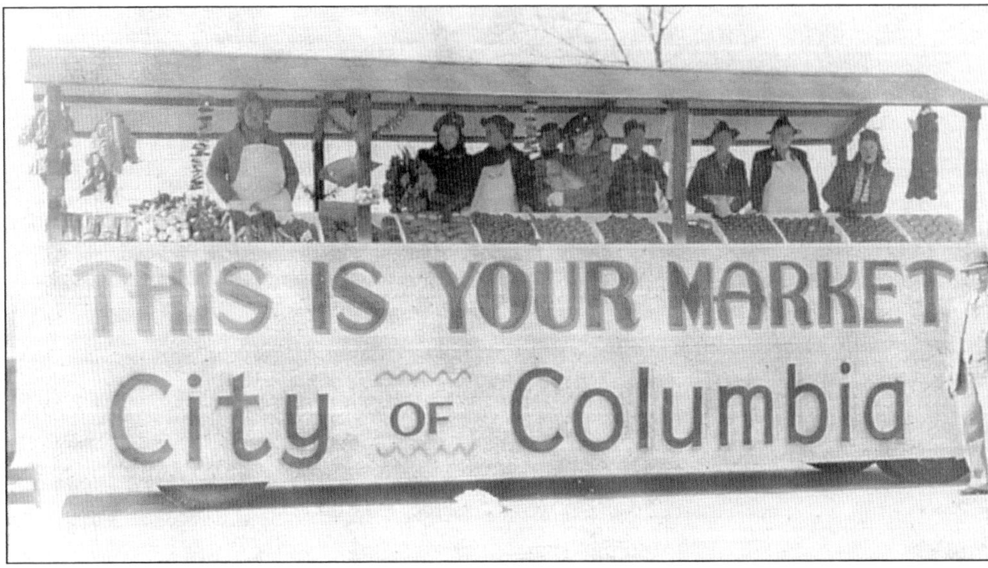

[This Is Your Market, City of Columbia, *c.* 1920.] This parade float placed on a flatbed truck displays some of the diversity of fresh produce that local farmers brought daily to the Assembly Street Market. The parade probably had floats from the City of Columbia departments such as the fire, police, schools, and other organizations.

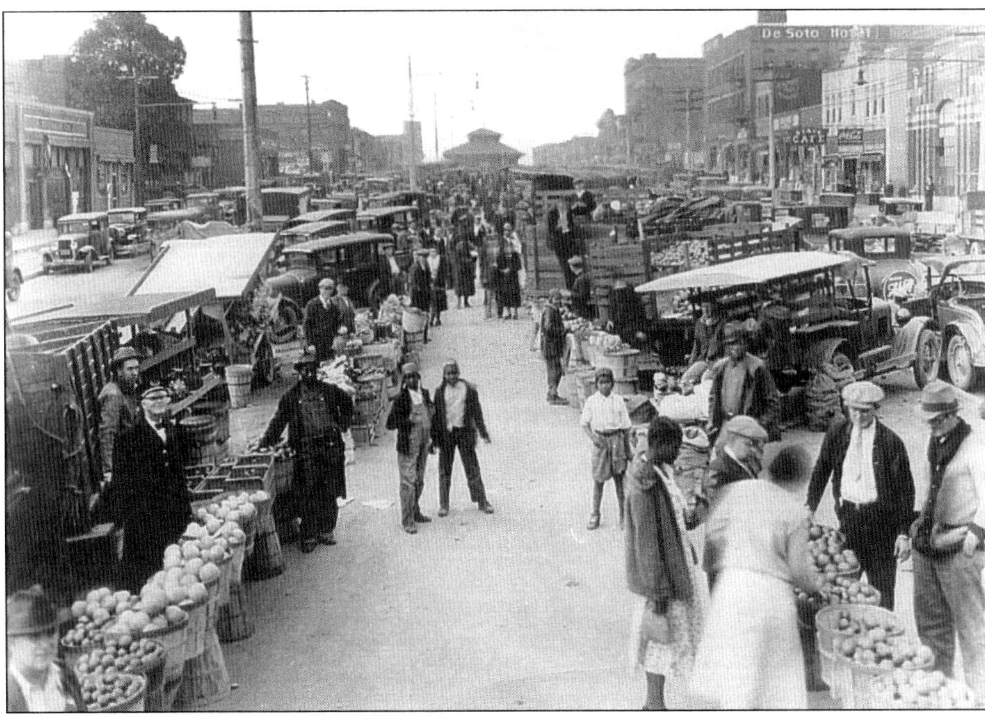

[Assembly Street Curb Market, *c.* 1930s.] Richland and Lexington County farmers continued the practice of parking their vehicles in the center of the street and selling their harvest from baskets beside their trucks. Many Columbia shoppers enjoyed the tradition of buying fresh produce at wholesale prices.

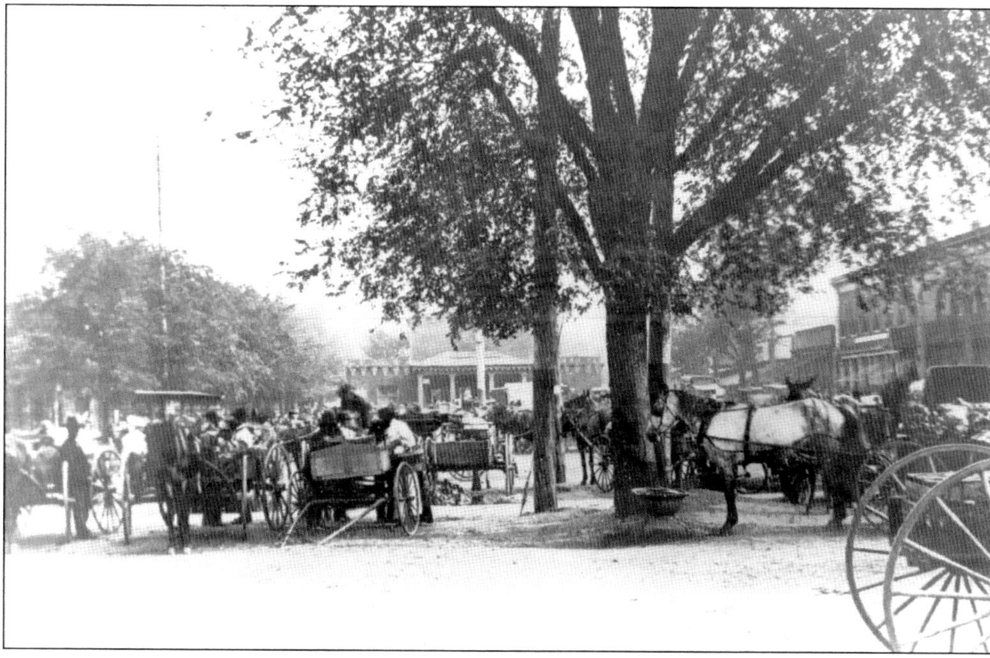

[Early Market Scene, *c.* 1910.] This reprint of an earlier image documents a turn of the century scene, when many families visited the Assembly Street market to buy their daily volume of fresh agricultural produce that would be carried home and stored in the ice box or pantry shelf.

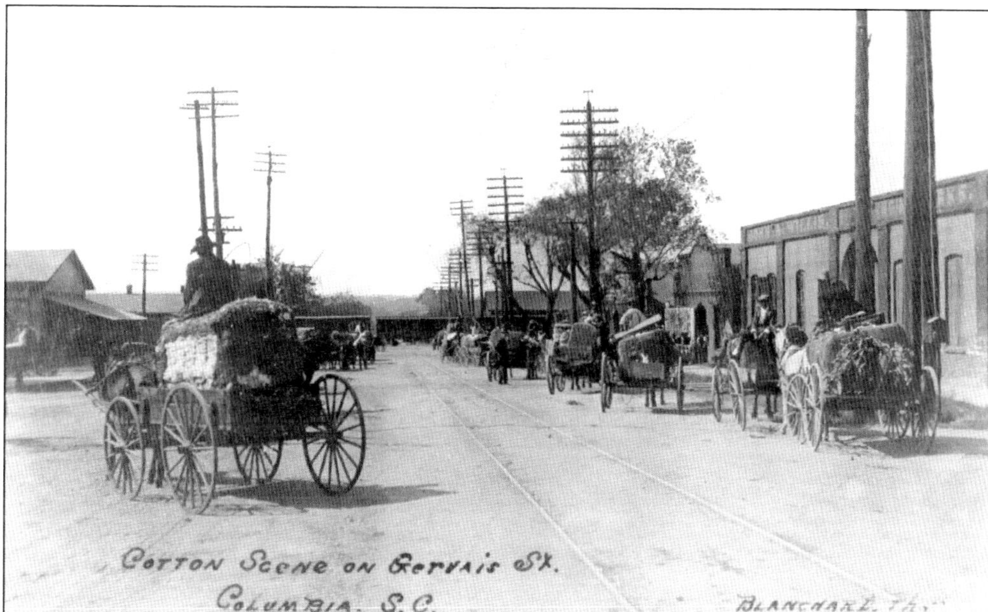

Cotton Scene on Gervais Street, Columbia, SC [*c.* 1910]. Columbia became a central market for cotton planters. Farmers would place their bales of cotton on wagons and take them to the cotton agents. This view looks down Gervais Street toward the box cars that block the street at the Seaboard Air Line tracks.

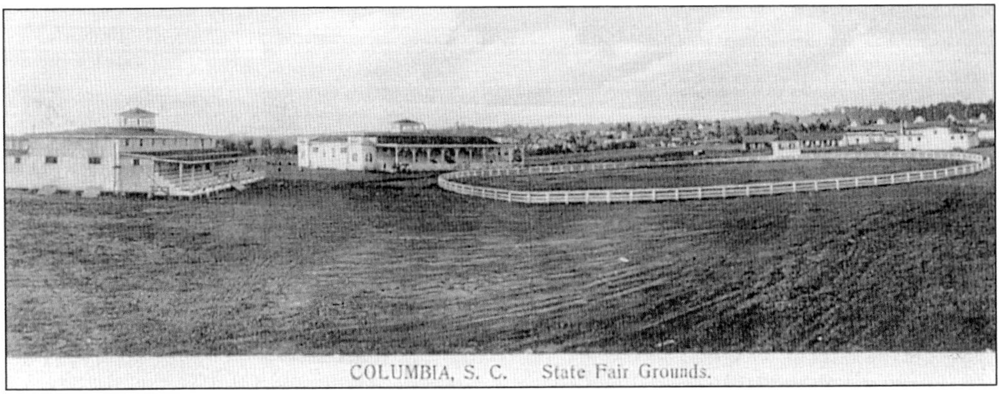

STATE FAIR GROUNDS, COLUMBIA, SC [C. 1907]. The first fair was held in 1869 on the Elmwood Avenue land where the Logan School now stands. In 1903 The State Agricultural and Mechanical Society of South Carolina, a private eleemosynary organization, decided this site was too small for future use and moved to a site off Bluff Road. This postcard shows the 1907 race track, stands, and facilities at the new fair site. In 1908 the society obtained the Steel Building from the Jamestown Exposition and it became the main building for exhibits. It was destroyed by fire in 1966.

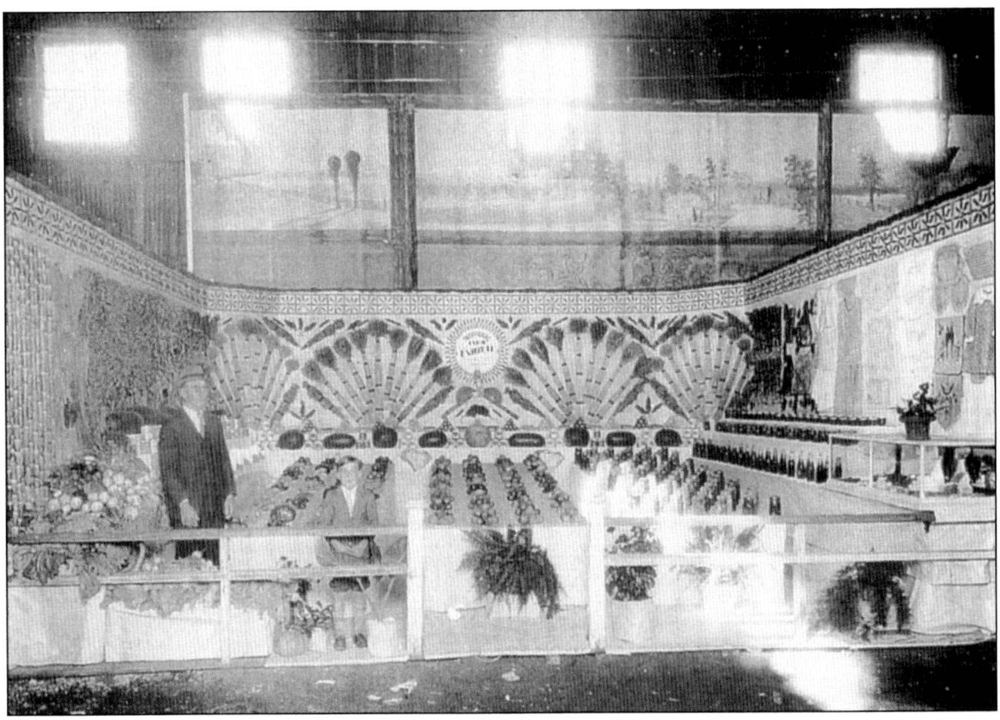

[INDIVIDUAL FARM EXHIBIT, *C.* 1930S]. W.A. Kleckley of Lexington County presented this exhibit in the Steel Building at a South Carolina State Fair in the 1930s. The annual fair is sponsored by The State Agricultural and Mechanical Society of South Carolina. Initially, the main events, activities, competitions, and prizes related to rural activities.

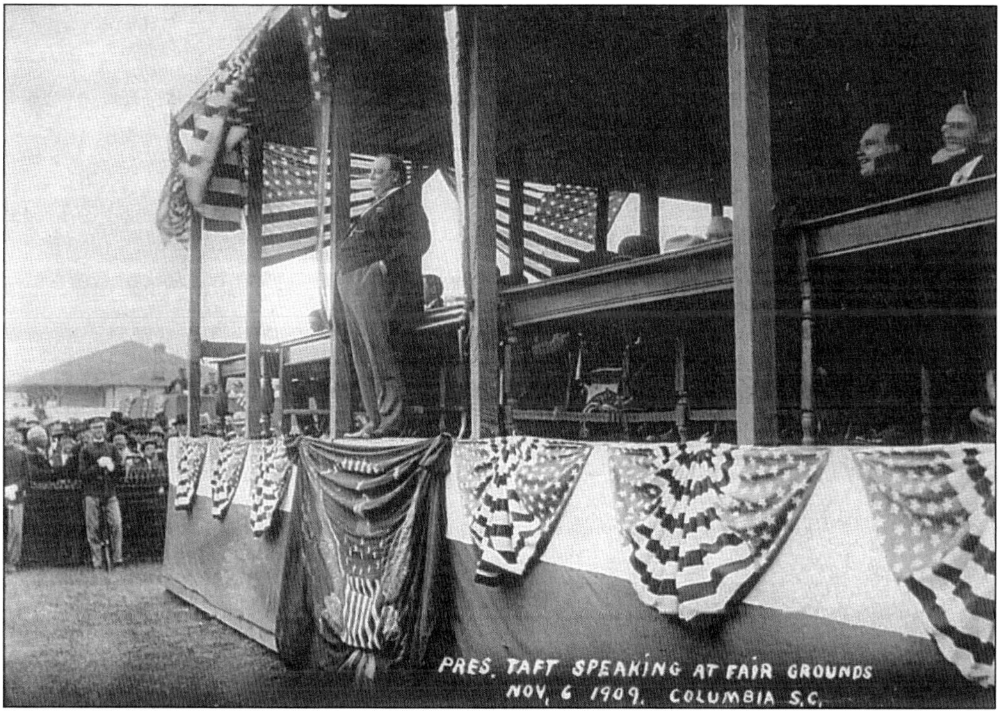

PRES. TAFT SPEAKING AT FAIR GROUNDS, NOV. 6, 1909, COLUMBIA, SC. Many political, religious, military, cultural, and educational visitors to South Carolina have used the fairgrounds as a venue for large public events.

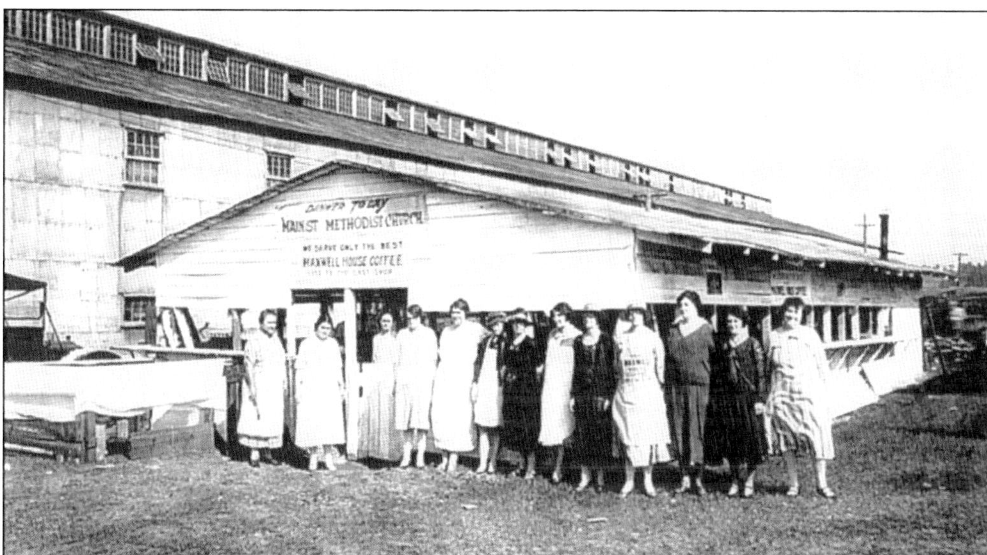

[SNACK BUILDING, STATE FAIR, c. 1920s.] The Main Street Methodist Church women, who served the community with various outreach activities, served refreshments at the annual state fair outside the Steel Building in the 1920s. The ladies making coffee and snacks included Mrs. E.C. Brown, Mrs. C. Gibson, Mrs. L. Newman, Mrs. W.B. Fulton, Mrs. A.J. Roberts, Mrs. G.C. Kirby, and Mrs. Boney.

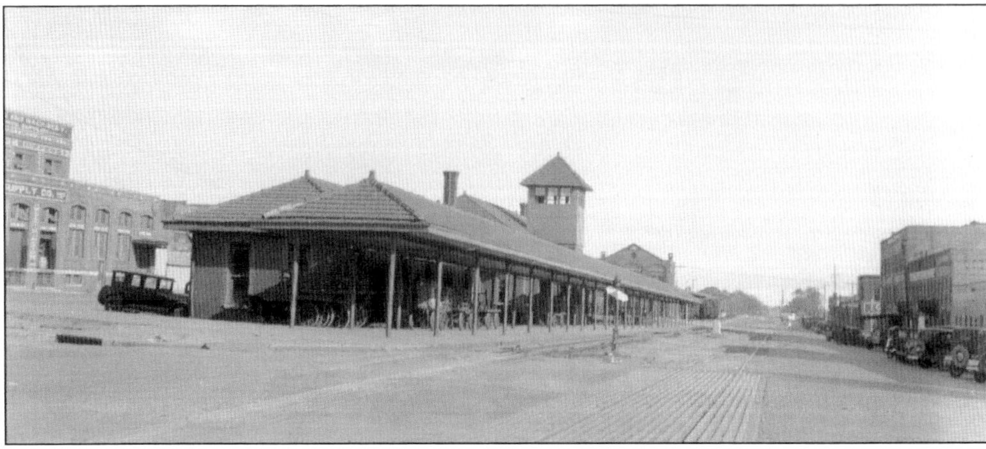

[SAL Station, Columbia, SC, *c.* 1930.] Columbia's railroad service from Charleston first extended to Gadsden and then to Hopkins. Columbia passengers ending at these "turnouts" needed to take a stagecoach ride to finish their trip. The first train to reach Columbia was in 1842, when the South Carolina Railroad crossed the Congaree River near McCord's Ferry and took the path later used by the Southern Railroad that connected Lower Richland to Charleston. The next improvement came in 1871 when the Wilmington, Columbia and Augusta Railroad completed the tracks from Sumter over the Wateree River, through the Wateree Swamp, and on to Columbia, which later became the route of the Atlantic Coast Line. The Seaboard Air Line Freight Office was built on Gervais Street in 1890. Their passenger depot, shown above at 1200–1230 Lincoln Street, was in use by 1905. In 2000, it houses restaurants.

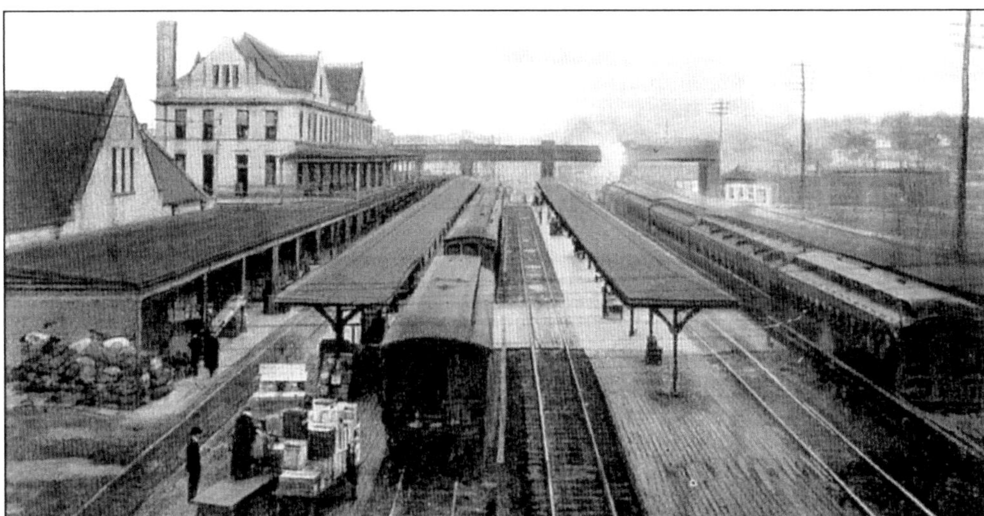

Union Depot, Columbia, SC [*c.* 1908]. This depot was designed by Frank P. Milburn of Charlotte and built by Nicholas Ittner Construction Co. of Atlanta in 1902. The Union Depot cost $150,000 and served both the Southern and the Atlantic Coast Lines. Columbia was situated on the main trunk lines with 65 trains entering and leaving the depots each day. By 1920, 11 separate lines intersected in Columbia, and over 200,000 freight cars loaded and unloaded annually. In 1972, railroads phased out passenger service. The depot still stands and is used as a restaurant.

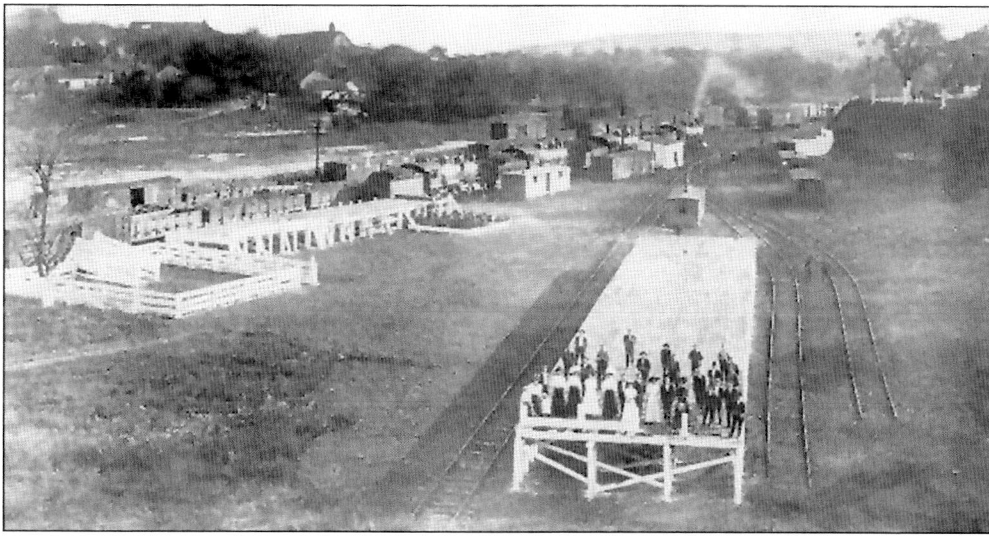

SEABOARD FREIGHT YARDS, OLD SIDNEY PARK, COLUMBIA, SC [*c.* 1910]. In the late 1840s, A. Sidney Johnston created a park by planting shrubbery and flowers and creating walking paths. The town council later named it Sidney Park. In 1899, the Seaboard Air Line Railroad claimed they needed the park for terminal facilities. When the park was destroyed, the railroad decided they did not need it, so they used it for warehousing activities.

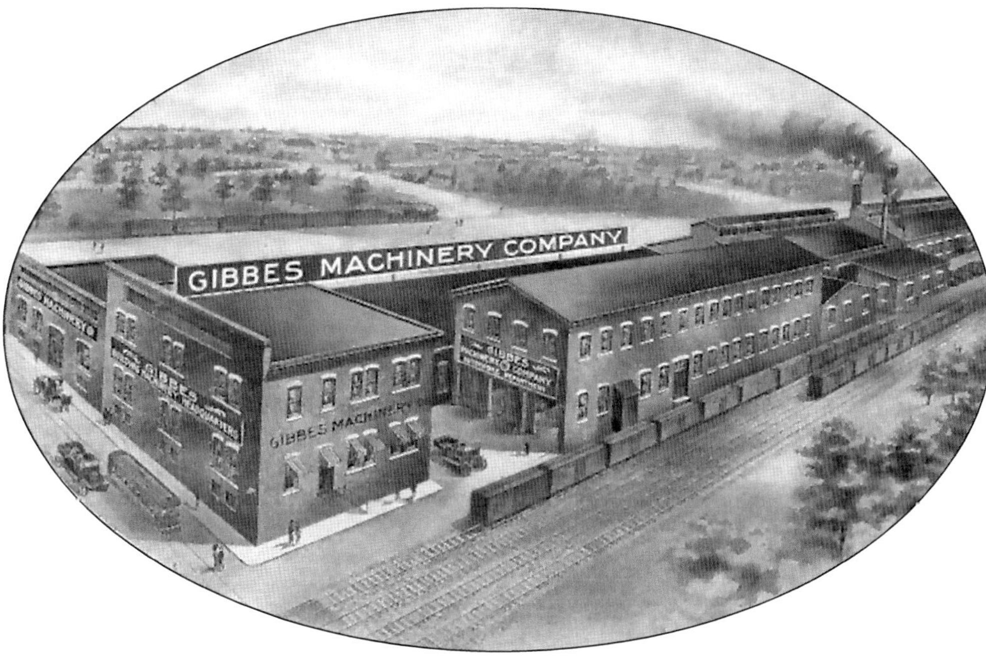

GIBBES MACHINERY COMPANY [*c.* 1913]. The Gibbes Machinery Company began selling machinery to the mills in the 1880s. Later, they sold automobiles. In 1913, they built a foundry and machine repair shops on the corner of Assembly and Blossom Streets. They also sold many brands of cars including Packards, Volkswagons, and Mazdas. In 1975, they moved from this site and it was later purchased by the University of South Carolina. The buildings have been razed for a new Strom Thurmond Fitness and Wellness Center.

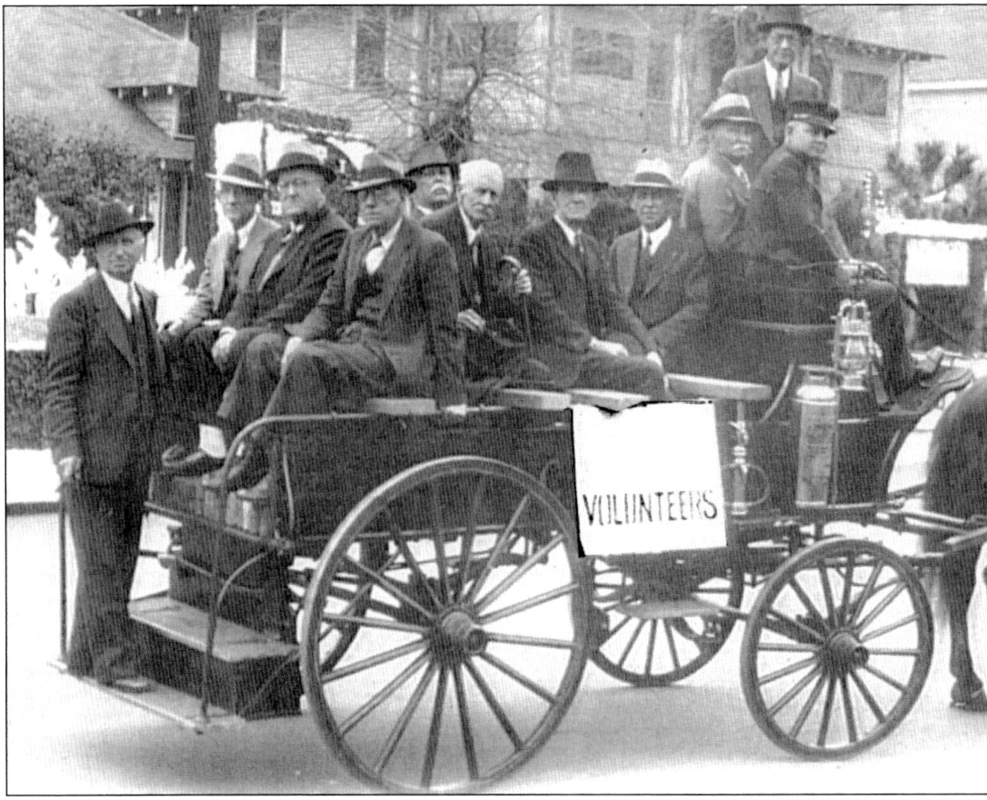

[Volunteer Fire Fighters, 1903]. These retired members of the all-volunteer Palmetto Fire Company were honored in a 1903 parade. They worked out of Blanding Street Station (1870s), which was likely built by William Byrd Stanley, president of the fire company from 1859 to 1888. In 1903, the volunteer firefighters were replaced by the first paid fire chief and 40-man crew.

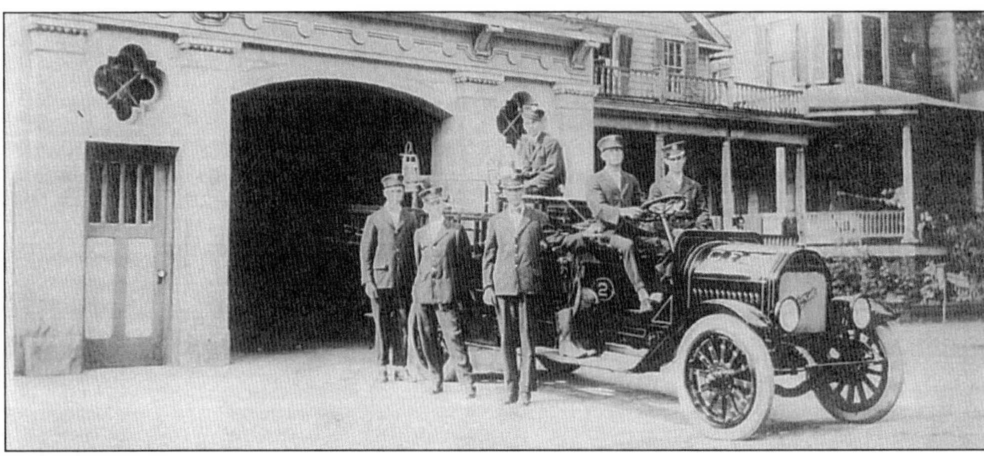

[First Fire Truck, 1917.] The first fire truck, a La France 750 g.p.m. pumper of the Palmetto Engine Company, was parked in front of the remodeled facade of the 1213 Blanding Street Station in 1917. The station operated until 1921 when the unit moved to the South Main Street Fire Station.

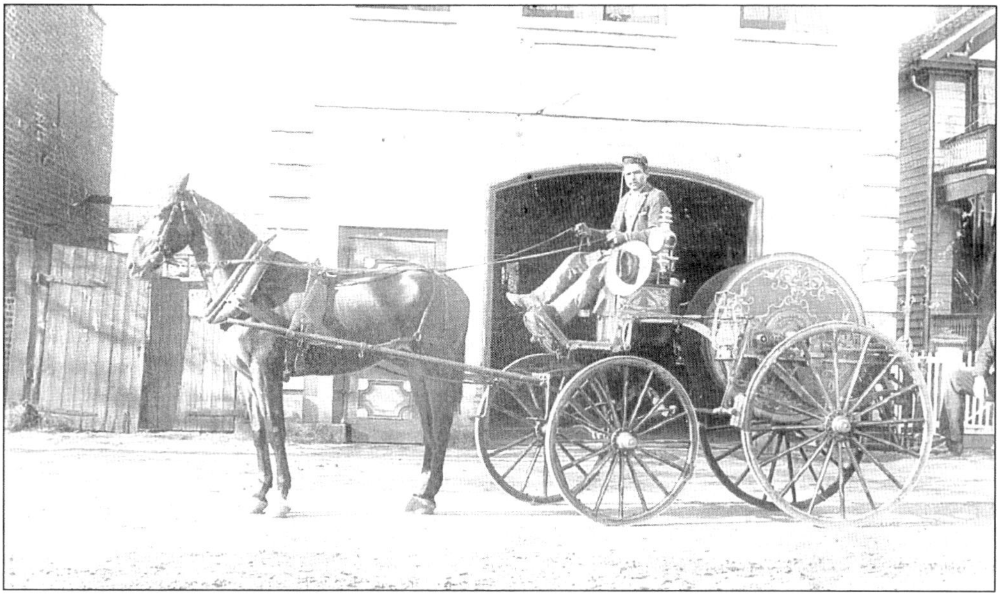

[**Horse-drawn Hose Reel Wagon, Fire Department, c. 1900.**] This Gleason and Baily Hose Carriage, obtained in 1890, was manufactured in Senneca Falls, New York. It was used for several decades, and in the picture above, it is in front of the 1213 Blanding Street Fire Station. The image reprint above was in use, *c*. 1907.

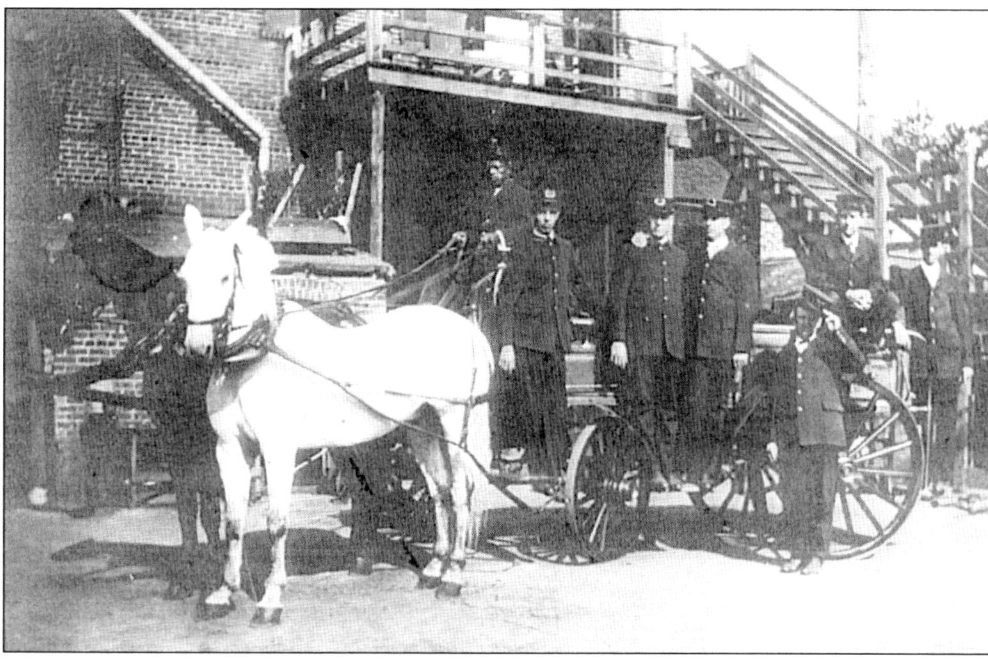

[**Horse-drawn Hose Wagon, 1908.**] By 1908, the fire department had a $25,000 annual budget for 3 stations—the Blanding, Lower Main, and Sumter Street Stations—equipped with 4 steamers, 1 hook and ladder, 4 hose wagons, 1 chemical engine, and 20 horses, which were all a part of the Palmetto Engine Company. This horse-drawn hose wagon was photographed behind the 1213 Blanding Street Station.

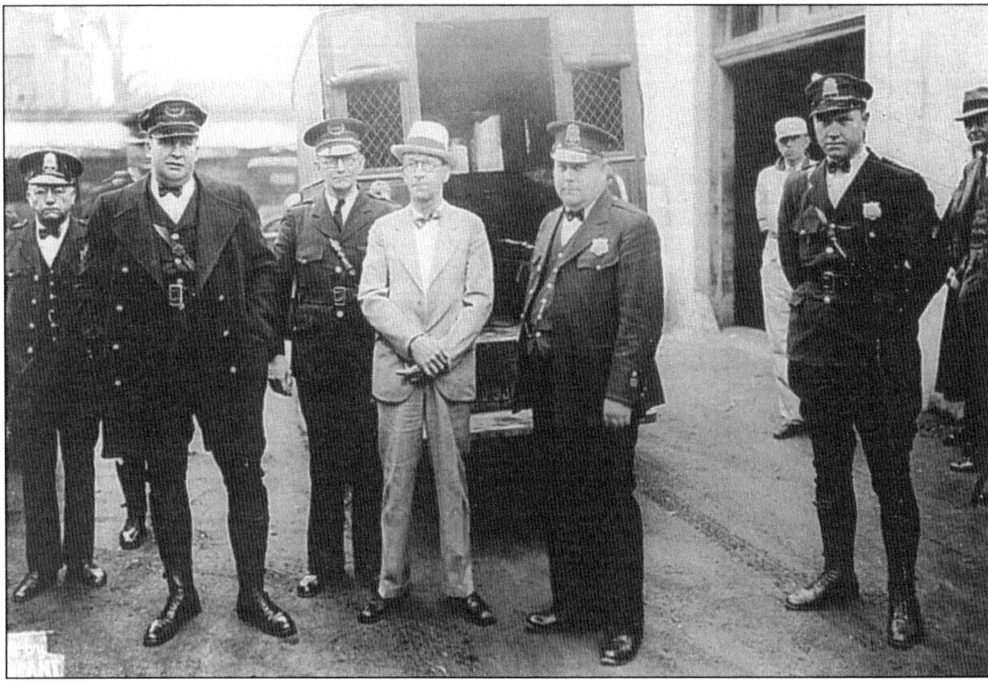

[Police and Prisoner Leaving the Old County Courthouse, 1934.] This image shows Robert H. Wiles, convicted of kidnapping and slaying Hubbard Harris Jr., standing by the patrol wagon at the back of the courthouse before being sentenced to die in the electric chair. Those police officers standing in the picture above are from left to right, unknown, C.K. Westcott, Sgt. E.D. Harrell, R.H. Wiles (prisoner), W.E. Helms (assistant jailer), and Chief L.J. Campbell.

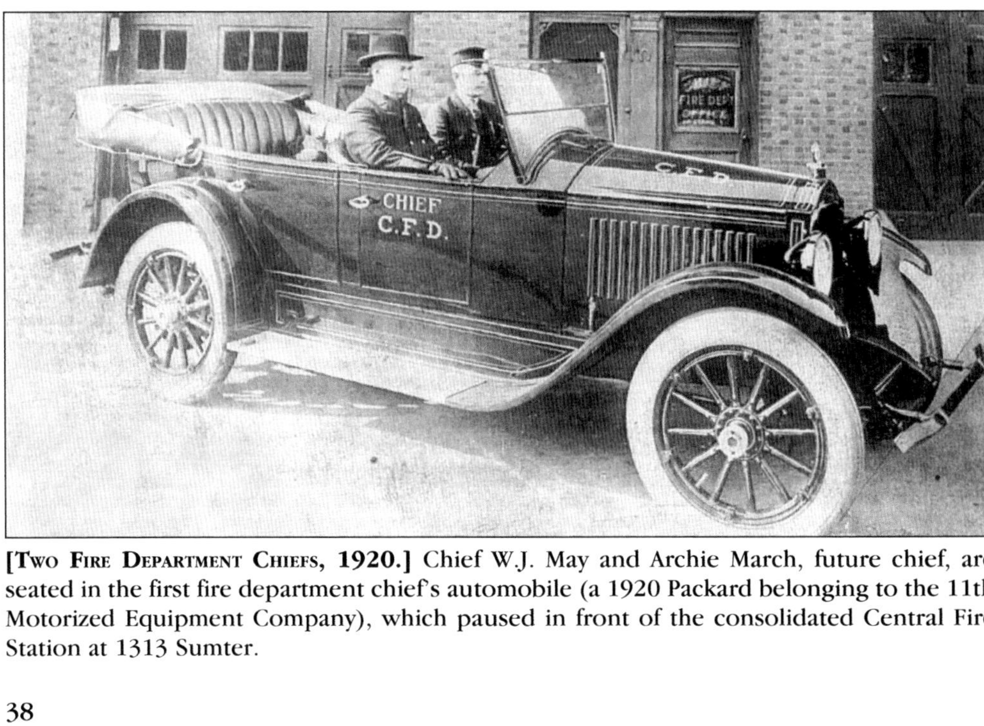

[Two Fire Department Chiefs, 1920.] Chief W.J. May and Archie March, future chief, are seated in the first fire department chief's automobile (a 1920 Packard belonging to the 11th Motorized Equipment Company), which paused in front of the consolidated Central Fire Station at 1313 Sumter.

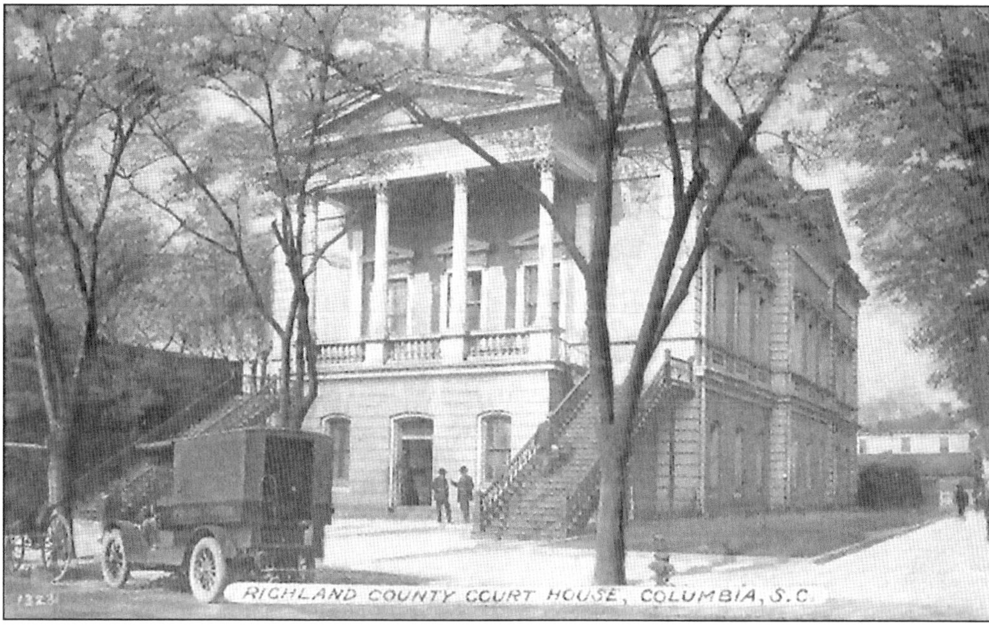

RICHLAND COUNTY COURTHOUSE, COLUMBIA, SC [1911]. The third Richland County Courthouse was erected in 1874 at a cost of $30,000 and was described as a handsome example of Corinthian-style Grecian architecture. This view from Washington Street shows the Sumter Street side. It was torn down in 1935 and replaced by the fourth courthouse. The city's first two patrol wagons were purchased in 1910. The 1913 sheriff was J.C. McCain.

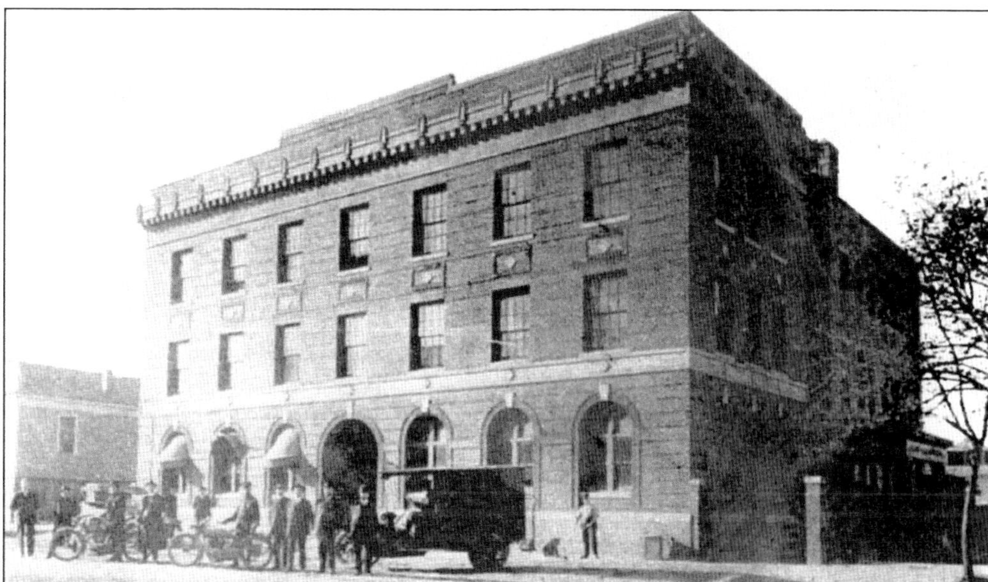

[COLUMBIA POLICE DEPARTMENT, 1914.] In 1908, the Columbia Police Department was on 1121 Gervais Street behind city hall. The building housed 45 policemen with an annual record of 4,800 patrol wagon runs, 5,000 arrests, and a budget of $32,186. Lafitte & Lafitte designed a new jail house in 1913, shown above, which was built in 1914 on 1415 Lincoln Street. J.W. Richardson was chief from 1914 to 1921 and Marion Kramer was the chief jailer.

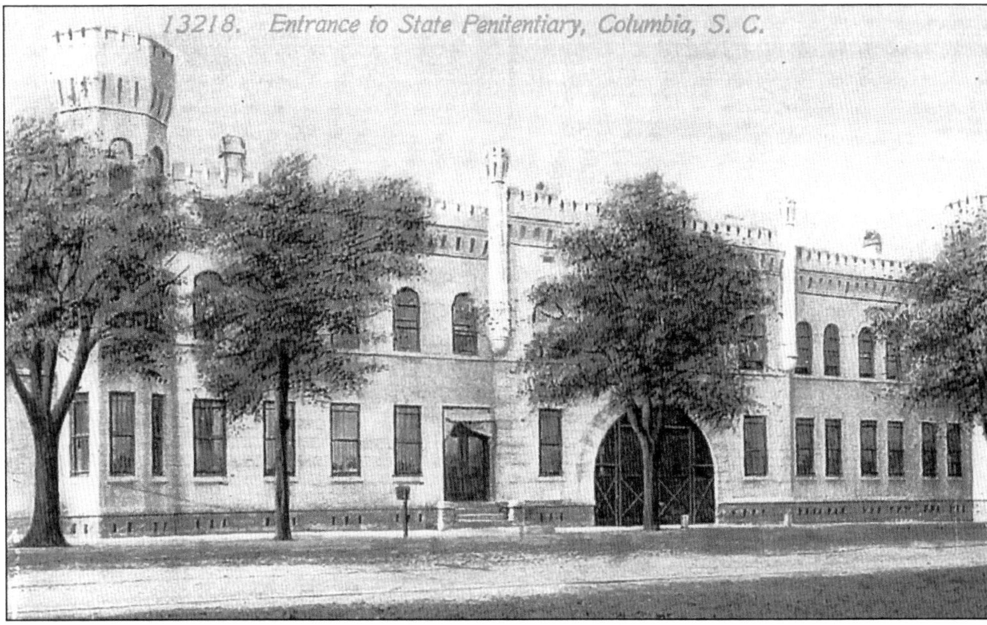

Entrance to State Penitentiary, Columbia, SC [*c.* 1907]. The General Assembly passed a State Penitentiary Act in 1866. Thomas B. Lee, architect, used convict labor in the granite quarries and prison work shops to construct the prison on 1515 Gist Street. Boundary walls were finished in 1882, and the west wing—a five-story granite structure— was completed in 1886. The administration building, shown above, and the east wing were finished later.

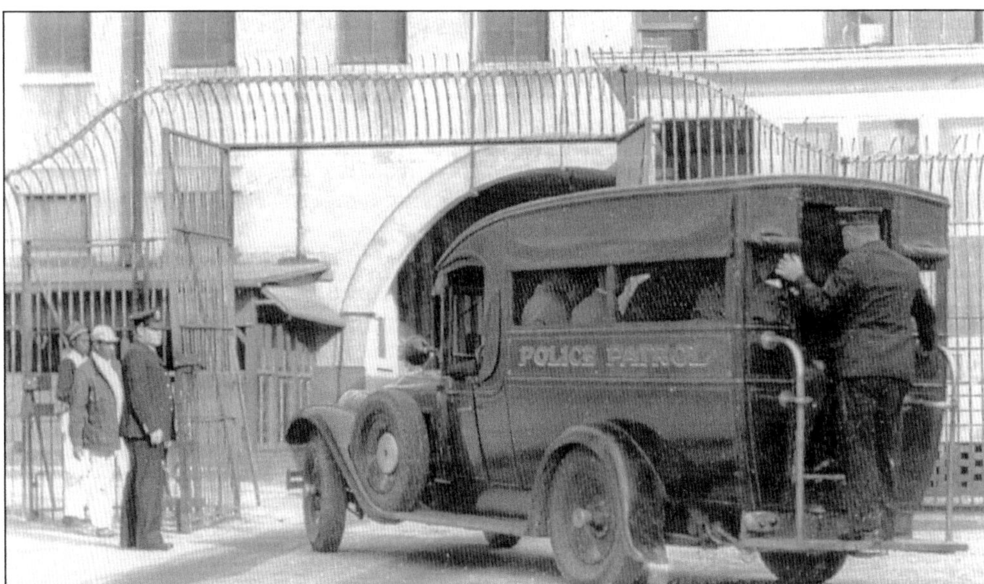

[Police Patrol Wagon, *c.* 1930s.] This view shows the police patrol entering the South Carolina State Penitentiary. The Columbia Police Department bought two automotive patrol wagons in 1910 to replace their horse-drawn vehicles. In 1915, the department had four horses and two motorcycles, with eight additional motor bikes obtained in 1917 to replace four bicycles.

Two

Views of Columbia Canal and Mills

The Columbia Canal became a significant industrial resource when it was redeveloped to produce electricity for mill and municipal use. Due to major industrial development, the city began to expand with new mill-village suburbs to its south and across the Congaree River in New Brookland for thousands of workers. By 1896, the Richland Mill had built homes for 400 employees on Wheeler Hill, inside the city limits. Olympia and Granby Mills had villages housing 1,500 workers in the southern area, while 1,500 employees of the Duck Mill lived in its New Brookland village. The average pay in 1902 was 75¢ for a 6 a.m. to 6 p.m. work schedule. Many new mill workers and their families moved to the mills in 1903, lured by the promise of jobs, steady pay, and a better life. By 1907, the six local mills had a payroll of $819,000 and employed 3,500 people. The mill district's population of 8,700 had 4,200 living in the city, which was 20% of Columbia's population and 33% of its white citizens. Columbia's cotton mills had a total of 237,056 spindles and 5,590 looms in 1908, consuming about 20,000 cotton bales annually. The conditions prevalent in mill villages inspired welfare work, educational reform, and progressive social campaigns.

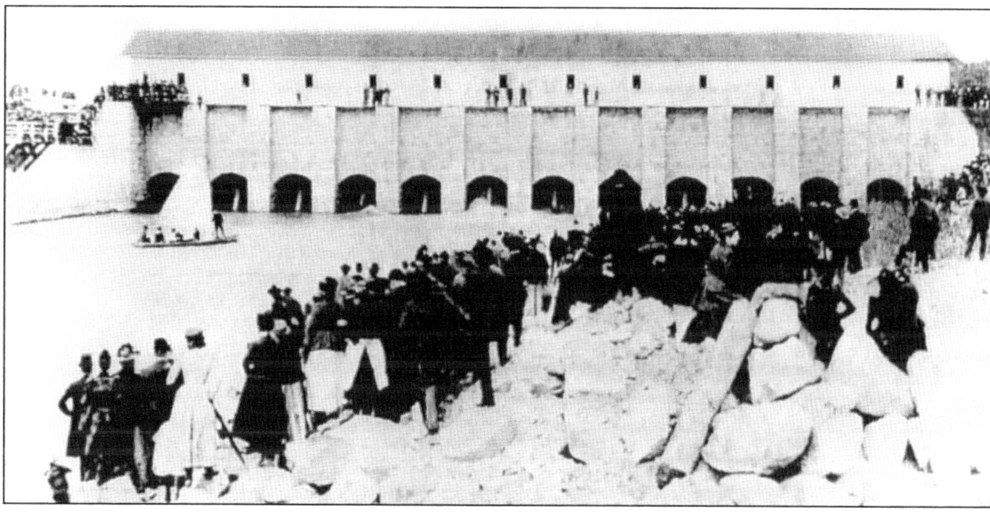

[Opening of the Locks, 1891.] The Columbia Canal opened in 1824, allowing river commerce to bypass the Congaree River's geographical fall line, but when railroad service connected Columbia to other regional towns, river traffic ceased. By the late 1880s, the idea of developing the canal for hydro-electric power was explored. This 1891 image shows the opening of the Columbia Canal, which was 150 feet wide and 10 feet deep, with its locks, gates, and wooden covered superstructure. The wooden structure no longer exists.

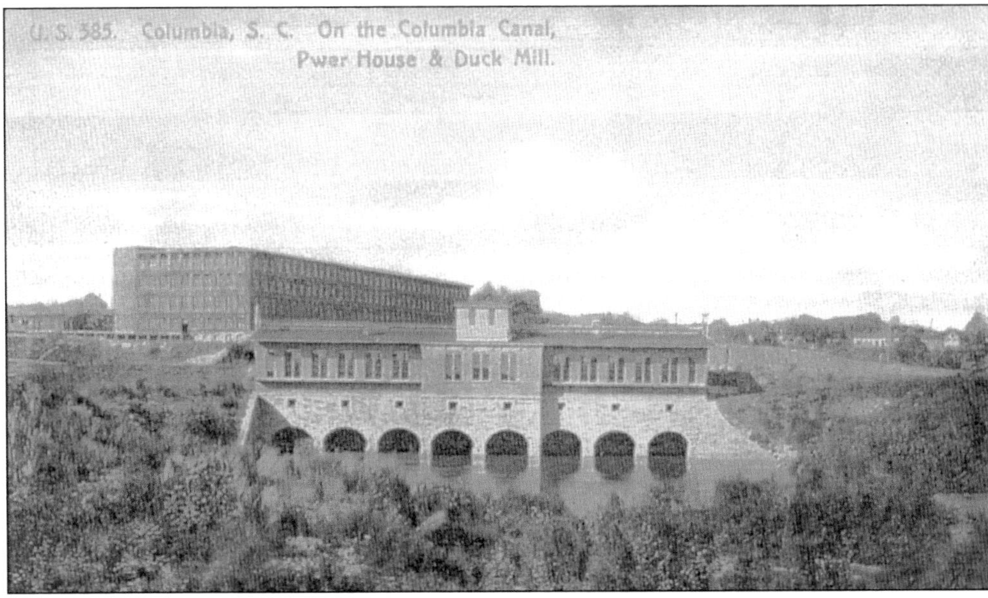

On the Columbia Canal, Power House and Duck Mill, Columbia, SC [*c.* 1908]. This view from the Lexington side of the Congaree River shows the hydro-electric powerhouse that was built in 1896. Its two 500 kw water wheel-driven generators would power seventeen 65-hp motors. The Duck Mill was the first mill to be operated by electricity. The electric power generated was used to run the street railway, for lighting the city, and for furnishing power to run the Duck Mill's 30,740 spindles and 498 looms.

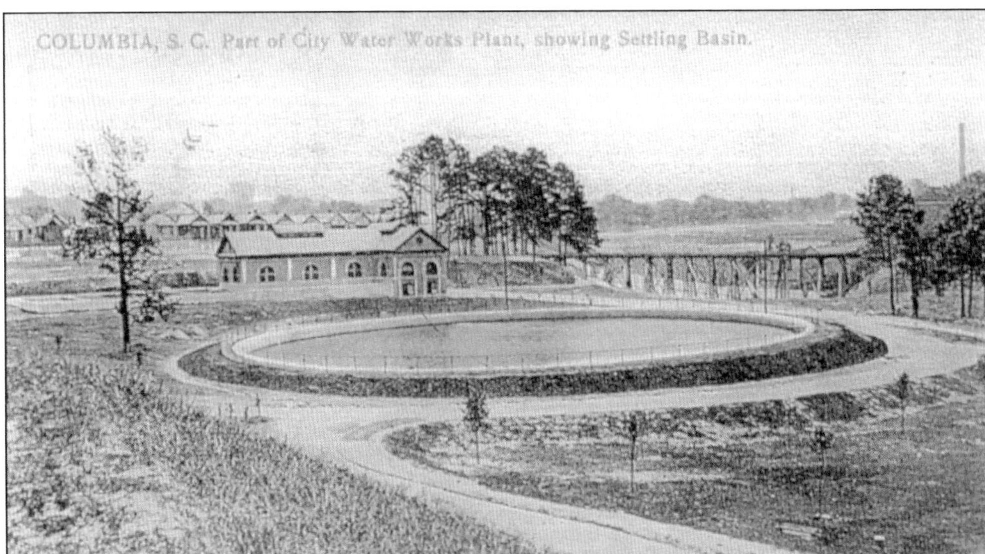

Part of the City Water Works Plant, Showing Settling Basin, Columbia, SC [*c.* 1908]. The first water works system opened in 1828 at a cost of $75,000 by Col. Abram Blanding. Unfortunately, it became a losing project and was sold to the city for about $25,000 in 1835. The city water works shown above was completed by January 1, 1907, at a cost of $400,000; in 1908, it had 42 miles of main pipelines with 240 fire hydrants. The sewer system had 32 miles of pipes and one station at a cost of $125,000.

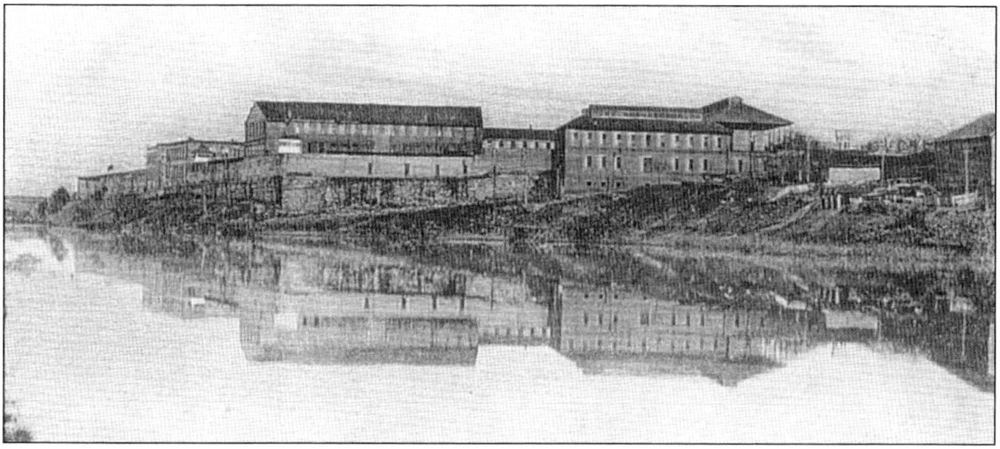

State Penitentiary, Columbia, SC [*c.* 1909]. This picture of the Columbia Canal shows the waterway and the back of the penitentiary with its reflection. The prison's work industries area was mainly next to the back boundary walls. They included a shoe factory operated by A.C. Dilbert, a broom factory operated by Lorick and Lawrence, a hosiery mill operated by Columbia Hosiery, and a chair factory operated by Fibercraft Chair Company. A 1932 fire destroyed the frame industrial building and a-third of the prison. The prison has been closed, the inmates moved, and much of the site razed in 2000.

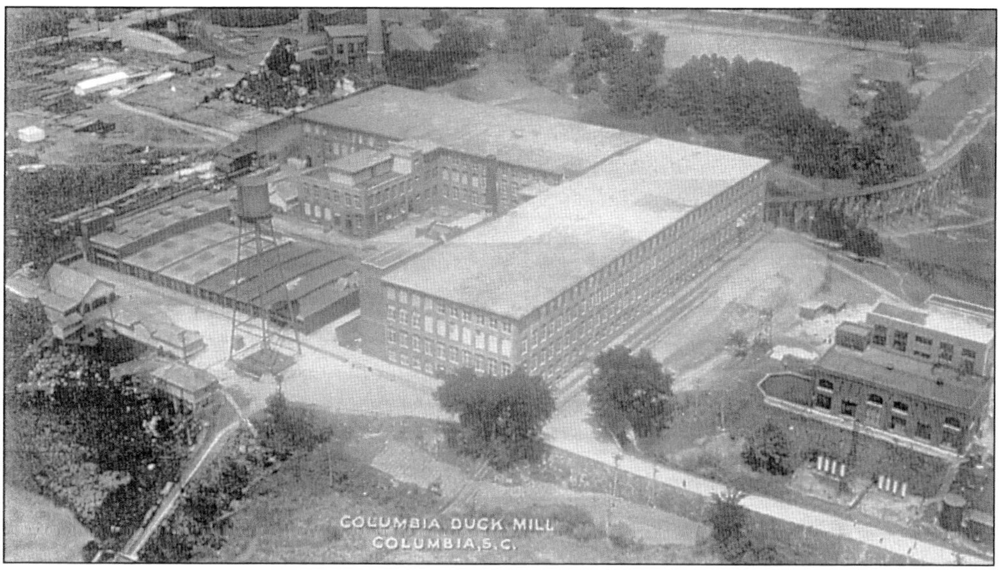

Columbia Duck Mill, Columbia, SC, [*c.* 1920s]. In 1893, Arethas Blood, president of Columbia Mills with a capital of $1 million—$700,000 for the mill and $260,000 for canal lock construction—began the mill construction with 300 workmen under the direction of S. Greene. The mill opened and employed 1,200 workers in 1894 and built a mill village across the Gervais Street bridge in New Brookland. In 1896, a new wing was added bringing the size of the mill to 325,000 square feet. Each day, the mill workers left the mill village in New Brookland, crossed the Gervais Street bridge to work at the Duck Mill, and returned to the village at night. Financial instability from the 1890s to the 1930s caused this mill and others to change ownership many times. The mill building now houses the South Carolina State Museum.

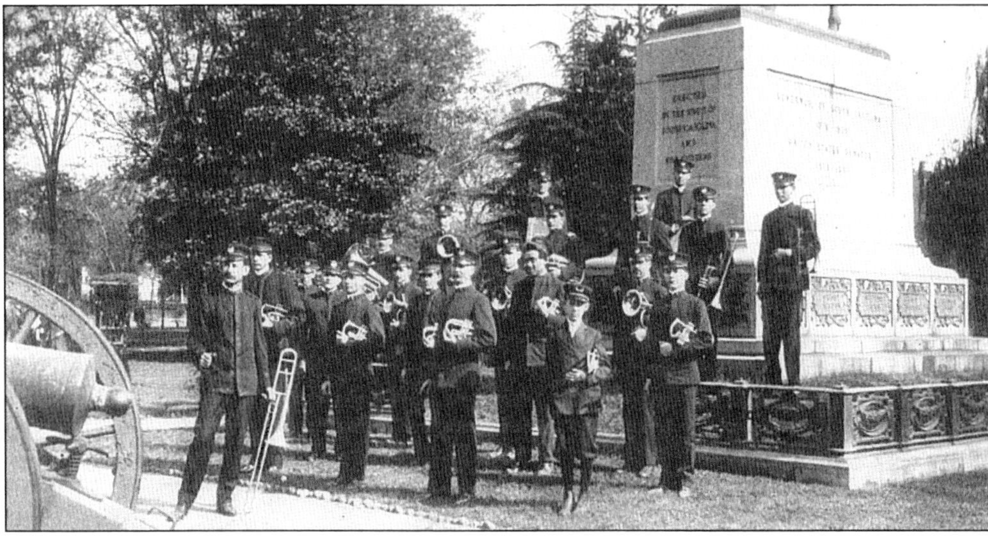

[Columbia Duck Mill Cornet Band, Duck Mills, Columbia, SC, 1913.] Annual labor day celebrations began in 1891 with parades, speeches, barbecues, and dances. The 1900 parade was supported by the local members of the National Union of Textile Workers, who assembled in a double-file line extending over a block long. In 1912, the Columbia Duck Mill workers' organized a cornet band that performed at city parades and entertained audiences at other venues.

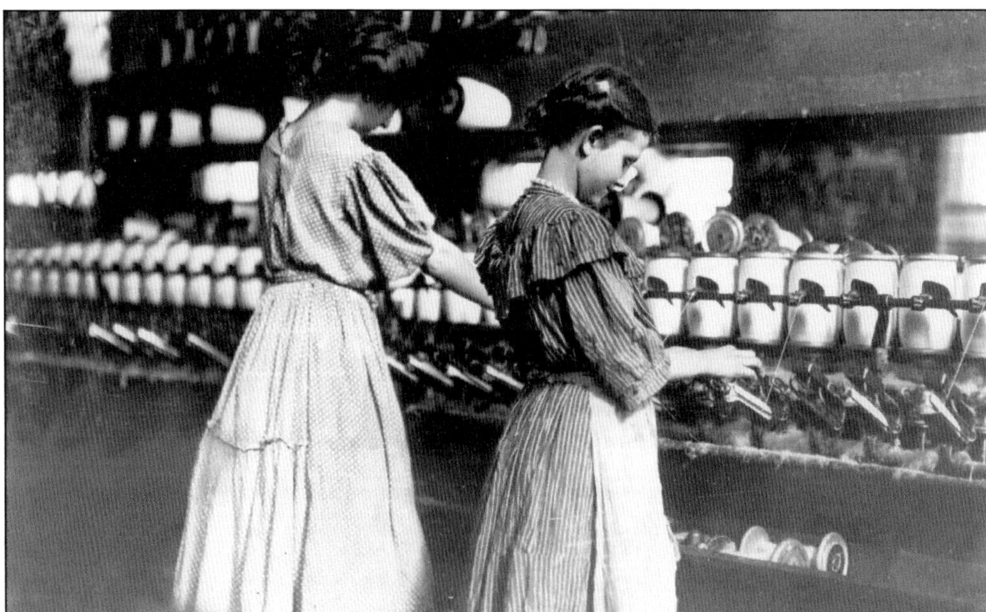

[Girls working in Cotton Mills, 1903.] The labor force of the cotton mills usually included young children in various hazardous work stations. Initially, South Carolina did not have child labor laws to protect the safety and health of those employees. In the view above, young girls worked in the spinning rooms of Olympia Mill in 1903; the mill had 104,000 spindles that moved at a speed of 9,000 rpm. The beginning wages for children was 60 cents a day.

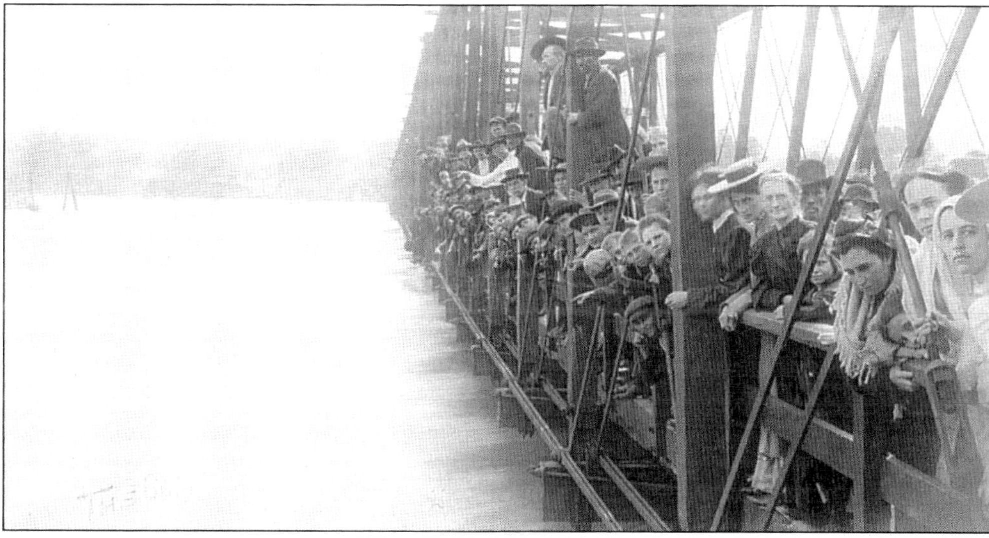

[Canal Bridge, 1908.] The Flood of August 27, 1908 was caused by a rain storm that lasted for days. The Congaree River crested at 35.8 feet. Fortunately, the Gervais Street and canal bridges withstood the deluge. Five people lost their lives and the flood caused $200,000 in estimated damages from railroad and public bridges being swept away, the repair of downed telegraph and telephone lines, and crop damage.

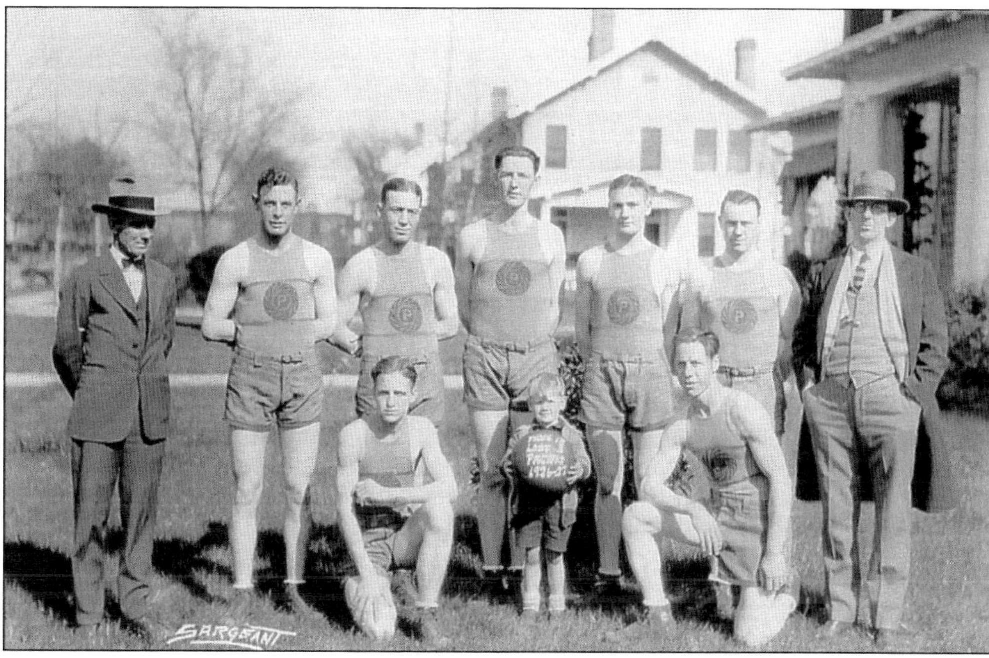

[Basketball Team, Pacific Mills, Olympia, 1927.] After working 64 hours per week, mill hands looked forward to Saturday afternoon ball games. Each mill fielded a team and played each other and other area teams in the Columbia City League. In 1909, Lewis Parker, the second manager, built a large YMCA with a gymnasium, a swimming pool, showers, pool tables, bowling alleys, and a theatre. Athletic activity grew in all sports including baseball, football, and basketball; the image above shows the 1926–27 basketball team.

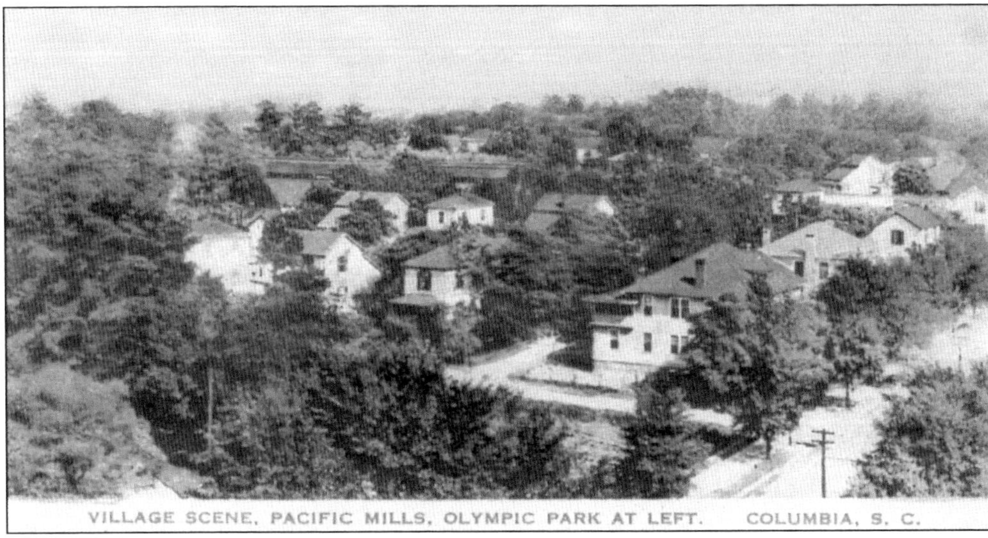

VILLAGE SCENE, PACIFIC MILLS, OLYMPIC PARK, COLUMBIA, SC [*c.* 1916]. W.B. Smith Whaley, the initial manager of Olympia Mills, erected a public hall, a library, and a school, and he contributed land for a church. Having a concern about malaria, along with a new interest in hygienic and health care programs in 1906, the management appropriated $25,000 from the Granby Mills for the drainage of a swamp behind Olympia and Granby Mills, built a sewerage system, and hired a trained nurse.

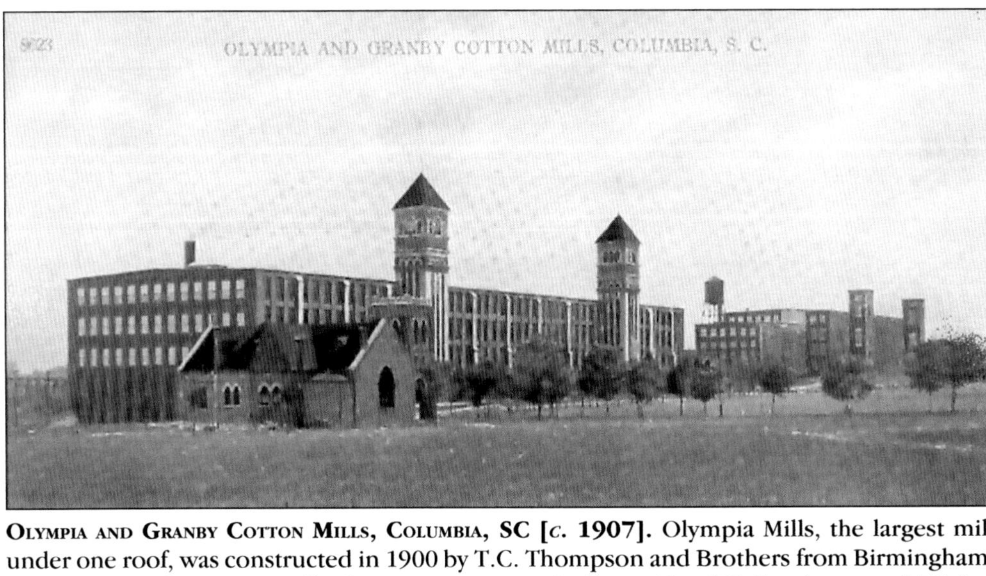

OLYMPIA AND GRANBY COTTON MILLS, COLUMBIA, SC [*c.* 1907]. Olympia Mills, the largest mill under one roof, was constructed in 1900 by T.C. Thompson and Brothers from Birmingham, Alabama. The four-story mills dimensions were 151 feet wide, 553 feet long, and 75 feet high with two front towers standing 140 feet high on 400 Heyward Street, a 104-acre site beside Granby Mills (1896). In 1907, Olympia Mills had 100,320 spindles, 2,250 looms, 1,000 workers, and a pay role of $246,000. Granby Mills had 57,000 spindles, 1,542 looms, 536 workers, and a pay role of $135,000. Olympia, Granby, Richland, Capital City, and Glencoe Mills, all created by Whaley, later became Pacific Mills due to financial problems. The Southside Baptist Church, left foreground, was organized in 1897; the initial sanctuary was built in 1901.

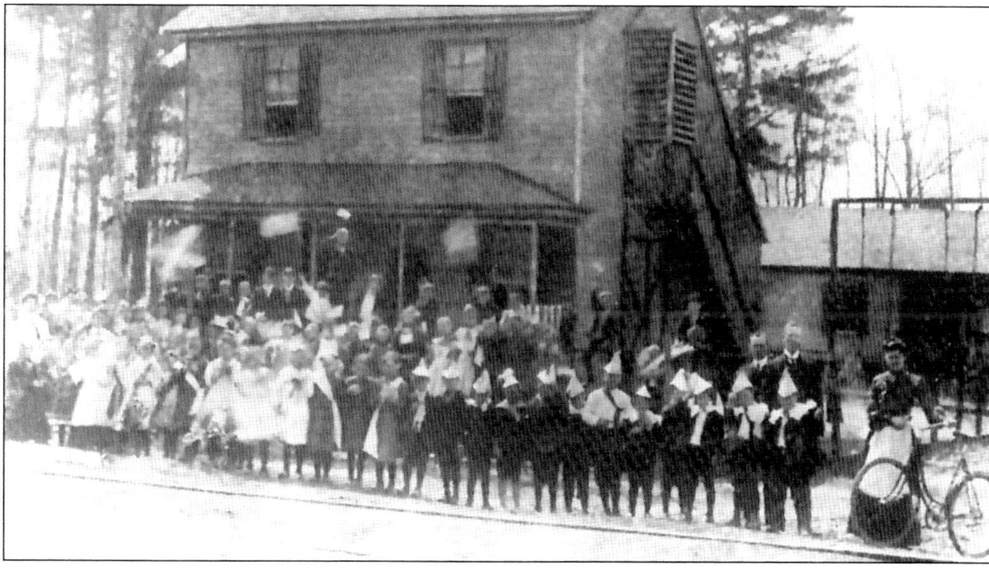

[Olympia School, 1903.] The school started in October 1901 with Miss Mamie Boozer, at right with bike, as its first teacher. Grades one through three were on the first floor, and grades four through six were on the second floor with outside stairs added for a fire escape. Miss Marion Means was an assistant. By 1905, enrollment rose to 115 students. The Olympia School District #4 included the adjacent county area to the south and east of Columbia. This initial residential-style school building still stands.

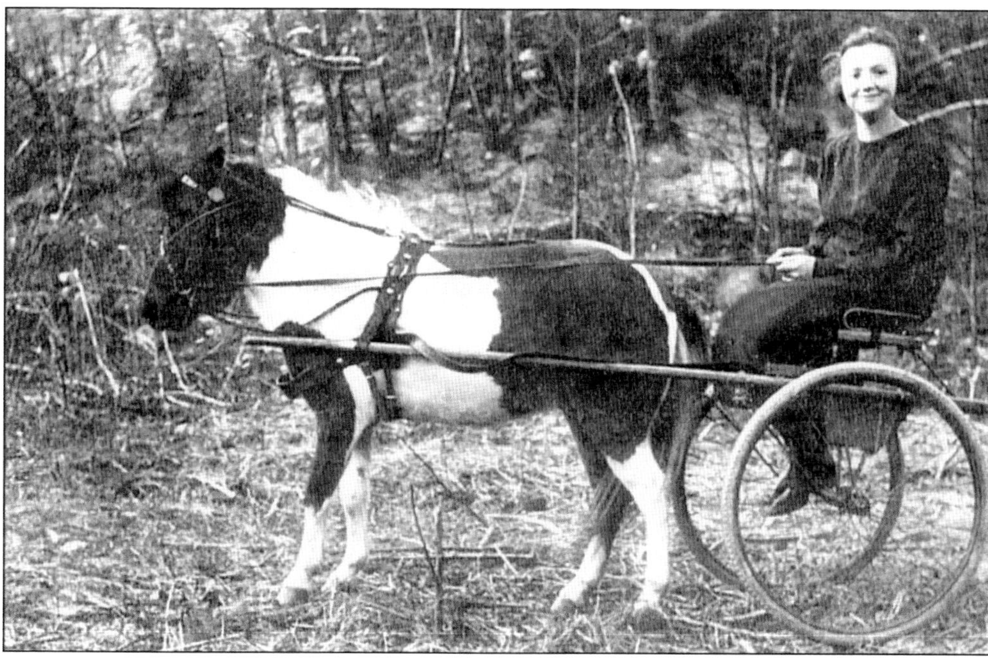

[Pony Cart, *c.* 1907.] A cart was an ordinary vehicle for short errands in small quiet neighborhoods like Olympia during this era. During the lean years before and during the Depression, this transportation was used in rural locations by families on the farms and in small towns.

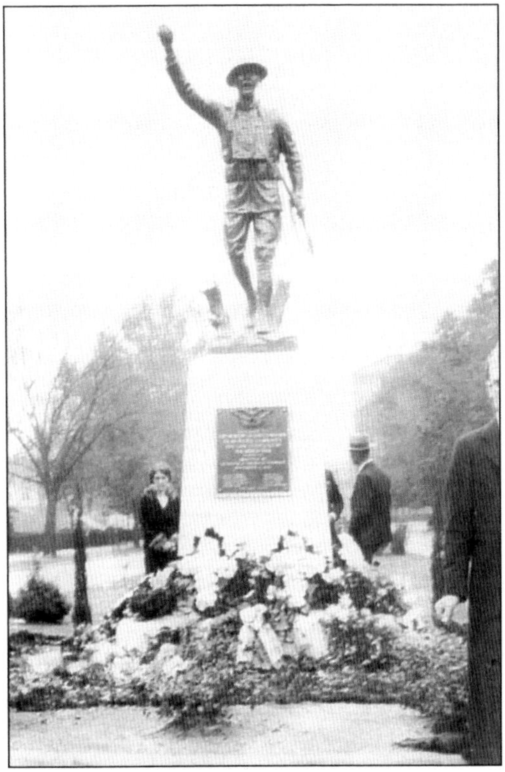

[Dedication of the Doughboy Statue, 1930.] Over 250 Olympia Pacific men saw action in World War I with 11 fatalities. Olympia village families raised $3,000 for a bronze statue, "The American Doughboy," that would honor those veterans. It was the first monument erected in the South by a mill village. The unveiling occurred on November 11, 1930 (Armistice Day) at the intersection of Wayne and Whaley Streets. A large crowd attended the ceremonies along with John G. Richards, governor, and Dr. L.B. Owens, mayor of Columbia.

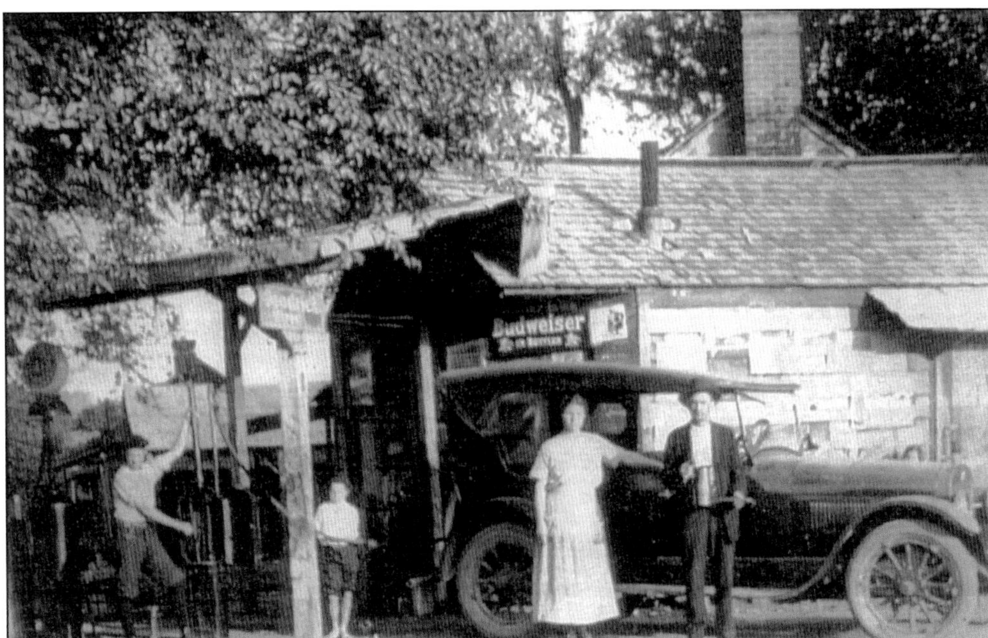

[Jaco Store & Gas Pump, Olympia Village, 1926.] Doyle J. Jaco operated the store on the corner of Olympia Avenue and Bluff Road until his death. It stocked standard and specialty items not carried by the mill store. He was an active member of the community.

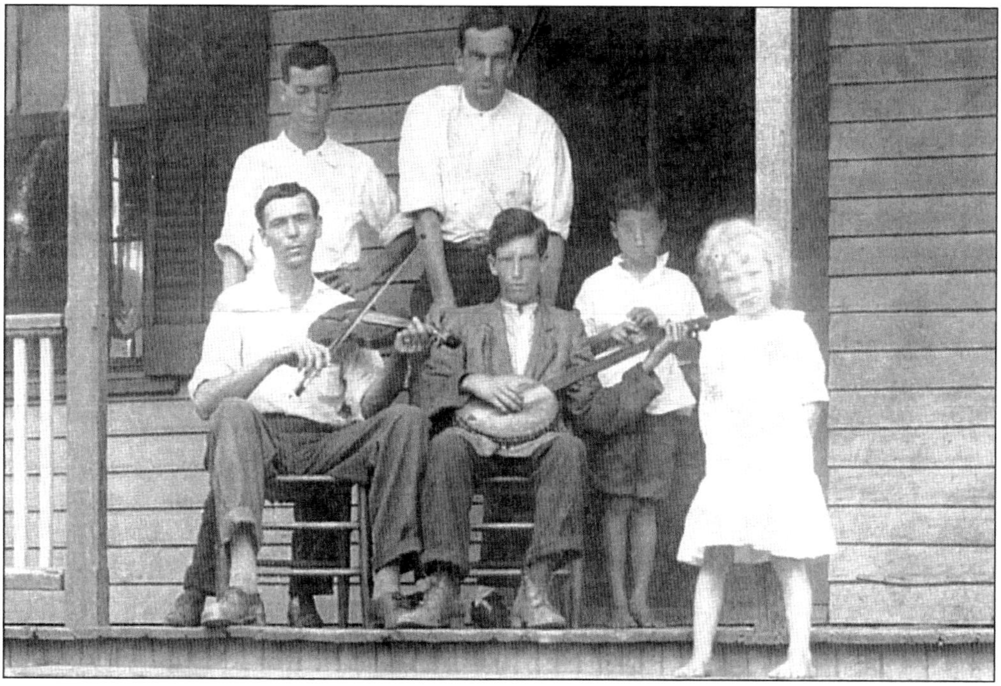

[Walter Webb and Friends, *c.* 1907.] In the early 1900s, farmers and other rural families left their financially depressed areas and migrated to mill villages in search of a more stable life. Walter Webb and friends sit on the front porch of a mill house in Olympia village, either entertaining themselves or practicing for an upcoming event.

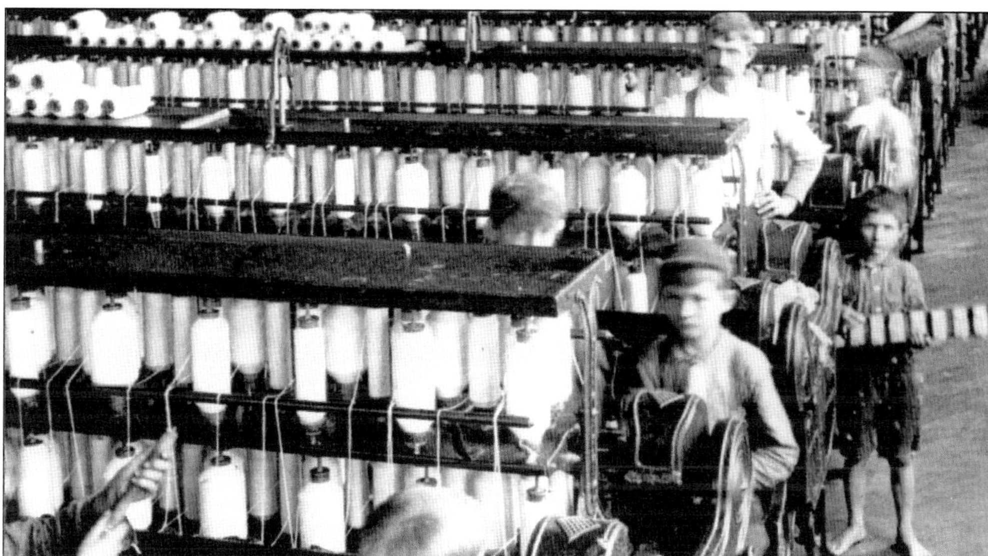

[Boys Working in the Spinning Room in Olympia Mill, 1902.] In 1902, children as young as five years old worked in the spinning rooms on work shifts lasting from 6 am to 6 pm. Legislators became concerned about it and passed "A Child Labor Bill," preventing children under age 12 from working in the mills and limiting the mill shifts to 10 hours per day. A lax enforcement of the bill allowed some boys to work 12-hour night shifts.

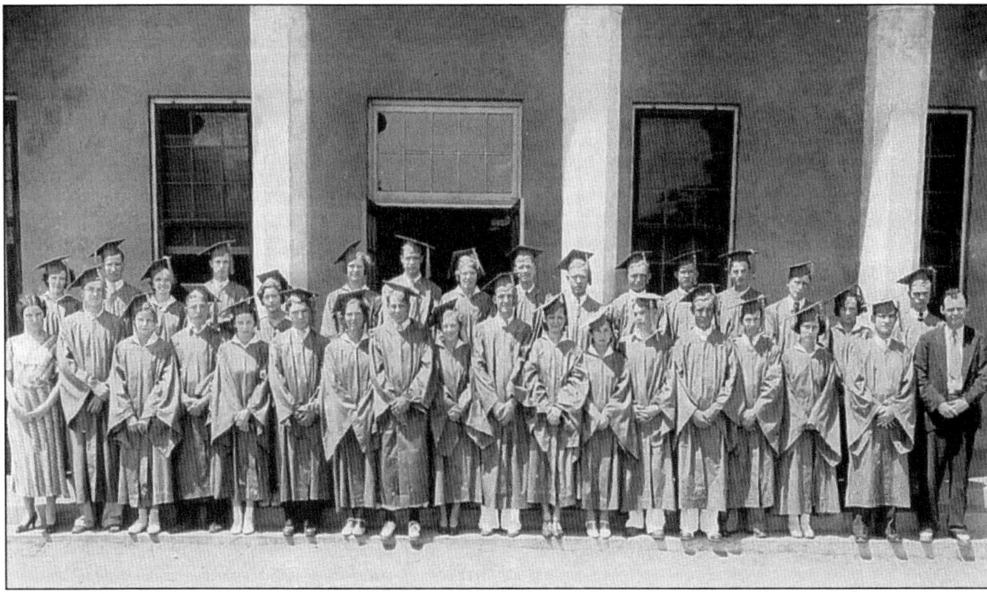

[GRADUATING CLASS AT OLYMPIA HIGH SCHOOL, 1933.] In 1910, the Olympia Grammar School had 8 classrooms, a library, and a principal's office. It had been built at a cost of $11,000 and housed 200 students. Wings were added in 1913 for $20,000, and in 1915 the school had 8 teachers and 533 students. A high school was built in 1925 at a cost of $67,000. The 1933 graduating class above had 33 eleventh-grade seniors and Mr. H.D. Lewis was principal.

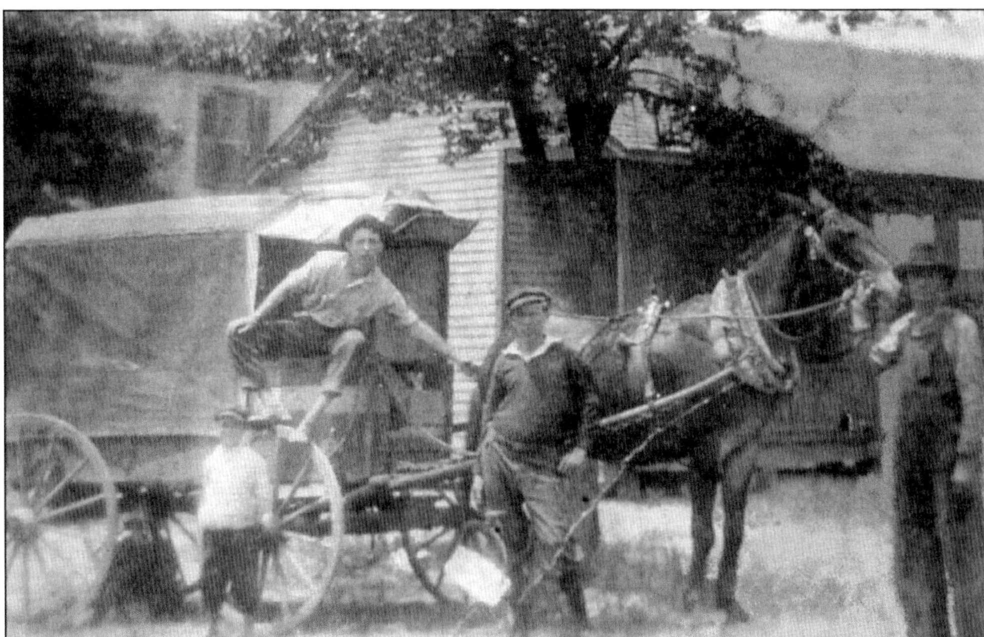

[JACO ICE WAGON., *c.* 1910.] Doyle J. Jaco was born June 17, 1908 in Huntsville, Alabama. The Jaco family came to live in the Olympia Village on Ohio Street. The father ran a small grocery and delivered ice to families in the village.

Three

CULTURAL VIEWS OF COLUMBIA

This chapter shifts to Columbia's social and cultural sides, and begins with postcards of the initial churches in the inner city. These images are followed by those of schools, colleges, and the University of South Carolina. Education has always played a significant role in preparing Columbia's children for their future, and in 1900 the county's public school system had 13 districts, 88 schools with 7,685 students (2,847 white and 4,838 black), and expenditures of $43,504. The initial city limits expanded during this era, and images of Eau Claire and Waverly and Shandon (1913) are contained herein. As the city evolved, the cultural climate reflected the artistic growth of the nation. The Opera House became a stage for national touring performances, while the Town Theatre highlighted the talents of local actors. Local painters traveled on an international level and displayed their art in Paris and London. In addition, the amateur and professional sports scene captured the attention of all of Columbia's society.

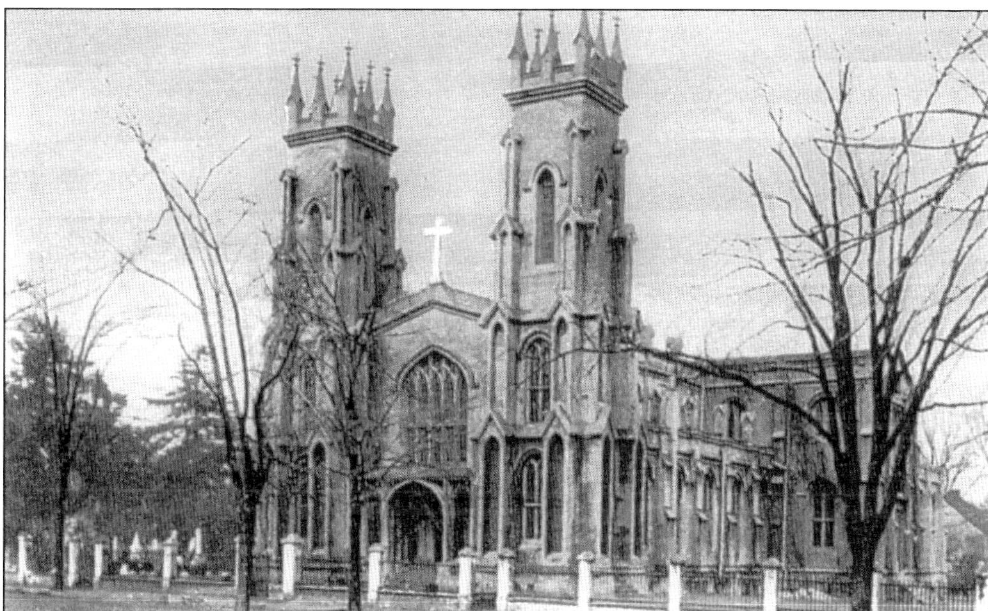

TRINITY CHURCH, COLUMBIA [1905]. Trinity Church at 1100 Sumter Street was organized in 1812. Col. Edward Brickell White was the architect and builder of this 1846 Neo-Gothic structure that uses "crossing" transepts and was designed after Yorkminster Cathedral. General Sherman spared the church in 1865. In 1900, the present edifice was finished.

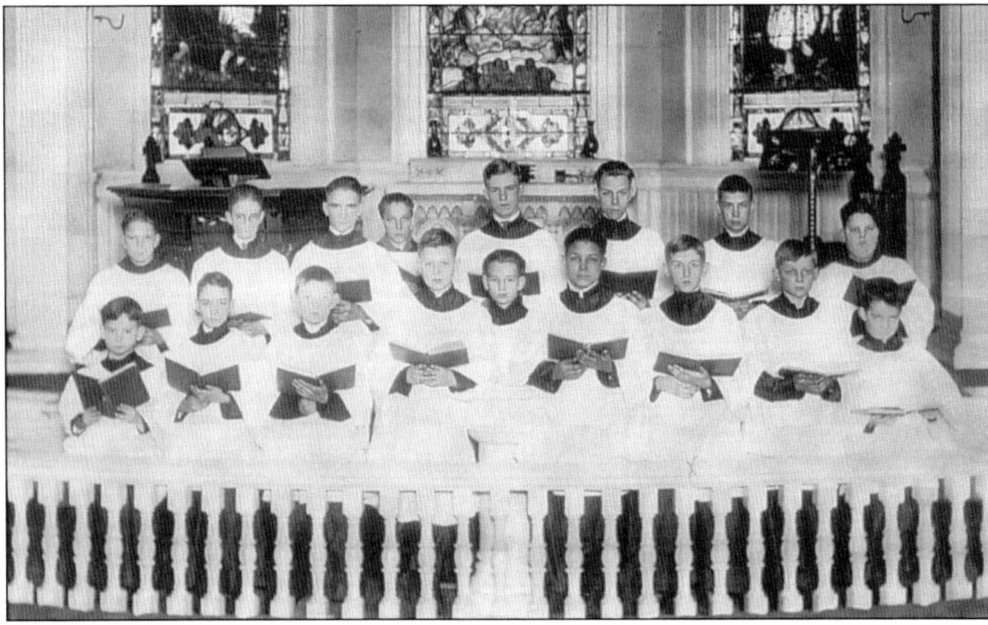

[Boy's Choir, Ebenezer Lutheran Church, 1930s.] This image of the boy's choir was taken in the choir's section, positioned in front of the church's stained-glass windows.

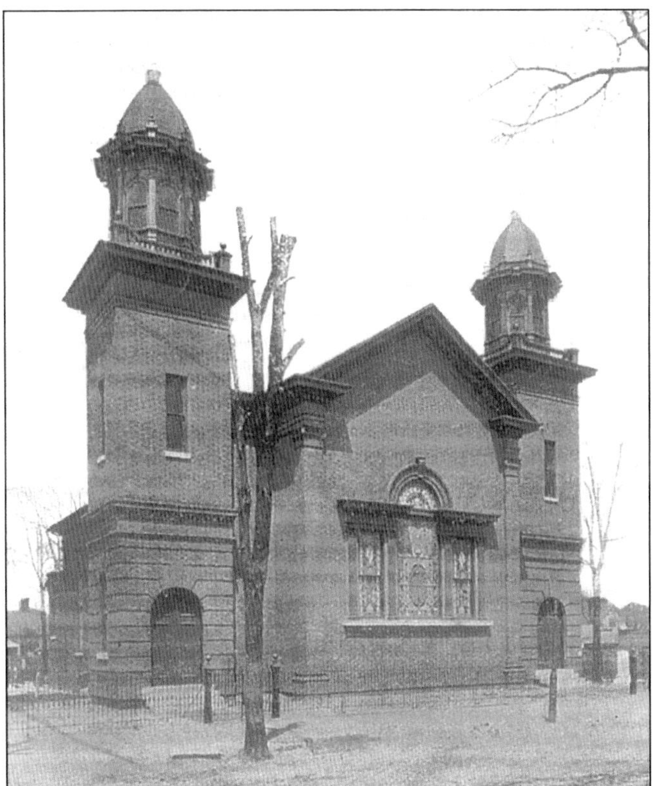

[Ebenezer Lutheran Church., Columbia, SC, *c.* 1920.] Ebenezer's congregation was formed in 1830 and a small brick structure was built that year. It was destroyed in 1865. In 1870, with the help of northern Lutherans, a brick edifice designed by G.T. Berg, the assistant architect for the State House, was built by G.C. Bell. Located at 1307 Richland Street, it had a seating capacity of 275. In 2000, the structure, without its twin cupolas, is called Friendship Hall and is used as a Richland County Senior Citizen's Center.

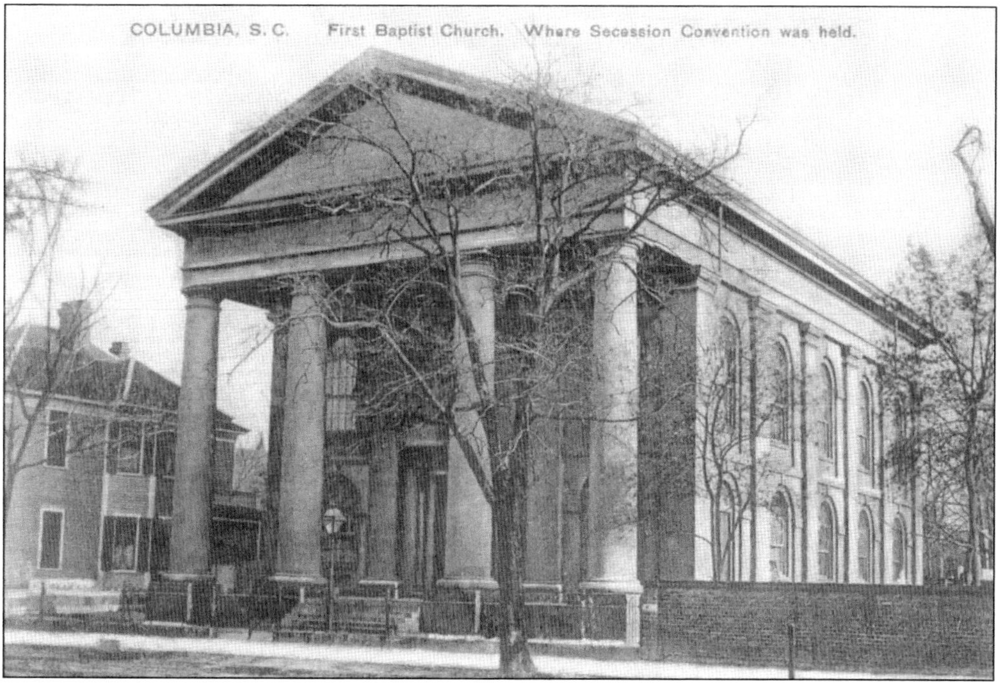

FIRST BAPTIST CHURCH, WHERE SECESSION CONVENTION WAS HELD, COLUMBIA, SC [*c.* 1907]. The First Baptist Church was established in 1809 with 13 members. Its initial edifice was a frame structure. The present brown brick building with four large Greek Revival columns at 1306 Hampton Street was completed in 1859. The architecture, with an interior slave gallery, was influenced by Robert Mills. On December 17, 1860, the South Carolina Secession Convention met in this hall to resolve the issue of secession from the union.

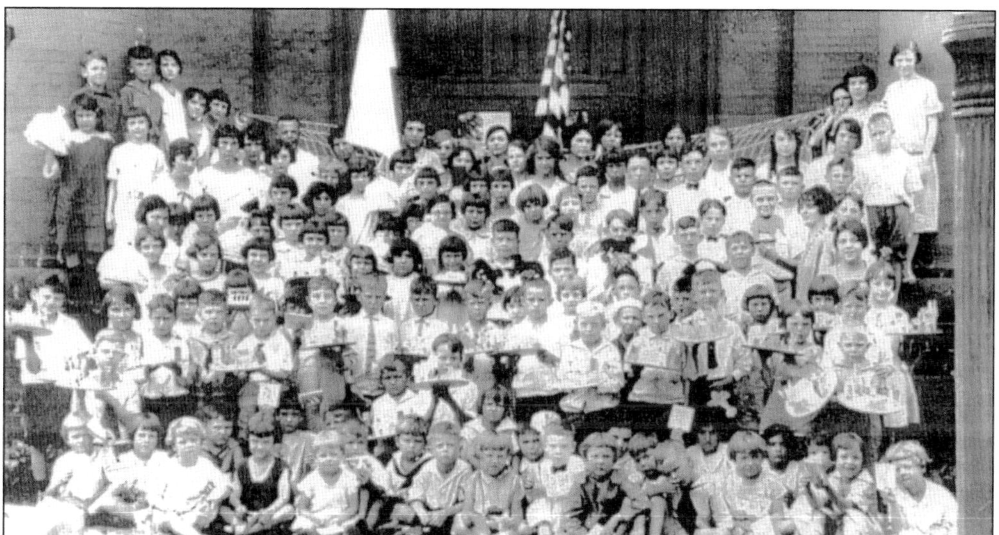

[VACATION BIBLE SCHOOL, FIRST BAPTIST CHURCH, *c.* 1930s.] This picture of the Vacation Bible School shows the young children and leaders of the congregation seated on the front steps of the First Baptist Church.

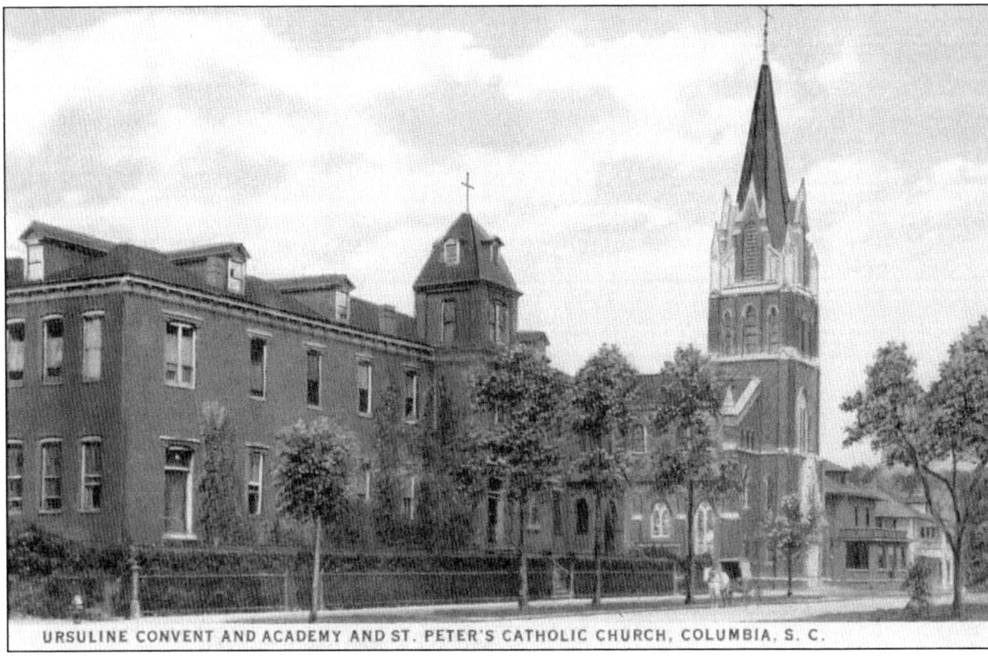

URSULINE CONVENT AND ACADEMY AND ST. PETER'S CATHOLIC CHURCH, COLUMBIA, SC, [*c.* 1909]. The Ursuline Convent opened in 1856 and was destroyed in the fire of 1865. In 1889, the Ursulines built their Victorian-style convent and school at 1513 Assembly Street by St. Peters Catholic Church. In 1908, the academy had 12 teachers, 82 residential students, and 22 others. The convent conducted classes on the ground floor until 1919, when St. Peter's Parochial School for boys and girls was built between the church and convent.

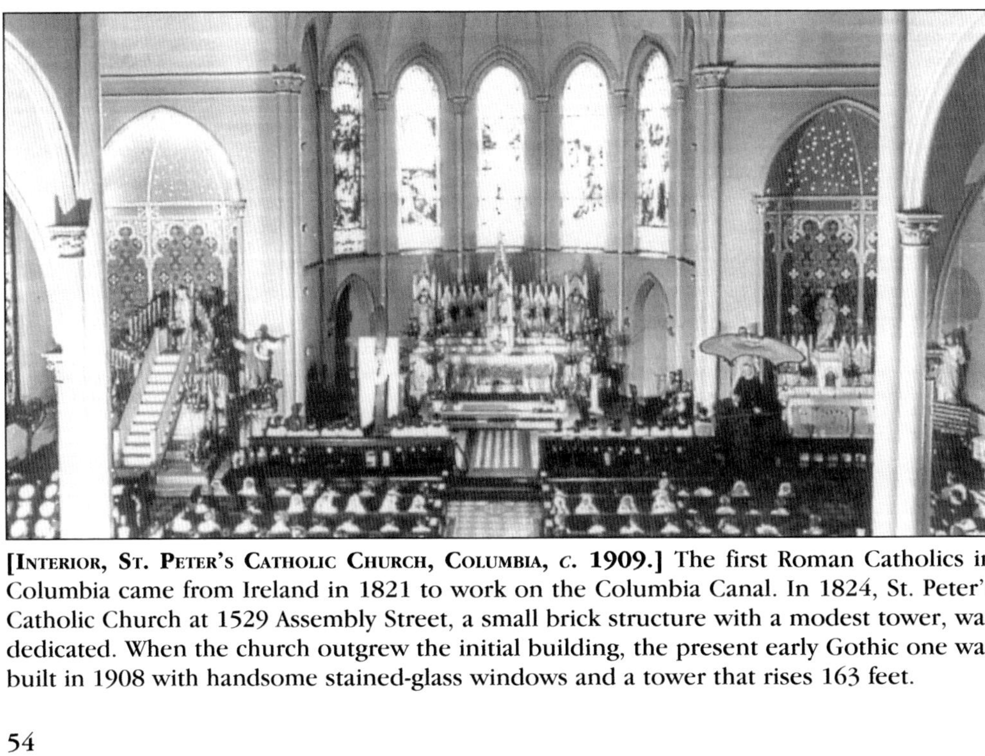

[INTERIOR, ST. PETER'S CATHOLIC CHURCH, COLUMBIA, *c.* 1909.] The first Roman Catholics in Columbia came from Ireland in 1821 to work on the Columbia Canal. In 1824, St. Peter's Catholic Church at 1529 Assembly Street, a small brick structure with a modest tower, was dedicated. When the church outgrew the initial building, the present early Gothic one was built in 1908 with handsome stained-glass windows and a tower that rises 163 feet.

First Presbyterian Church, Columbia, SC [1920]. The First Presbyterian Church was established in 1795, and the present structure was erected at 1324 Marion and Lady Streets in 1854. Its early English Gothic–style with rose beige stucco, pointed arches, and vaulted ceilings suggests that the possible architect was N.G. Starkwealter of Boston. The 188-foot steeple was blown down in 1875, and caught on fire in 1910.

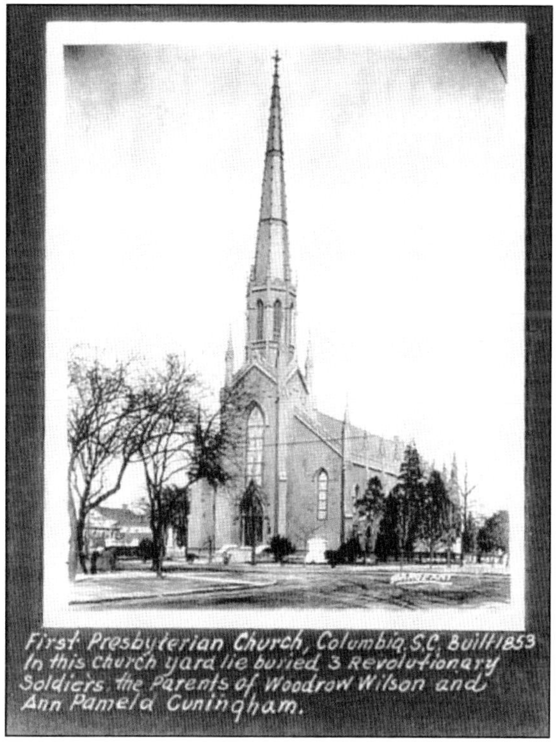

[Basketball Team, First Presbyterian Church, 1928.] The First Presbyterian Church's basketball team became the 1928 champions of the Basketball League of Columbia Churches. This team image was a popular one to enlarge and frame, or to print at postcard size, so that the families could mail them to friends elsewhere.

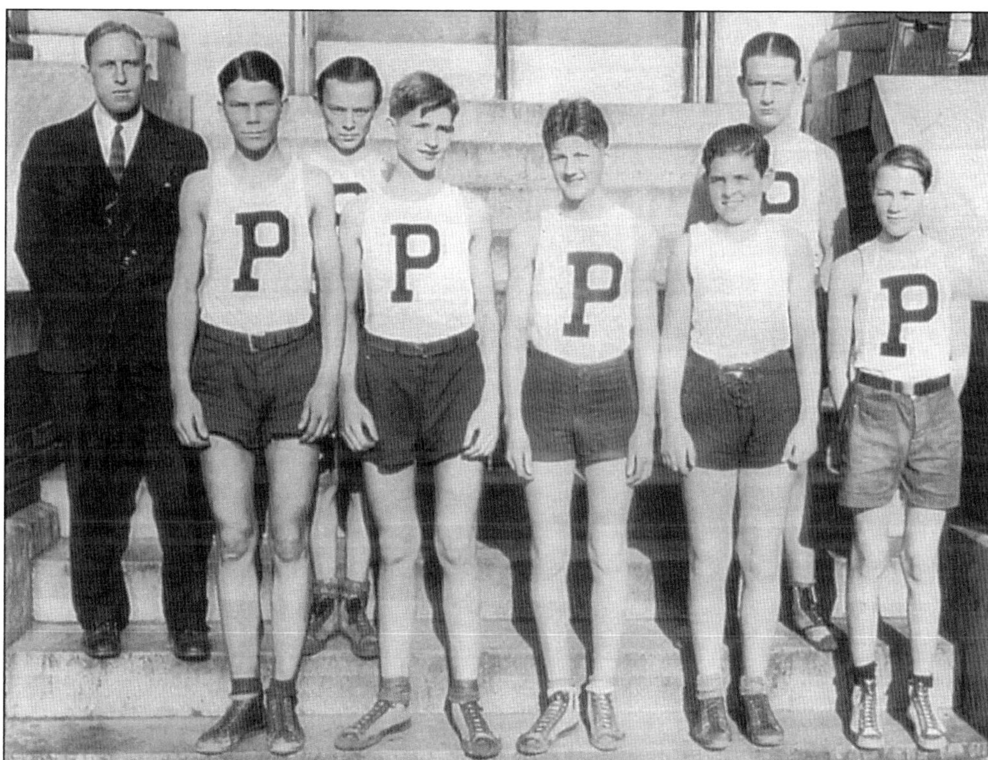

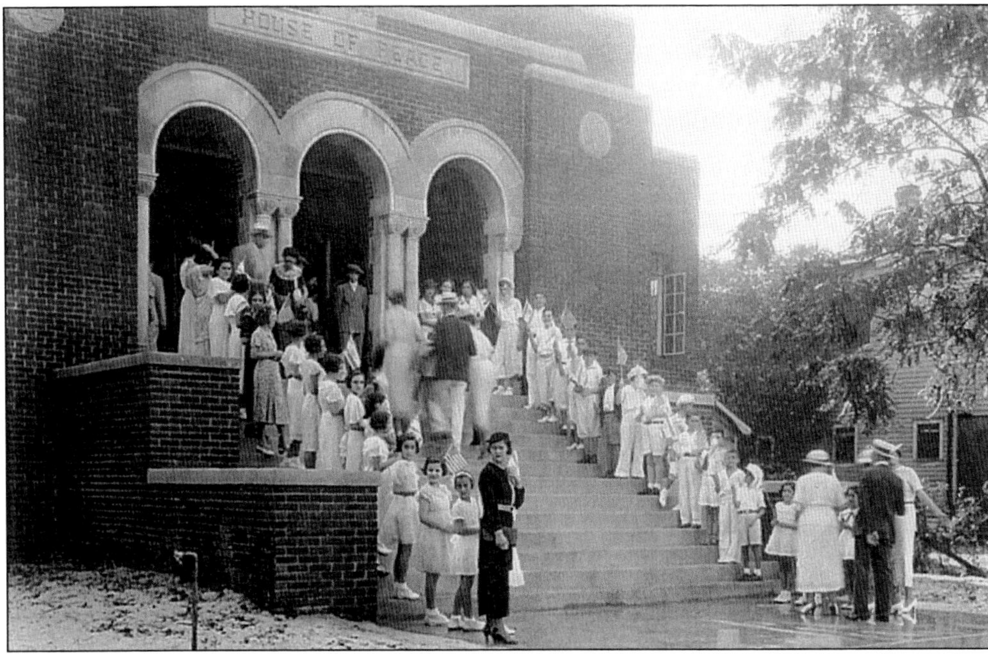

[House of Peace Synagogue, 1935.] The enlarged congregation of the Park Street synagogue caused them to build a new edifice at 1719 Marion Street that was designed by Lefaye and Lefaye and built by M.B. Kahn. The view above shows the membership attending the first service held in the new synagogue. It was demolished in 1973.

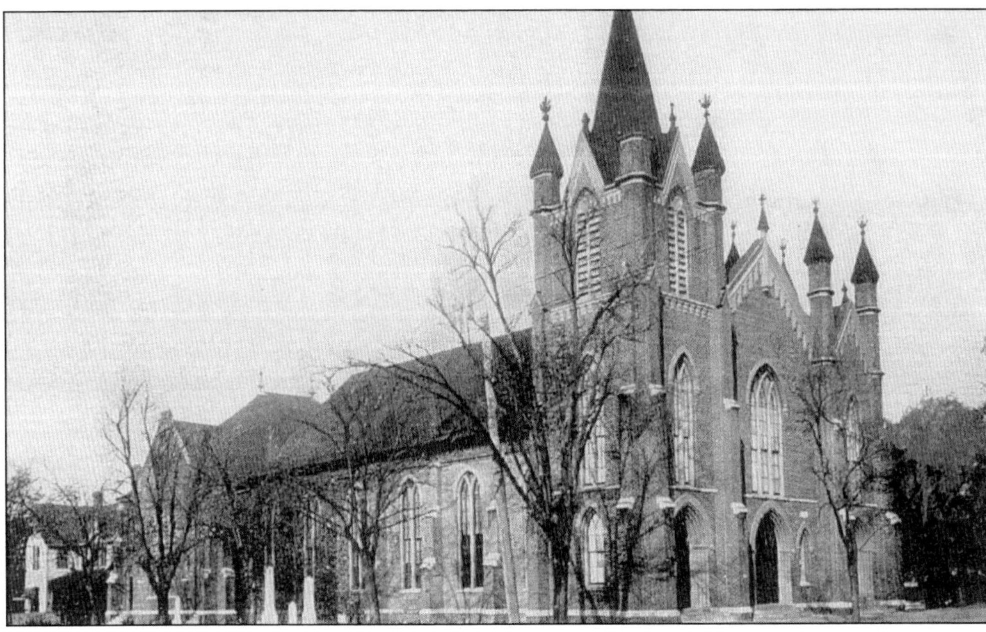

Washington Street Methodist Church, Columbia, SC [*c.* 1908]. The Methodists organized their church in 1803 and built a wooden structure on the corner of Washington and Marion Streets, which was followed by a brick structure in 1831. It was destroyed in the fire of 1865 with the present structure rebuilt in 1875.

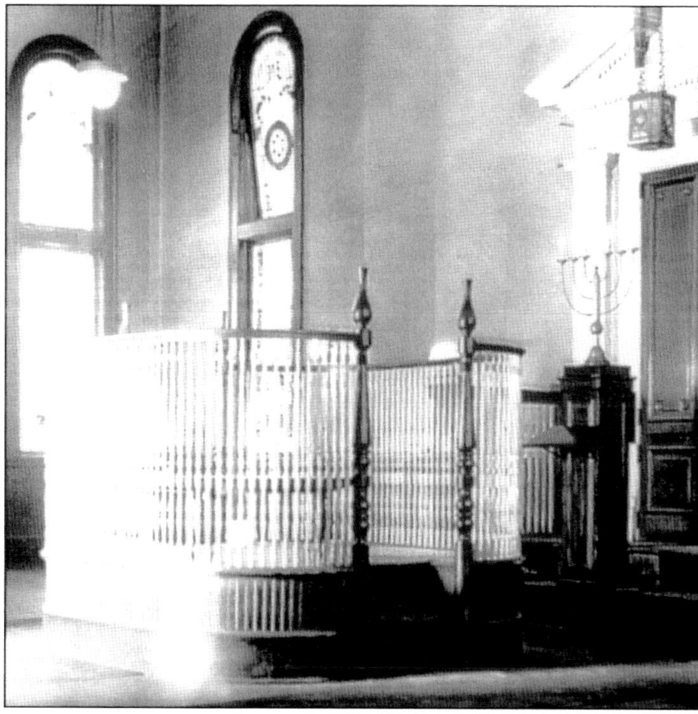

[House of Peace Synagogue, Interior, 1928.] Columbia's Orthodox Jewish members built a small, square, two-story frame edifice at 1318 Park Street in 1916. The synagogue had the features of Eastern Jewish architecture and became a center for Polish and Russian-Jewish immigrants. The sanctuary had leaded, stained-glass windows and a balcony where the women members could stand and watch the religious ceremonies. When this building was vacated, it became The Big Apple Night Club.

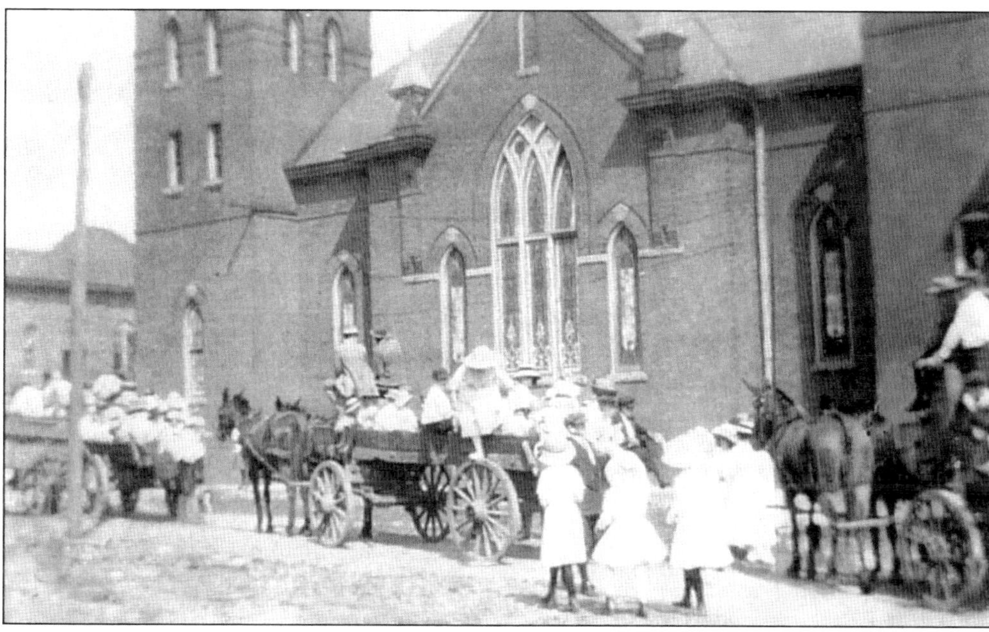

[Methodist Children on a Field Trip, *c.* 1907.] The Main Street Methodist Church was an outgrowth of the Washington Street church that first moved to a Marion Street site and then to the corner of Main and Richland Streets. Architects Hayden, Wheeler, and Schevend of Atlanta designed the two-towered brick structure, which was built by H.M. Johnson of Charlotte in 1900. The image above shows children dressed in their Sunday clothes, seated in several wagons, as they prepare to take a church field trip.

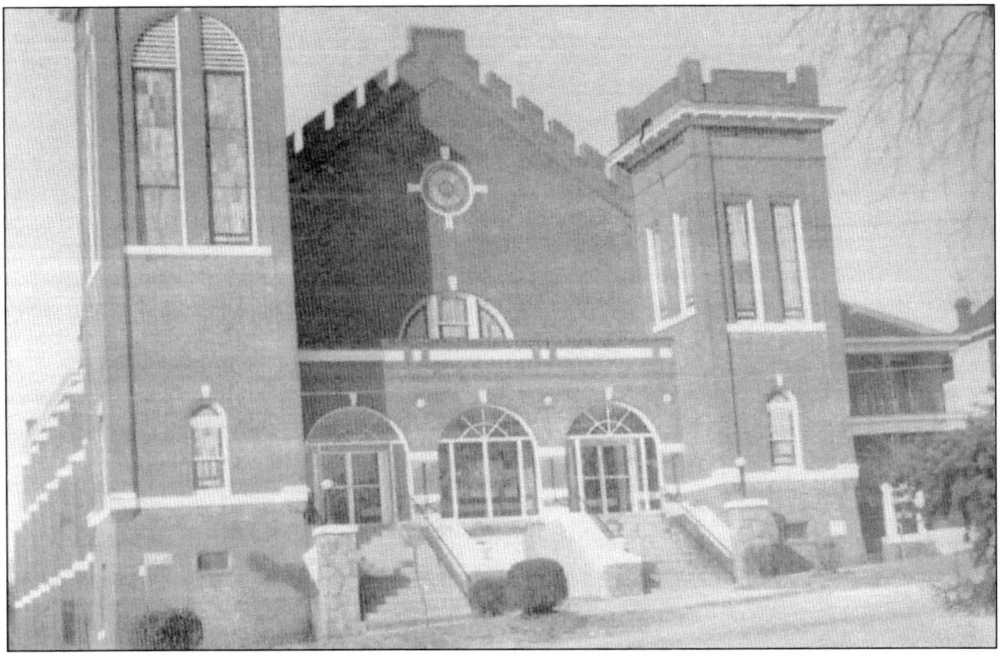

[ZION BAPTIST CHURCH, *c.* 1930s.] The Zion Baptist Church was founded in 1870 with Rev. F. Dobbins as the pastor. The 801 Washington Street sanctuary was rebuilt in 1916 by J.H. Cooper, contractor, during the pastorate of Rev. J.C. White.

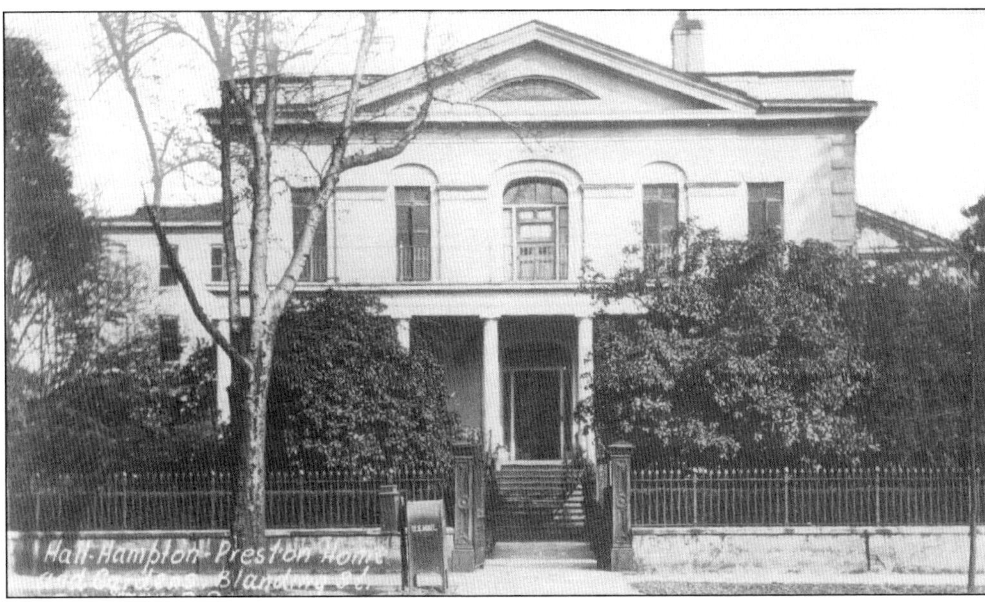

HALL-HAMPTON-PRESTON HOME [*c.* 1910]. The Hampton-Preston Mansion (1818) at 1615 Blanding Street reflects the elegant antebellum society of that early era. The South Carolina Presbyterian Institute for Women opened there in 1890 under the direction of Rev. William R. Atkinson. The 1908 student body was 270 girls, with 90 living in their dormitory. In 1910, they changed its name to College for Women and merged with Greenville's Chicora College in 1914, which lasted until 1930 when it combined with Queen's College in Charlotte.

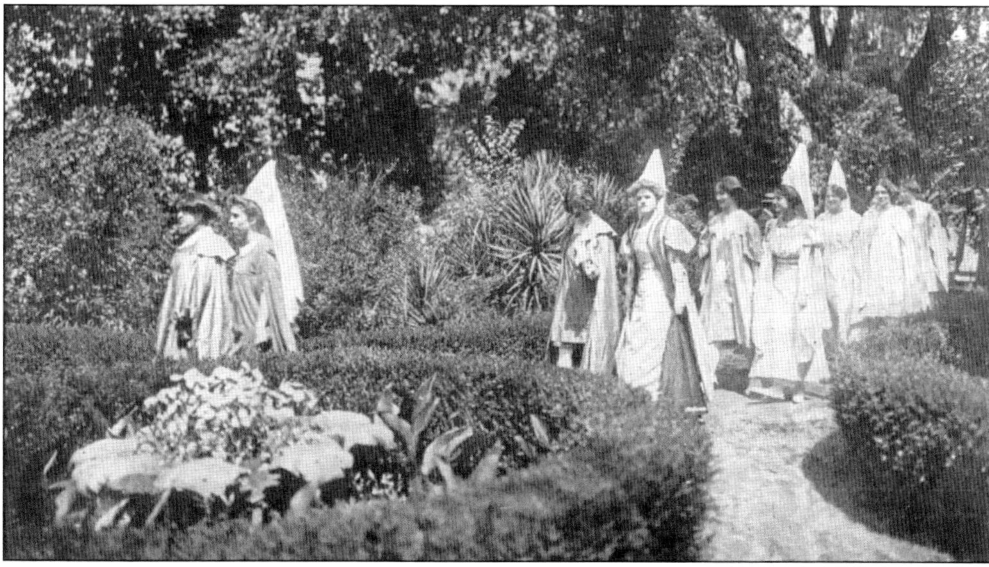

[**Joan of Arc Pageant, Womans College,** *c.* **1911.**] This image of young ladies in costume parading through the gardens illustrates some of the classical themes the young women studied and performed in theatrical productions. Other activities included tennis and basketball.

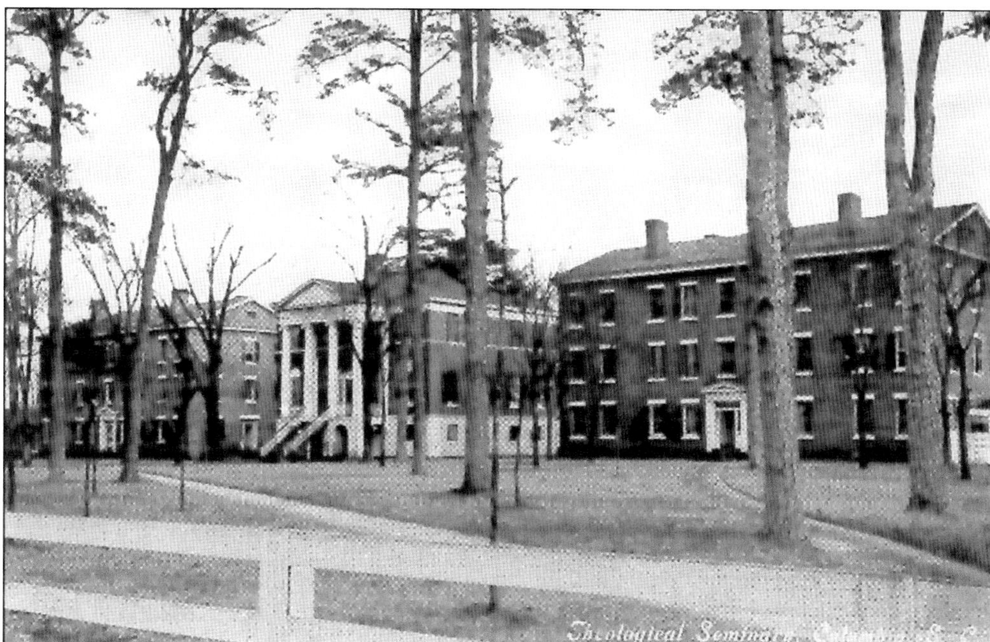

Theological Seminary, Columbia, SC [1907]. The Theological Seminary was founded in 1828 by the Presbyterian Synod of South Carolina and Georgia; it moved to this site in 1830. The central building was designed in 1823 by Robert Mills. The house was flanked by two dormitories, Simons Hall and Law Hall, and a brick carriage house that was converted into a chapel. In 1908, it had 4 teachers and 22 students. Woodrow Wilson's father and uncle were on the faculty. In 1925, the seminary vacated the site and moved to Decatur, Georgia.

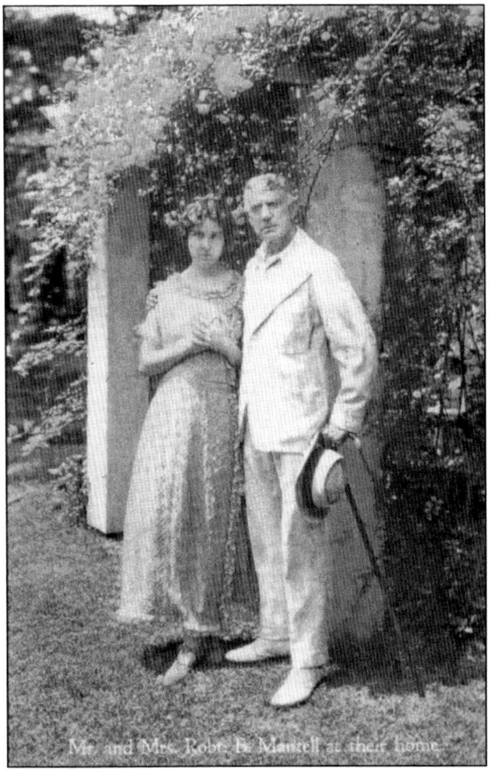

Mr. and Mrs. R. Mantell, Columbia, SC [1925.] This postcard image of the Mantells, actors in Shakespearean plays at the Columbia Theatre, was used to briefly reply to inquiries or to invite friends to performances.

Columbia Theatre, Columbia, SC [1905]. The Columbia Theatre-Opera House-City Hall was built at 1201 Main Street at Gervais in 1900. This third city hall was designed by Frank P. Milburn of Charlotte in a European style and constructed by W.J. May. City offices were on the ground floor front with the remainder of the building used by the Opera House. It was razed in 1936 and the Wade Hampton Hotel was built there. It was demolished in the 1980s for an office building.

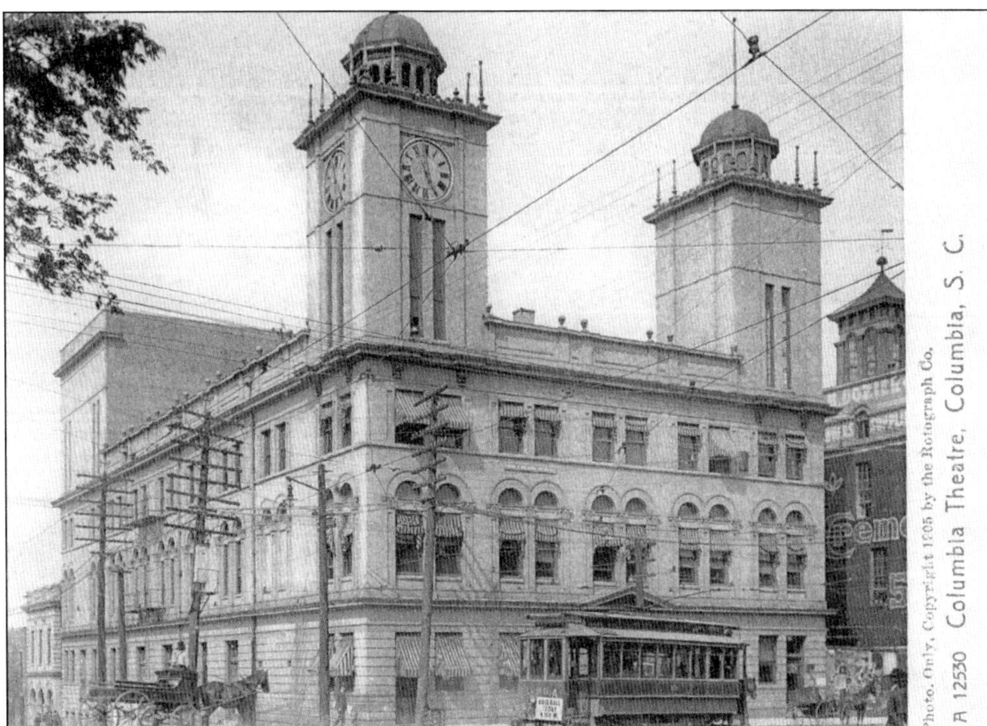

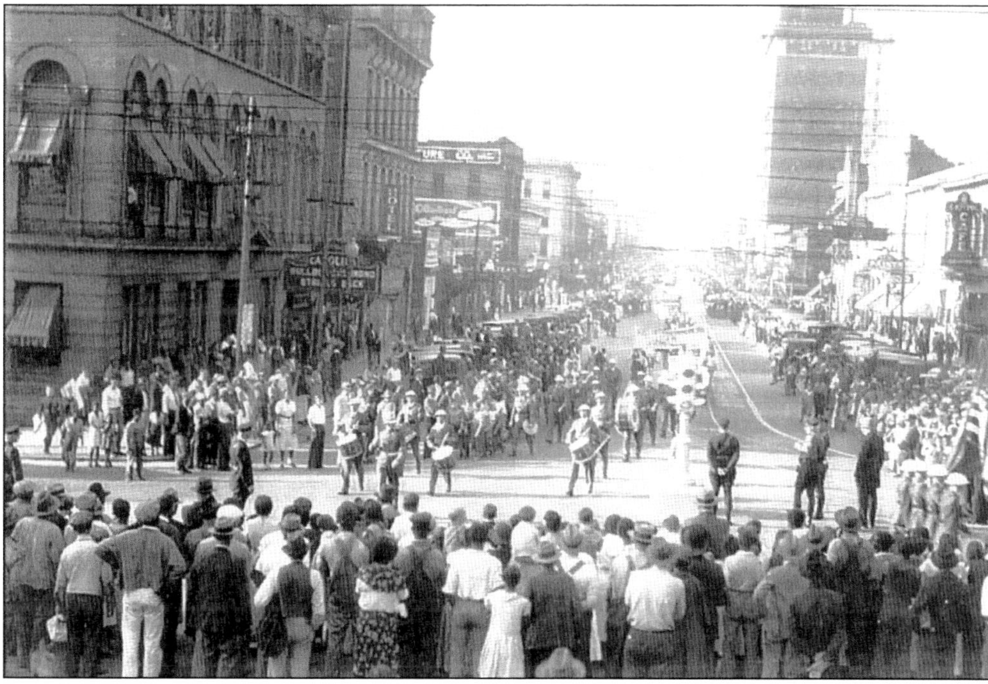

[Main Street Parade at Gervais Street, Fire Prevention Parade, 1934.] The Fire Prevention parade followed the general parade route for most celebrations and events. Lining up on Laurel or Richland Street, they proceeded from the 1800 block of Main Street towards the State Capitol and turned on Gervais Street to a disassembling area.

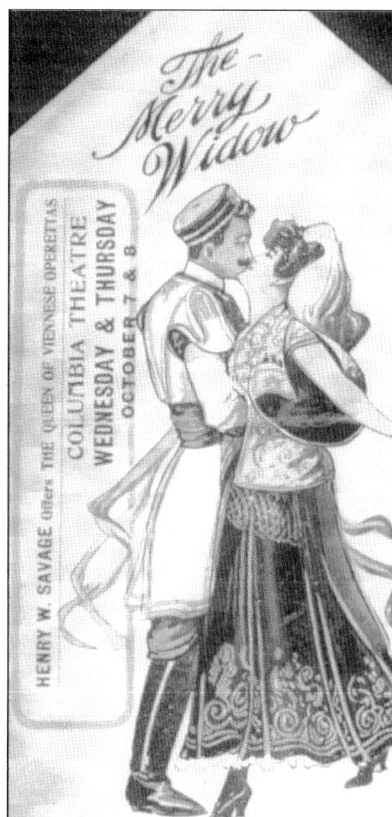

***The Merry* Widow [Columbia Theatre, Columbia, SC, *c.* 1910].** This generic postcard advertising *The Merry Widow* was sent to each venue with the theatre, adding the local data. The touring Viennese Operettas scheduled two performances at the Columbia Theatre on a route following the railroad lines south.

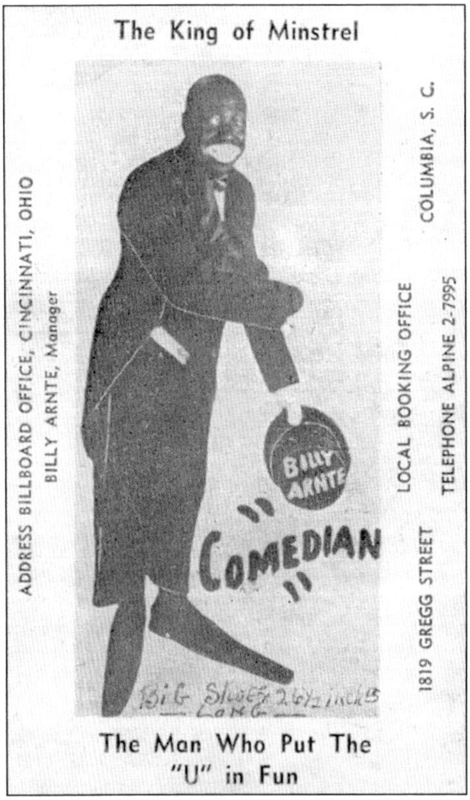

[Billy Arnet, *c.* 1930s.] The black comedian, Billy Arnet, took his minstrel shows to African-American audiences across the eastern region of the country. His Cincinnati office created this generic postcard with an exaggerated image, slogans, office address, and that of the local booking office.

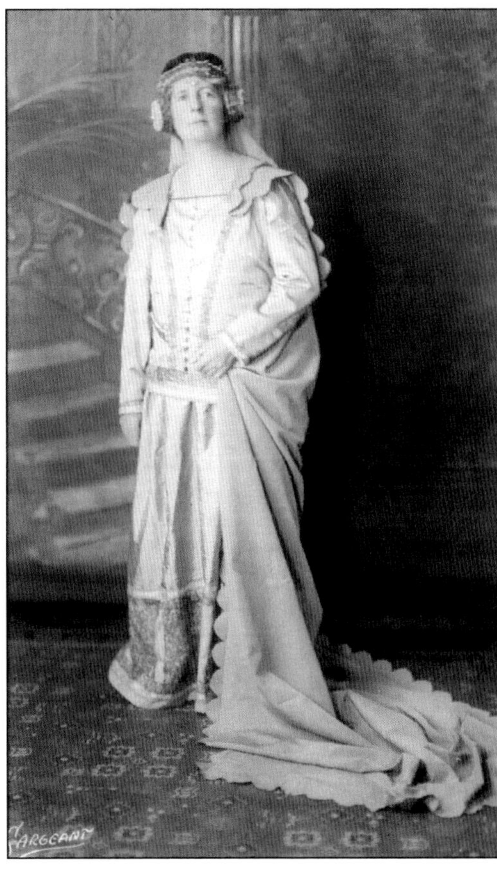

[Mother of Hamlet, Town Theatre, 1932.] This portrait of Mrs. Robert Gibbes as Gertrude, Queen of Denmark and mother of Hamlet, was the image used to promote the 1932 play of *Hamlet* performed in the new Town Theatre on the initial site. Theatres used mailers and posters of all types.

[Portrait of Blondelle Malone, 1911.] Blondelle Malone (1877–1951) was born in Georgia; she moved to Columbia in 1883 and studied art in South Carolina and New York at the New York School of Applied Design, New York School of Art, and the Arts Students League until 1900. Malone traveled to Japan and Europe and became known as "the Garden Artist of America" as she visited, painted, and exhibited pictures of gardens in Paris (1911), London (1913), and the United States. Financially supported by her parents she traveled and lived a charming, luxurious life as a single unmarried woman. She died in Columbia in 1951.

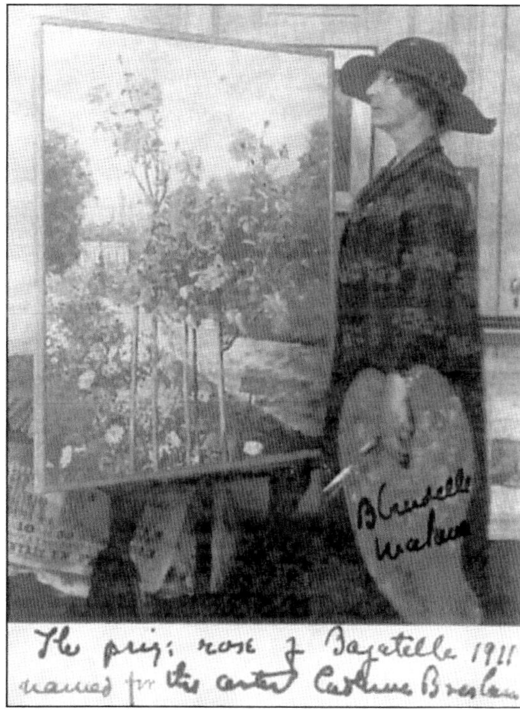

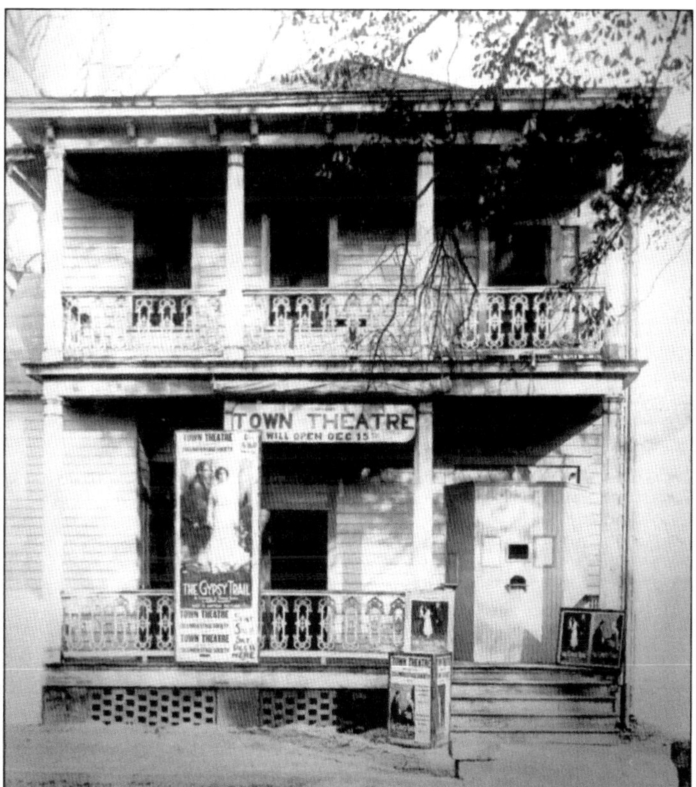

[Town Theatre, *c.* 1919.] The Columbia Stage Society was founded in 1919. Their first facility was the R.B. Sloan home at 1012 Sumter Street, and Arthur Hamby, architect, converted it into a theatre building. The present building, designed by Chicago architect Harry Jenkins, was built in 1924. This theatre is the nation's oldest continuously performing community theatre.

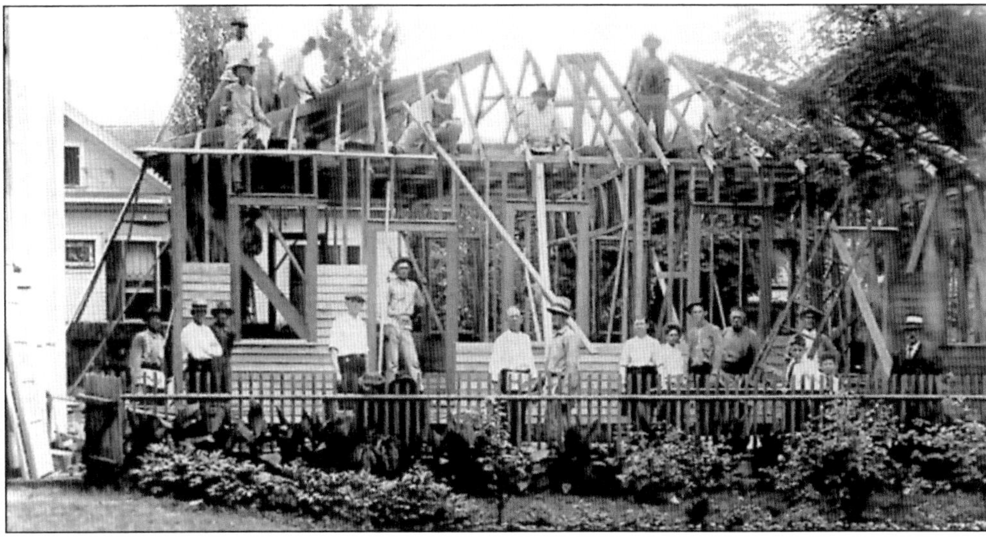

[SHANDON METHODIST CHURCH'S SUNDAY SCHOOL BUILDING, 1921.] The Shandon Methodist Church, organized in 1909, built their initial frame sanctuary in 1910. The men of the church built the frame Sunday School building, shown here, which was erected in one day during June 1921 on the church's lot at the corner of Maple and Preston Streets. The women gave encouraging support and made the day's meals.

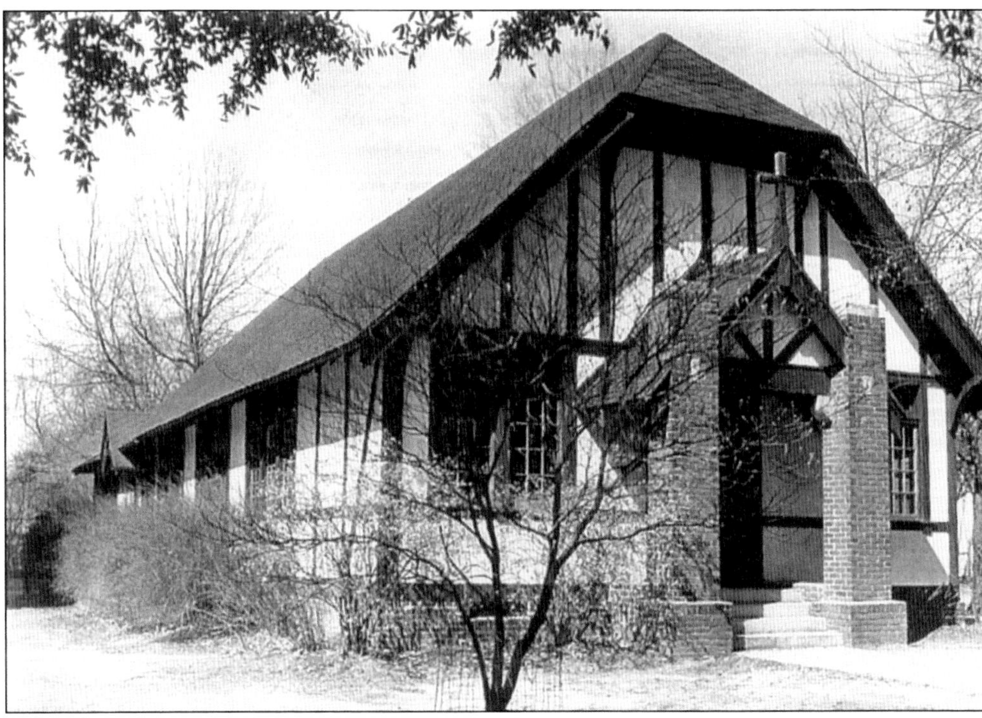

[ST. JOHN'S EPISCOPAL CHURCH, *c.* 1916.] St. John's Episcopal Church was organized in 1912 and used this edifice, which was built in 1914, as its sanctuary until 1926. With the construction of the current building, the older one was used as a parish hall until it was torn down *c.* 1949.

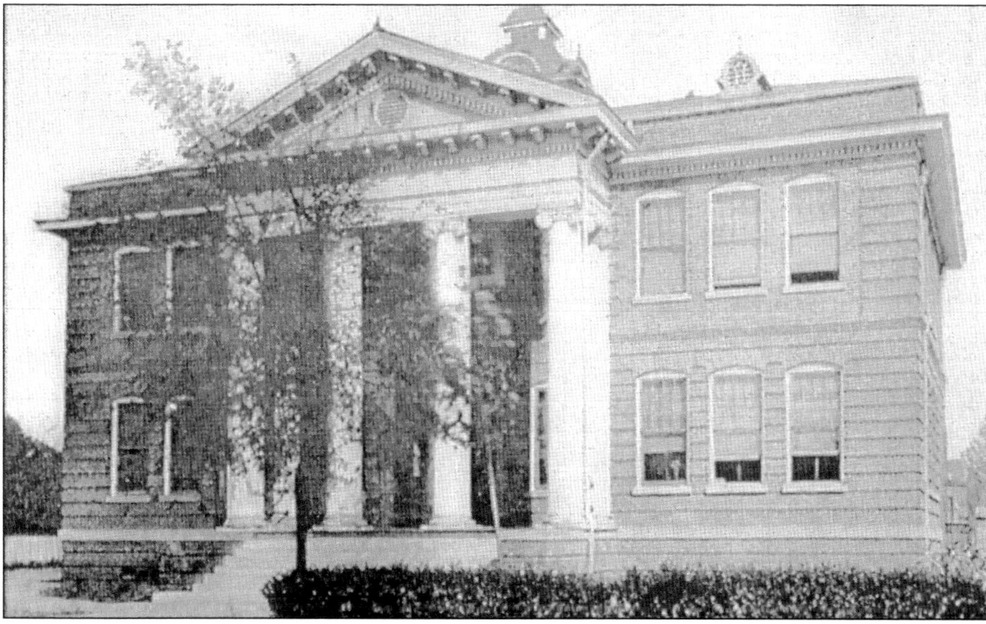

[SHANDON SCHOOL, 1909.] The brick six-classroom Shandon School at Devine and Maple Streets was built in 1909 at a cost of $10,000 to serve the expanding new suburb. The school's first principal, S.M. Busby, and six teachers taught grades one through seven. Shandon was annexed into Columbia in 1913, at which time it had 274 students. The school's name was changed to honor Samuel D. Schneider in 1937. It was closed at the end of the 1975–76 school year and later converted into apartments.

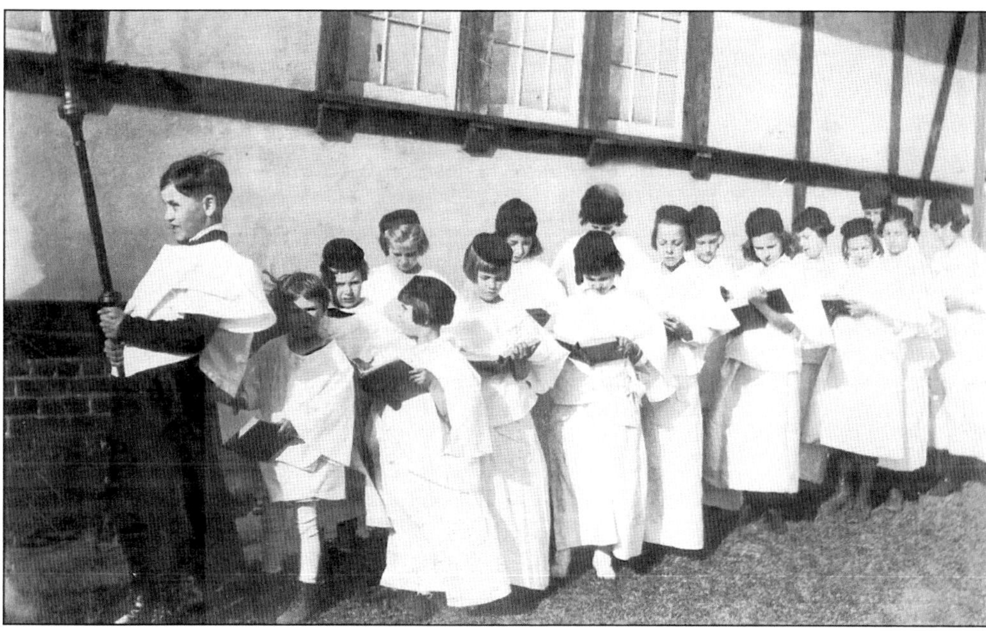

[ST. JOHN'S EPISCOPAL CHURCH'S JUNIOR CHOIR, 1922.] This scene shows the junior choir lining up outside St. John's Episcopal Church awaiting the signal for the procession into the sanctuary to begin.

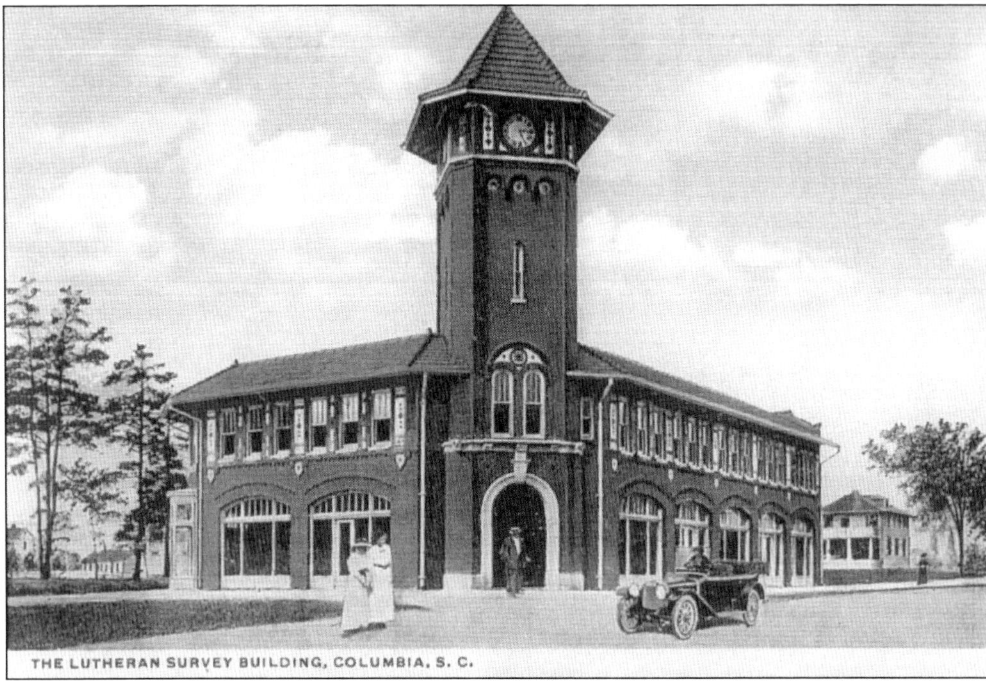

LUTHERAN SURVEY BUILDING, COLUMBIA, SC [*c.* 1925]. The Lutheran Survey Building, located at 3904 Monticello Road in Eau Claire and incorporated in 1899, was designed by architect J.B. Urquhart and constructed between 1912 and 1914. It served as the offices of the American Lutheran Survey, who published a weekly national publication edited by Dr. W.H. Greever until 1928. The two-story brick structure with a four-story peaked tower then became the Eau Claire Town Hall from 1928 to 1955.

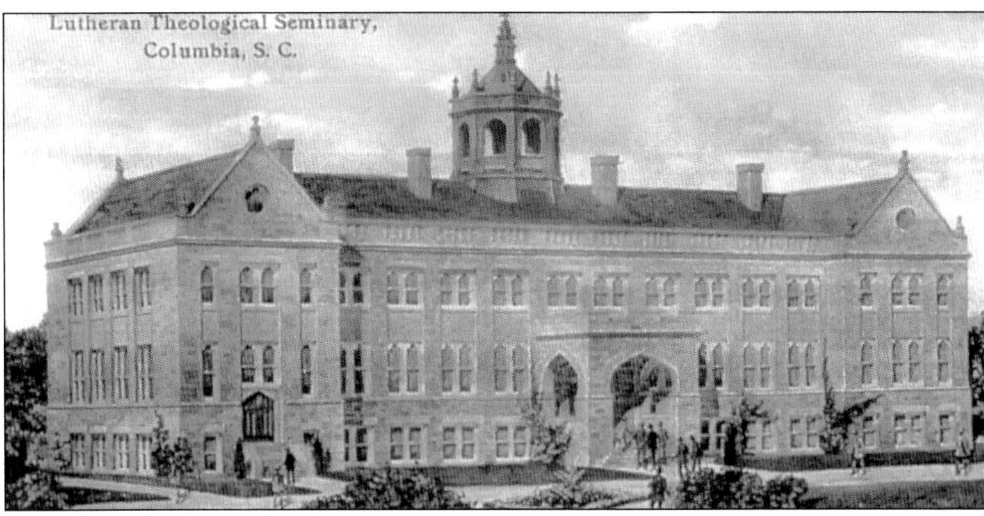

ADMINISTRATION BUILDING, LUTHERAN THEOLOGICAL SEMINARY, COLUMBIA, SC [*c.* 1911]. This elegant three-story building at 4201 Main Street was designed by C.M. Robinson and erected in 1911 by Wise Granite Company on six acres in Eau Claire. It was operated by five Lutheran Synods in eight southern states. It originally contained classrooms, a chapel, faculty offices, and a dormitory.

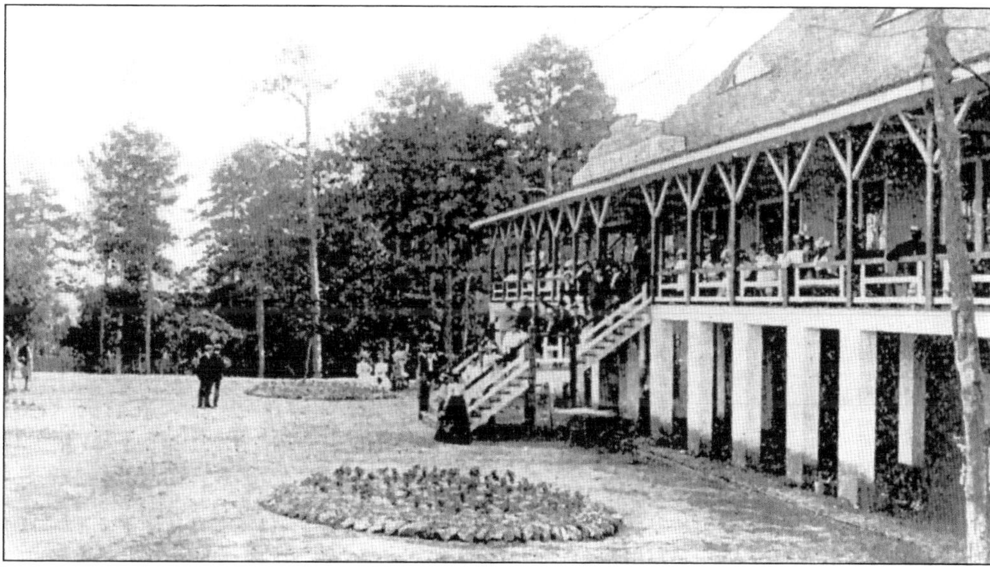

[Hyatt Park Auditorium, c. 1907.] F.H. Hyatt presided over the evolution of the new Eau Claire community north of the Columbia boundary. The Casino opened in July 1897 in the center of Hyatt Park by the end of the trolley line. It had an East Indian–bungalow architectural style with a broad staircase entrance. It led to a piazza that encircled the hall, which had an 80-foot-long auditorium with numerous windows. The structure had a ground level area for dressing rooms, bowling alleys, shooting galleries, etc.

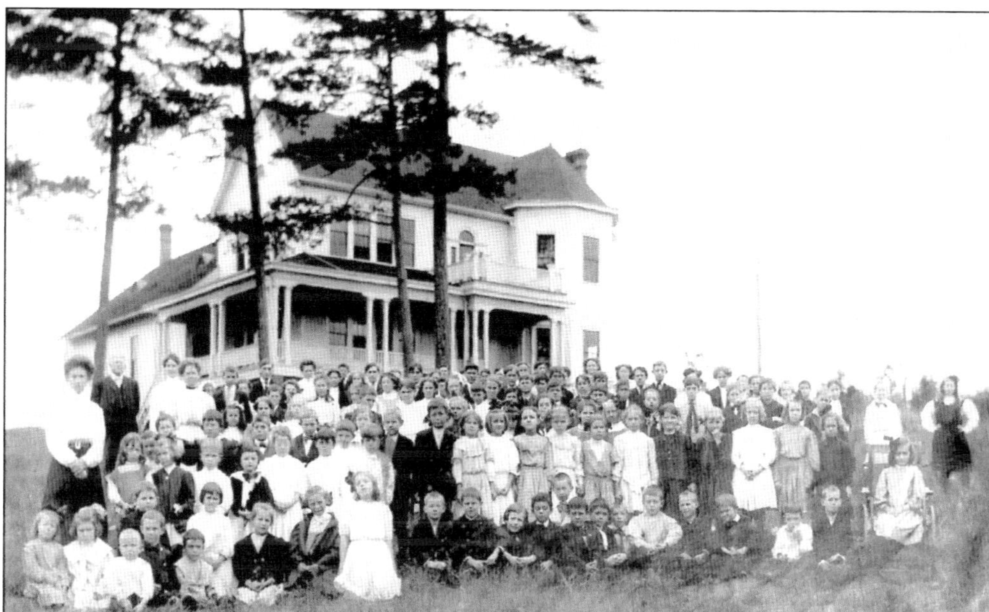

[Hyatt Park School House and Children, c. 1903.] F.H. Hyatt donated a lot on Lamar and Johnson Streets for a school in 1899; it was a large white frame house on a wooded hill site. In 1910, Hyatt Park School had two full-time and two part-time teachers, with eight students graduating. A new brick building was constructed in 1913. By 1915, the school had 11 teachers and 412 students. Eau Claire was annexed into city in 1929.

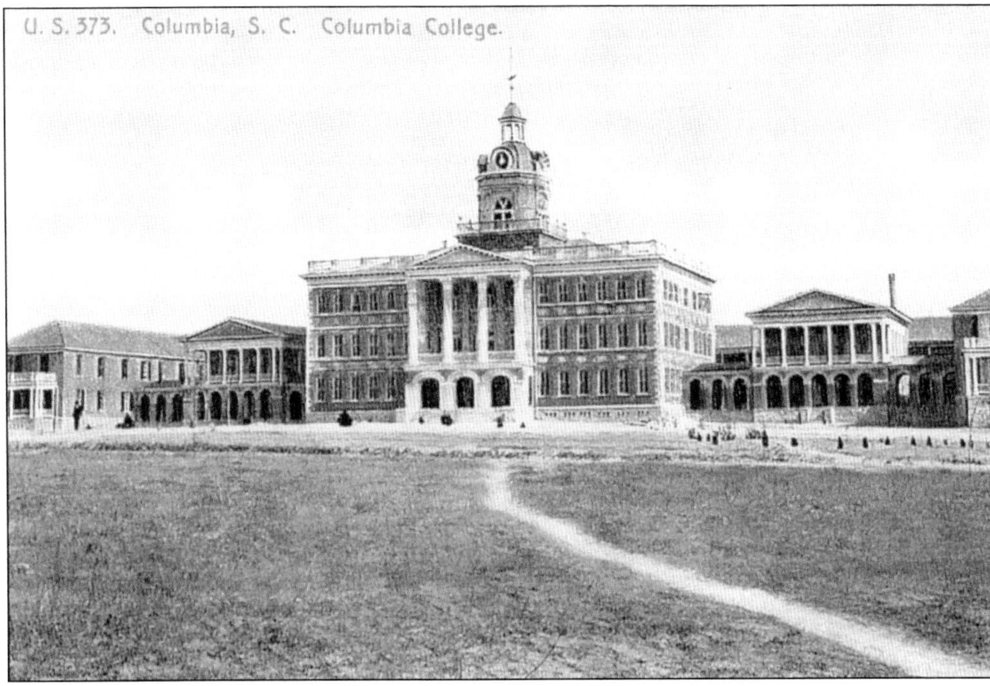

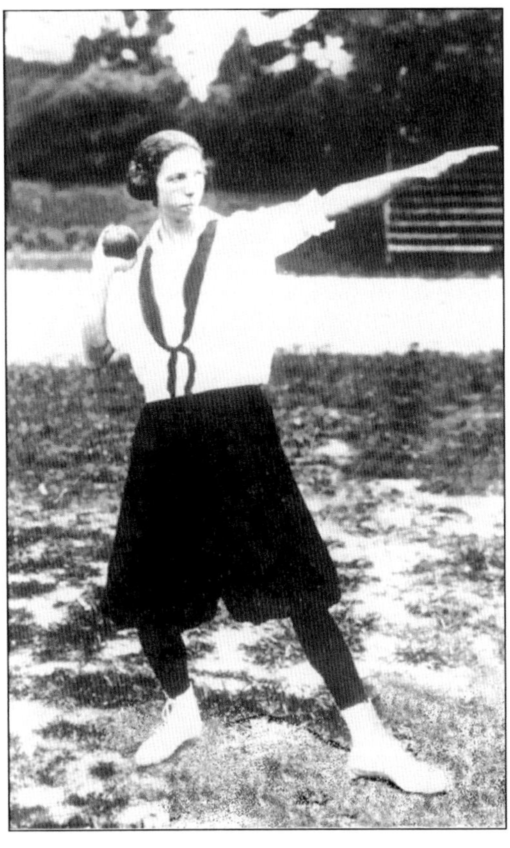

Columbia College, Columbia, SC [*c.* 1905]. Columbia Female College, a Methodist Episcopal Church school, was founded in 1854 and their first building erected on Hampton Street in 1859. It had a faculty of 16 and 121 students. The school closed during the war years and reopened in 1873. In 1905, the school changed its name to Columbia College and moved to Eau Claire into a five-building campus designed by Lafaye and Lafaye, architects. Three years later it had 26 teachers, 63 dormitory residents, and 252 other students.

[Ludy Godbold, *c.* 1922.] Lucille ("Ludy") Godbold from Estill, established a spectacular record in both the Women's 1922 Olympics in Paris. At the John J. Pershing Stadium, Godbold set a new woman's world record and became an Olympic gold medalist in the shot put and in the hop, step, and jump events. She also came in second in the distance basketball throw and third in the javelin throw and the 1,000–meter race. She became head of the Columbia College physical education department in 1922.

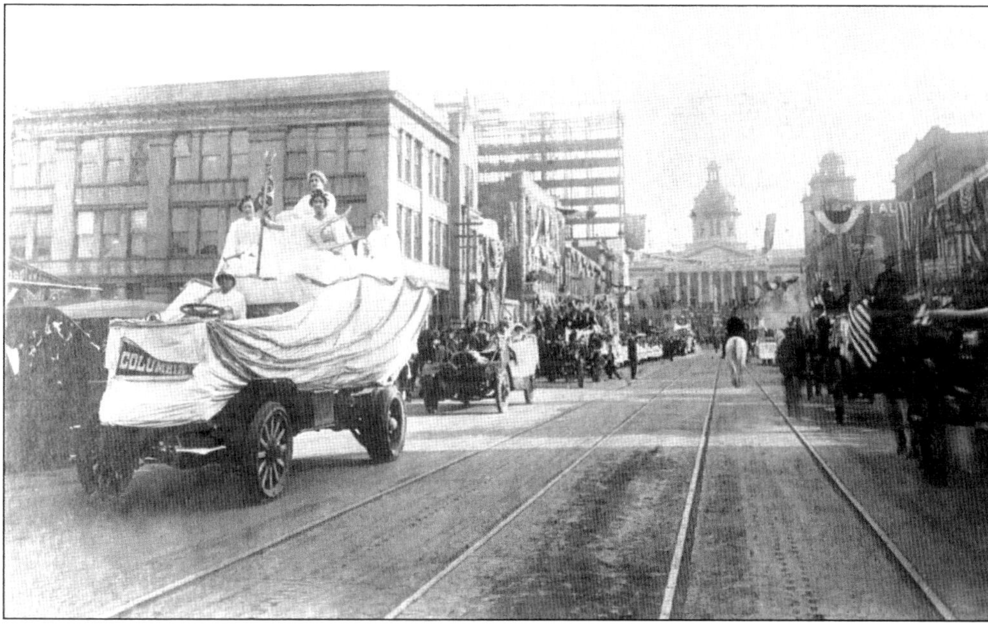

[SUFFRAGETTE FLOAT, COLUMBIA COLLEGE, 1913.] Students from the Columbia College demonstrated their support of the voting rights amendment in the United States Constitution as they rode on a float in the Corn Exposition Parade on Main Street in 1913. Congress passed the 19th Amendment to the Constitution on June 4, 1919, granting women the right to vote, and it was ratified by the states on August 26, 1920.

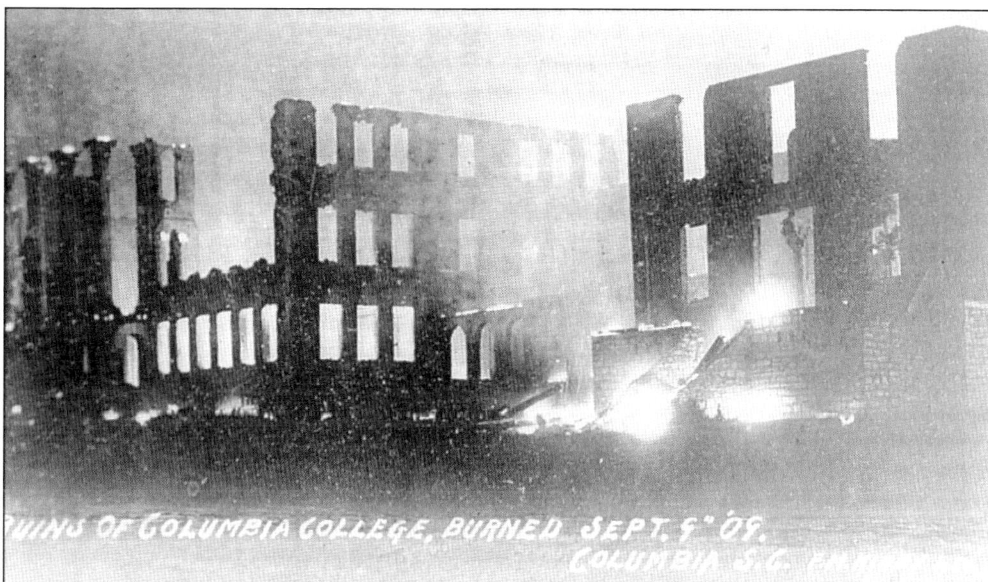

RUINS OF COLUMBIA COLLEGE, BURNED SEPT. 9, 1909, COLUMBIA, SC. On the evening of September 9, 1909, a major fire consumed the main college building and the adjoining East Wing with the students losing all their belongings. The students returned to their initial site, the remodeled Colonia Hotel, and continued their studies until the ruined buildings were rebuilt. They returned in 1910.

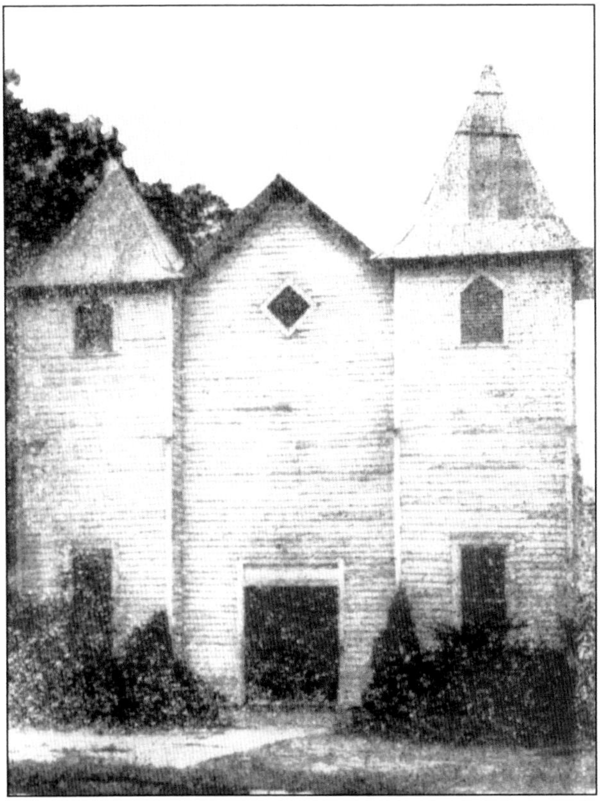

[St. Paul's Baptist Church, *c.* 1930.] The original congregation met on this site as early as 1865. In 1911, the Reverend J.M. Myers laid the cornerstone for a one-steepled frame structure at 4503 North Main Street, which preceded this two-steepled edifice that was dedicated in 1930 in this north Columbia community just south of Columbia College.

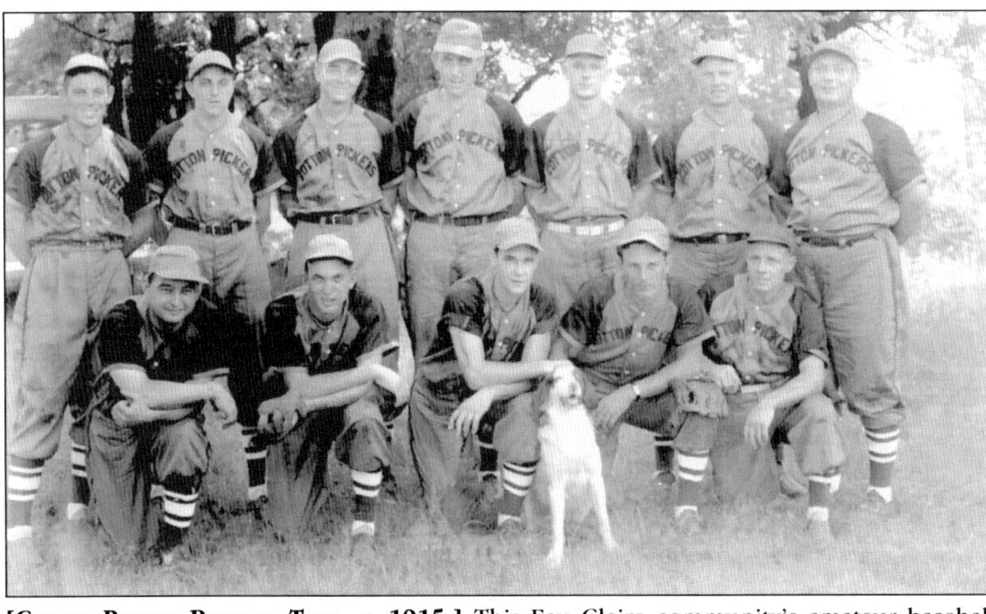

[Cotton Pickers Baseball Team, *c.* 1915.] This Eau Claire community's amateur baseball team was like others, formed by members of clubs and workers at schools, churches, businesses, or associations. The Cotton Pickers played their games on a baseball field on Sunset Drive, east of Main Street.

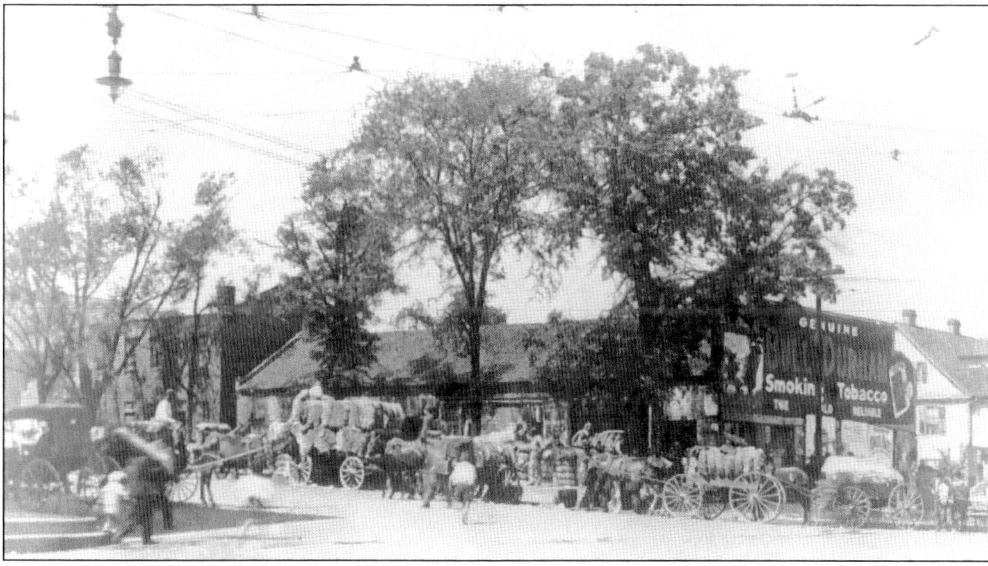

[COTTON WAGONS AT COTTONTOWN, *c.* 1907.] Cottontown was the name given to the area around Main and Elmwood Streets and it extended several blocks in each direction. Cotton was bought and sold at a cotton warehouse that stood on the site of the Jefferson Hotel, which gave way to Jefferson Square.

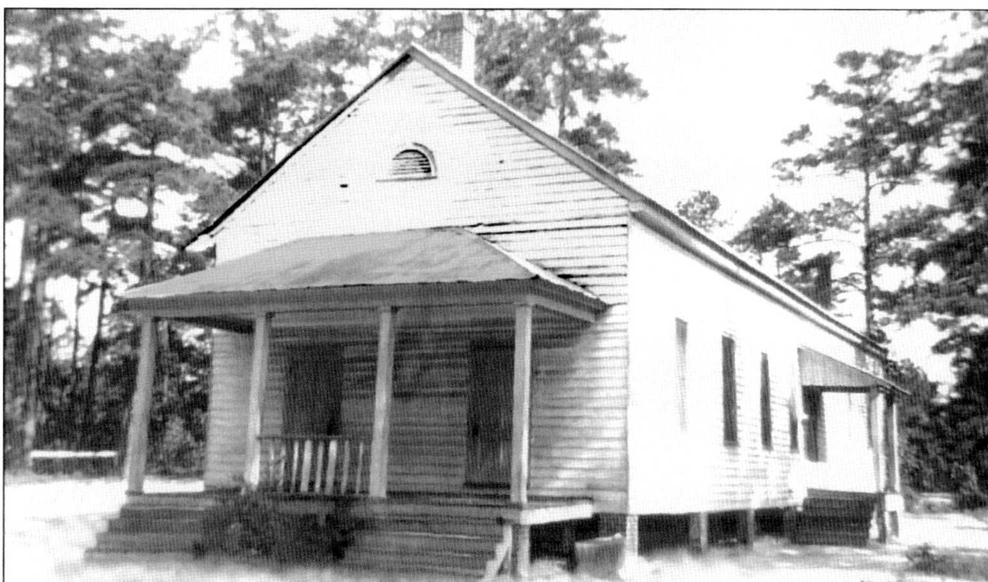

[MONTEITH SCHOOL, DISTRICT #2, 1922.] This school at 6500 North Main Street was established during the Civil War. R.N. Louis gave three acres for a church and school for African Americans. Lacking adequate financial support, the school closed in the 1880s. In 1921, Rachel Monteith reopened it for blacks and it stayed open for 26 years. It was absorbed by Richland County District #1 in 1941, and had three teachers covering grades one through seven. Students who passed a readiness test could go to Booker T. Washington High School. In 1947, the district consolidated one and two room schools into larger central schools. Monteith was closed; the property was sold for $3,000 in 1949.

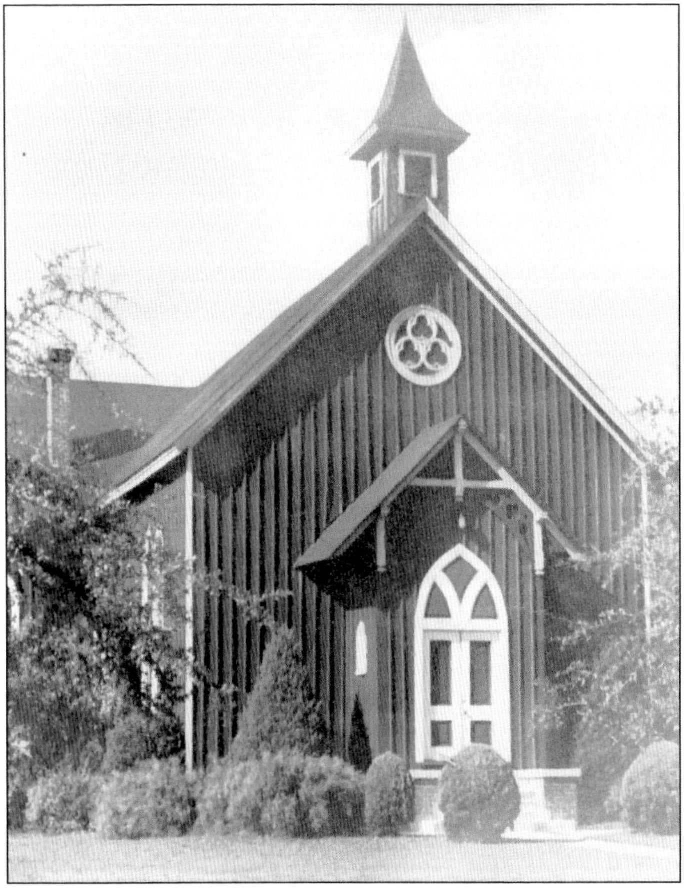

[Eau Claire Presbyterian Church, *c.* 1913.] On October 13, 1912, the Reverend Dr. R.B. Ginnan dedicated the new Eau Claire Presbyterian Church, located on the corner of Wildwood and Monticello Roads on property donated by Mr. L.T. Wilds. The structure was a gift of the First Presbyterian Church of Columbia, who erected this edifice on their grounds in 1813 at a cost of $8,000 and then moved it to its current location. The first service was held on May 19, 1912.

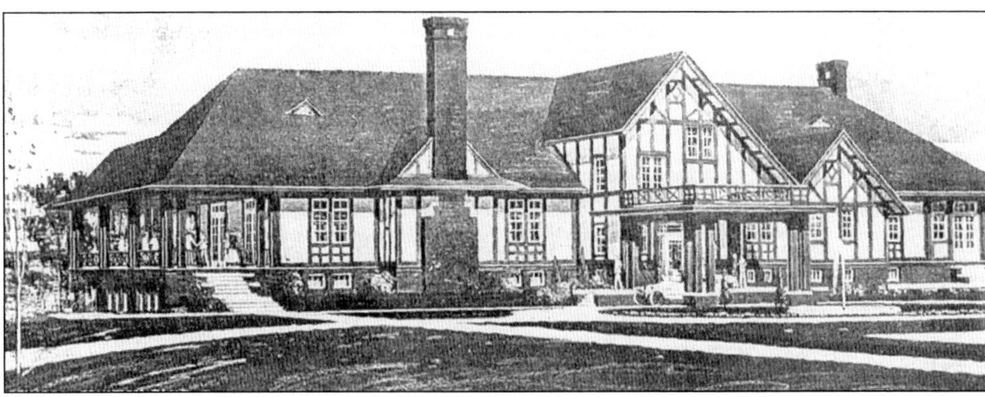

Ridgewood Country Club, Columbia, SC [1916]. The Ridgewood Club for men was formed in 1904 on a site near Monticello Road. Mr. E.W. Robinson, a Columbia banker, real estate speculator, and president of the street railroad system, was eager to extend the Columbia Street Railroad System beyond Hyatt Park in Eau Claire in order to develop that adjacent Columbia neighborhood. The membership of the Ridgewood Club with bowling alleys, pool tables, tennis courts, and golf courses quickly grew to 250. In 1915, the building burned down and was quickly rebuilt. The postcard image above shows the new facilities by Urquhart and Johnson.

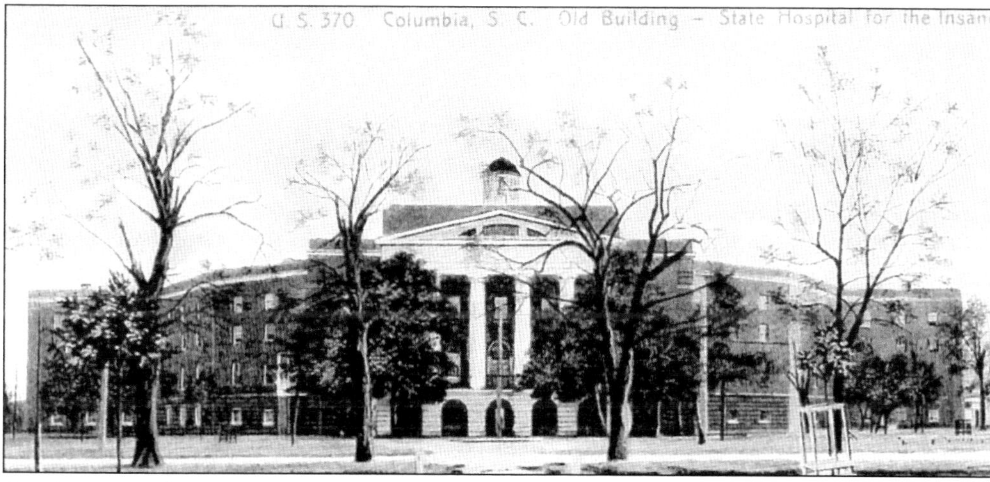

Old Building, State Hospital for the Insane, Columbia, SC [*c.* 1906]. The initial building at Bull and Calhoun Streets was erected in 1822 from plans drawn by Robert Mills. Samuel Farrow of Spartanburg, a member of the South Carolina House of Representatives, and William Crafts, a senator from Charleston, developed a legislative act to create a state hospital [Lunatic Asylum], which was completed in 1828.

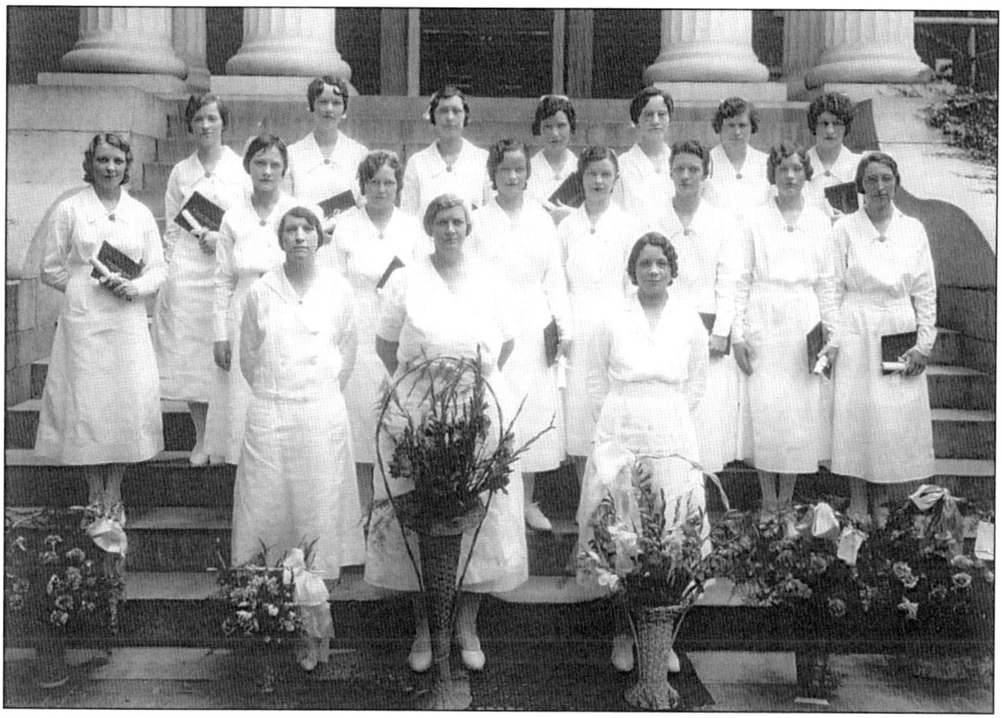

[Graduating Class of Nurses, State Hospital, 1932.] In 1892, Dr. James W. Babcock began a training school for psychiatric nurses at the South Carolina State Hospital. It was expanded in 1894 to include the Columbia Hospital so that the state hospital's nurses would have experience in the wards of a general hospital. The image above is a 1932 graduation portrait of the School of Nursing, taken in front of the Babcock Building on the state hospital grounds.

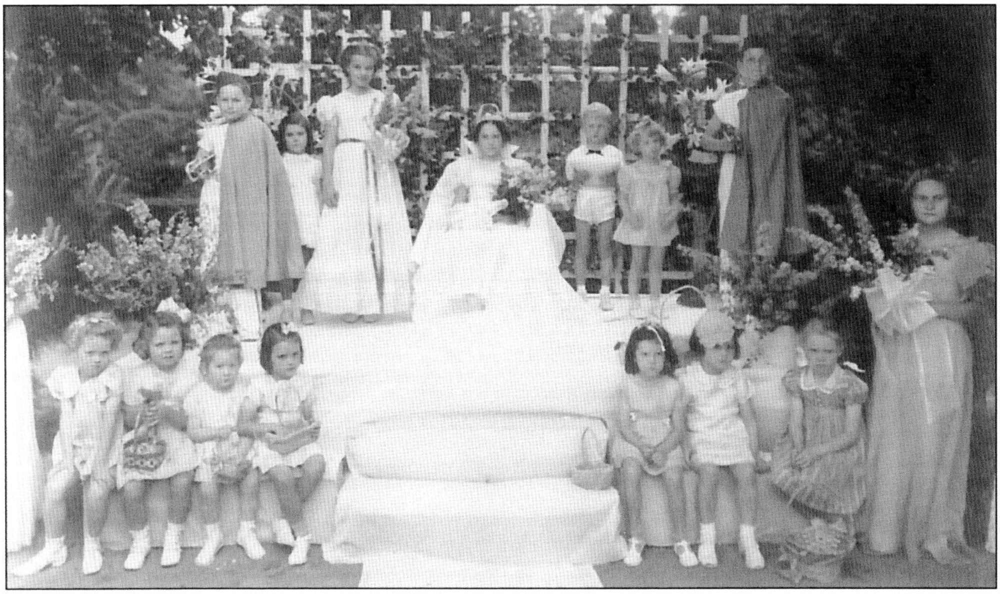

[May Court, Logan School, *c.* 1920.] This is a typical event held by the schools during this time. In 1908, the Richland County School System had 16 school districts with District #1 being Columbia. The city had 8 public schools, 59 teachers, and a budget of $27,310. The rural districts had 94 one-room school houses, 94 teachers, and a budget of $27,313. The 1908 city was divided into four white zones: a northern section was split into west and east zones, a middle zone, and a southern zone. Hyatt Park, Waverly, Shandon, and Olympia School served the respective communities outside the city limits.

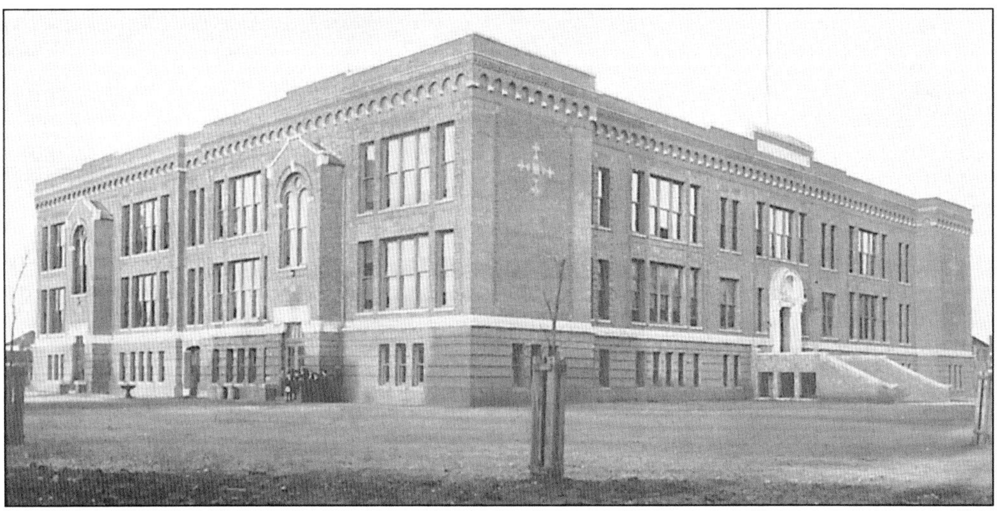

[Blossom Street School, 1916.] The Blossom Street School opened in 1898 on a one-half-acre lot on the southeastern intersection of Gates [Park] and Blossom Streets. W.B. Smith Whaley & Company were the architects and W.J. May was the contractor for a cost of $1,970. The school opened with an enrollment of 64 students. By 1913, Blossom Street School had 3 teachers and 194 students. Its zone borders were College to Main, Main to Devine, Devine to Laurens, and Laurens to the southern limits of the city. It burned down in 1915 and was rebuilt in 1916. The Blossom Street name was changed to Cella Dial Saxon in 1930.

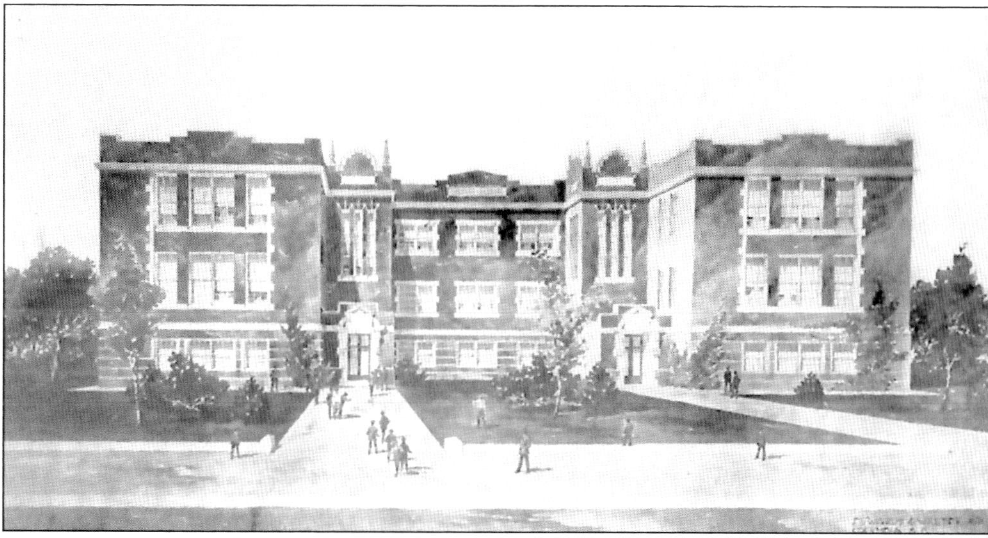

[**Taylor School, 1906.**] Ex-governor John Taylor gave four-acres of land for a public school. Edwards and Walters were the architects of the structure that cost $42,000. The Taylor School at 1615 Laurel Street opened on February 2, 1906, and had 12 class rooms, an assembly hall, a library, offices, and a recreation room. The school's initial capacity of 575 increased to 745 in 1913. Taylor School's northeast zone boundaries were from (Elmwood) to Laurens, Laurens to Hampton, Hampton to Main, and Main to Elmwood. It was torn down in 1965 to make way for Richland District #1 offices.

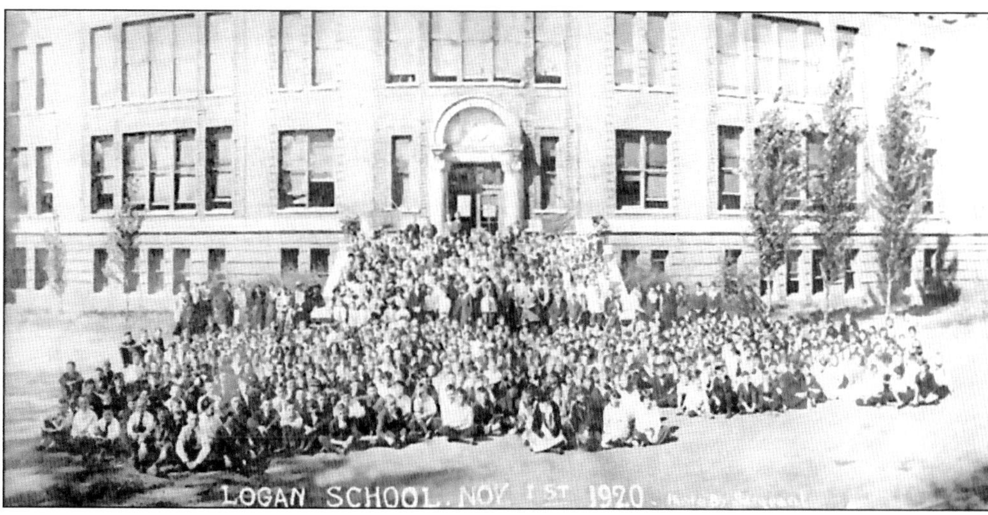

[**Logan School, 1920.**] In 1904, Charles Logan donated four-acres and $40,000 for a school on the 800 block of Elmwood Street. Wilson and Sompayrac, architects, designed this Italian-Renaissance structure, which was built by W.R. Harback, contractor, for a total of $59,242 in 1913. Its northwest zone region was bounded by the city's northern limits (Elmwood) to Main, Main to Hampton, Hampton to the river, and the river back to Elmwood. A.C. Flora was the first principal. The class picture above was taken in 1920.

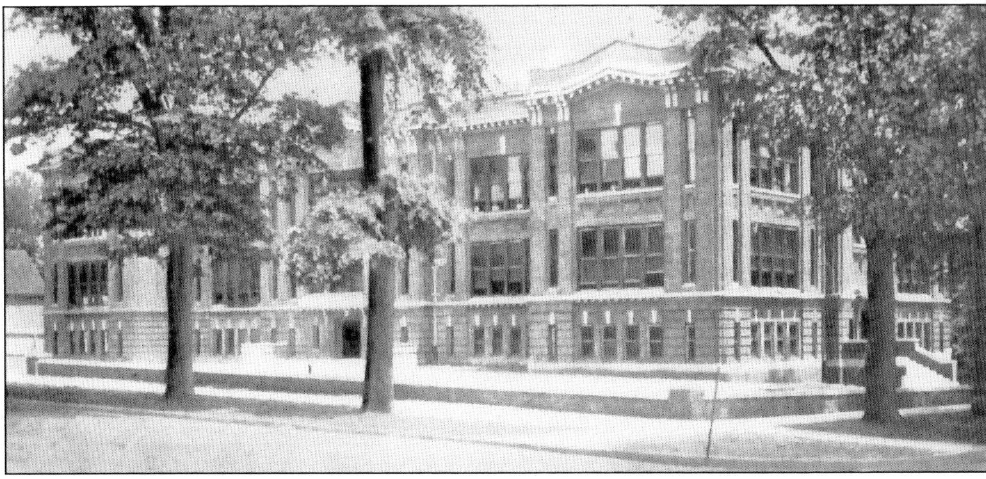

McMaster School, Columbia, SC [*c.* 1912]. Edwards and Walters, architects, designed McMaster School in 1910, and J.J. Cain, contractor, built the structure on lots on the corner of Pickins and Senate Streets. McMaster's total cost was $61,500, and the school was occupied on February 6, 1911. Its service zone (middle) was Hampton to Laurens, Laurens to Devine, Devine to Main, Main to College, and College to the river. In 1913, there were 13 teachers and 638 students.

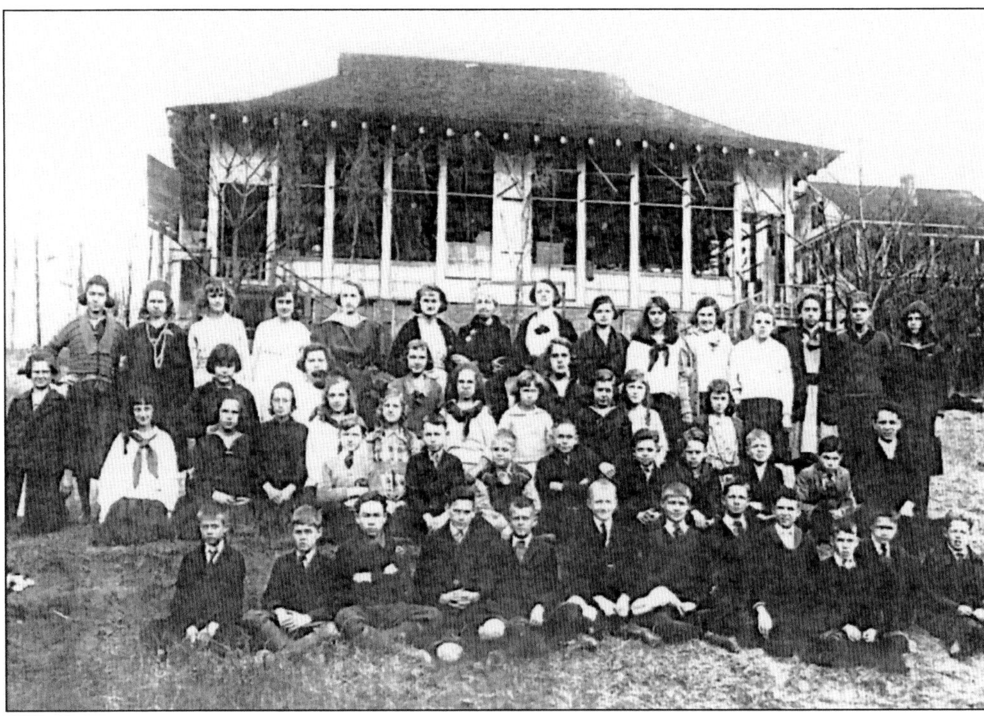

[Bon Air School, 1921.] The private Bon Air School began in 1896 and continued to 1932. Miss Annie Bonham began in the back rooms and porch of her house. In 1908, she had 4 teachers and 50 students, and liked to teach her classes in the open air outside. She built a school building on the corner of Green and Barnwell in 1912 that had window walls on three sides.

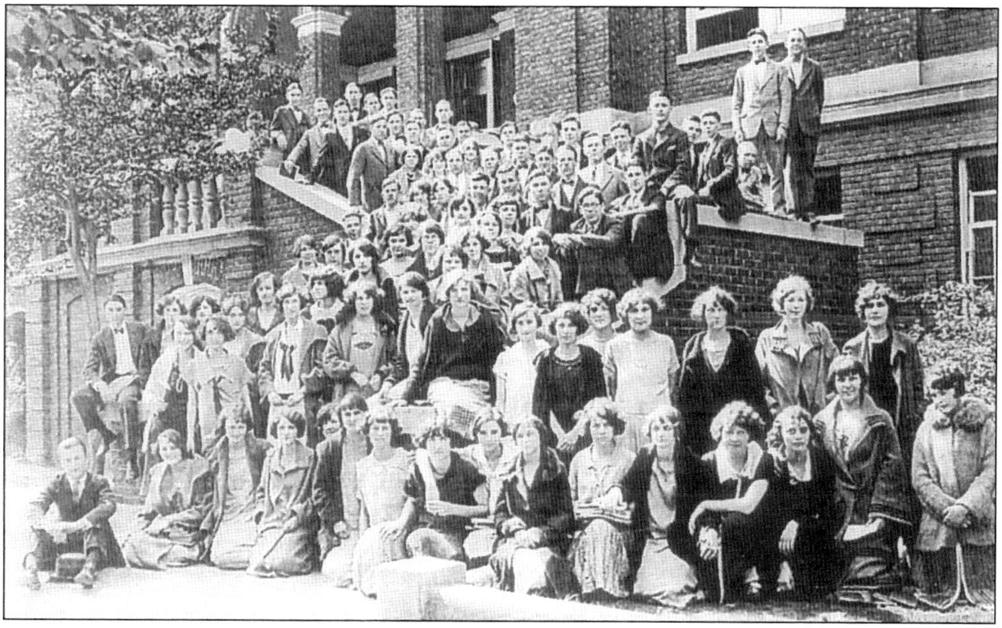

[**Columbia High School, Class of 1925.**] The Washington Street School—the only white high school—at the corner of Washington and Marion Streets opened in 1906 with 12 classrooms. By 1915, it had 11 teachers and 281 students in grades 8–11 with 41 students graduating. The new Columbia High School, replacing the Washington Street School, opened in 1916. The 1925 class had 154 students graduating. The last high school classes were held in 1975. The building was sold in 1983, and demolished in 1984. The First Baptist Church's new sanctuary now occupies the site.

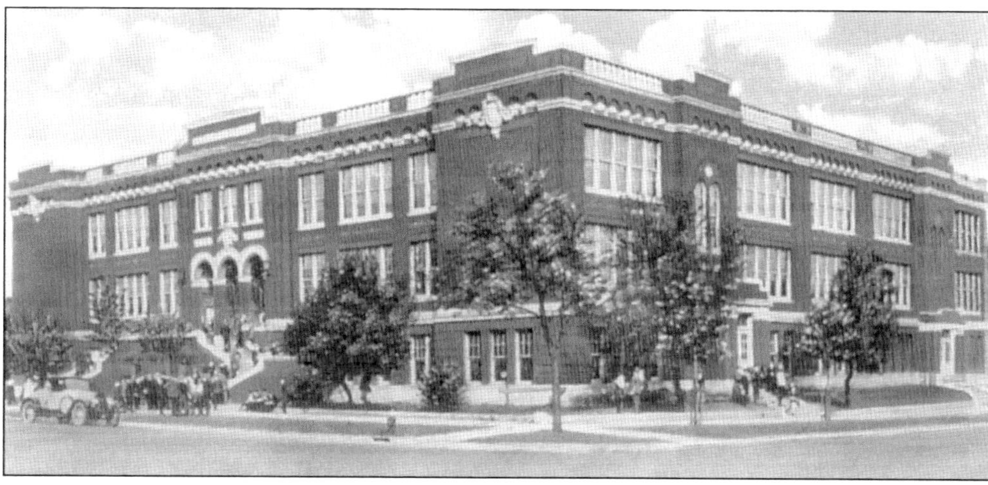

Columbia High School, Columbia, SC [*c.* 1916]. Columbia High School was designed in an Italian-Renaissance style by Urquhart and Johnson, architects, in 1915. George Waring was awarded the contract for the three-story brick structure at the corner of Washington and Marion Streets for a cost of $125,000. The ground floor contained: manual, domestic science, secretarial training, and the gymnasium; the first floor had eight classrooms, a library, and auditorium, and offices; and the second floor had eight classrooms and science laboratories. The design permitted future additions.

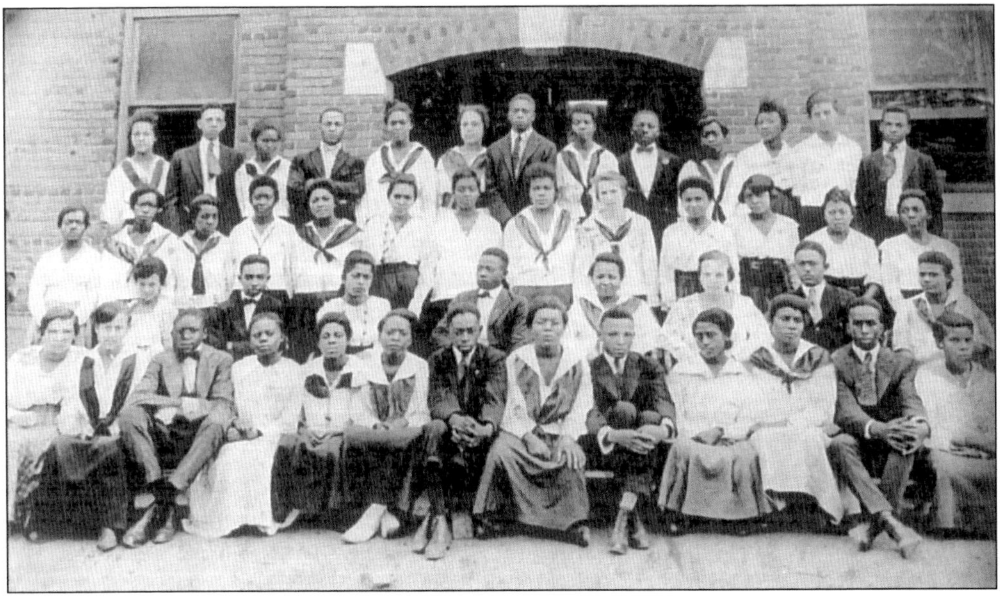

[**Booker T. Washington High School, Class Picture, 1919.**] Booker T. Washington was the third African-American public school built in Columbia. The school opened in 1916, and students could take vocational classes in carpentry, bricklaying, painting, and horticulture, along with academic studies and music. This class portrait includes students who began and graduated from this high school. In 1925, an industrial building was erected at a cost of $34,882.

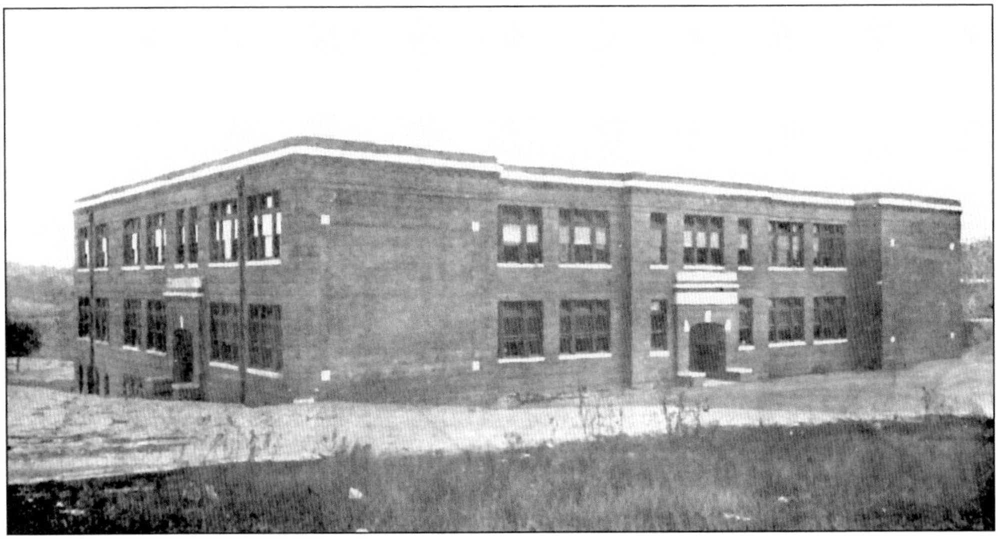

[**Booker T. Washington School, 1916.**] The school district bought a four-acre lot bounded by Bull, Marion, Wheat, and Blossom Streets for $1,200. J.H. Sams was the architect, and the Seastruct Company built the 17-classroom school for $16,175. The Rosenwald fund for black schools donated $25,000. In 1916, this 12-teacher school began taking elementary students, and in 1918, it became a high school where African-American students living south of Gervais Street attended.

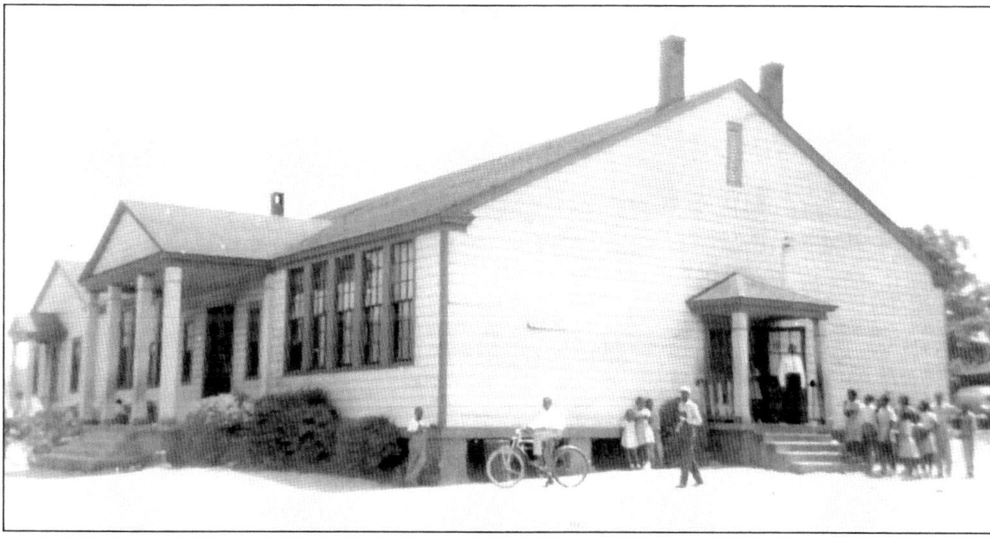

[Taylors School (Perrin-Thomas), c. 1930.] Taylors School for African Americans was located at 1034 Andrews Road, across the Southern railroad tracks from Assembly Street and the state fairgrounds. This site was inside the Olympia School District #4, which included the area to the south and east of the city boundary in 1910. The initial frame structure, having 2 teachers and 142 students in 1913, was expanded and altered over the years. In 1952, the school was renamed the Perrin-Thomas Elementary School. It stands as an abandoned school house in 2000.

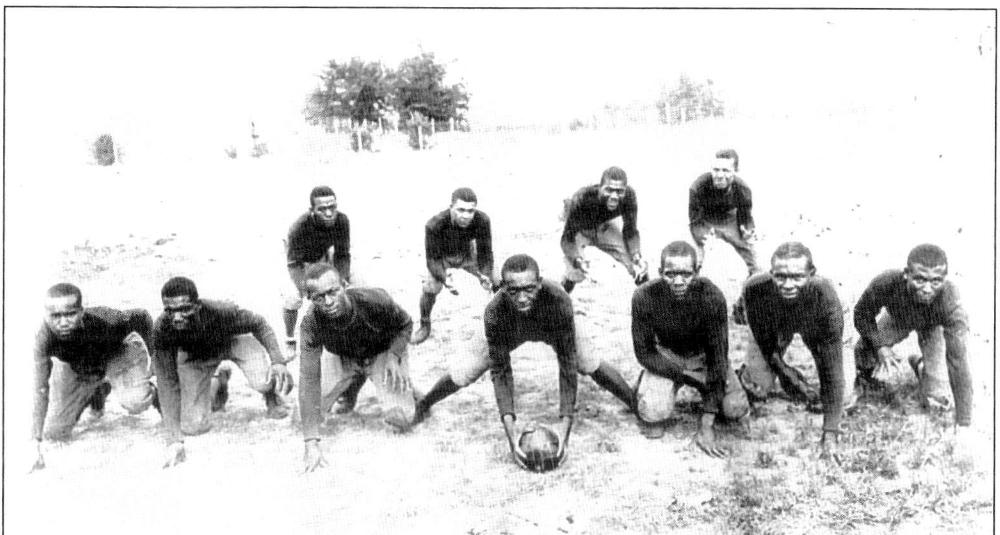

[Booker T. Washington's 1931 Champion Football Team.] Booker T. Washington's "tornadoes" football team were state champions in 1931 and champions of North Carolina, South Carolina, and Georgia in 1932. Team members, from left to right, were (front row) W. Lawson, G. Kershaw, A. Cooper, J. White, G. Phelps, M. Amos, and J. Byrd; (back row) M. Hopkins, L. Shelton, J.D. Robinson, and A. Walker. The school athletic programs were approved but not subsidized. Students sought discarded clothing and padding from other schools since the school and athletes could not afford new uniforms.

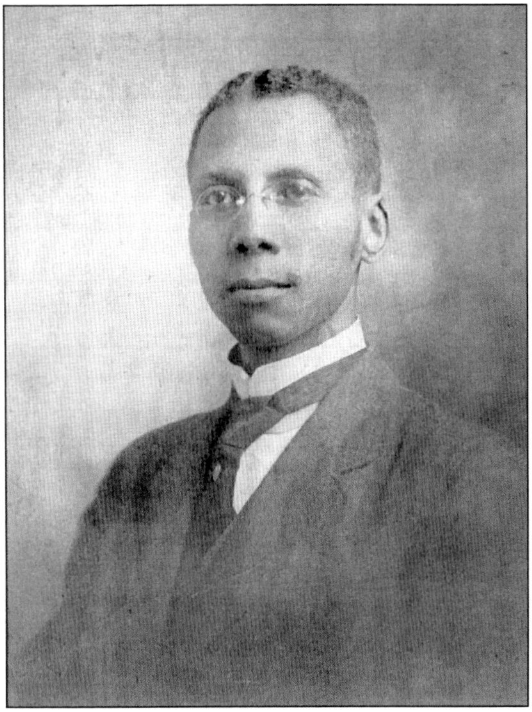

[Portrait of Nathaniel J. Frederick, 1907.] Nathaniel J. Frederick (1877–1938) was born in Orangeburg County, graduated from Claflin College with a B.A. in 1899, and studied at University of Wisconsin where he received an A.M. in 1901. Frederick became principal of Howard High School in the fall of 1902 and continued until 1918 when it became the largest black school in the South. Frederick was admitted to the S.C. Bar in 1913 where he could defend African Americans whose civil rights, jobs, or lives were in great danger. He was the editor of the Southern Indicator and the Palmetto Leader, and became a leader in black republican politics. He married Corinne Carroll and they had four children.

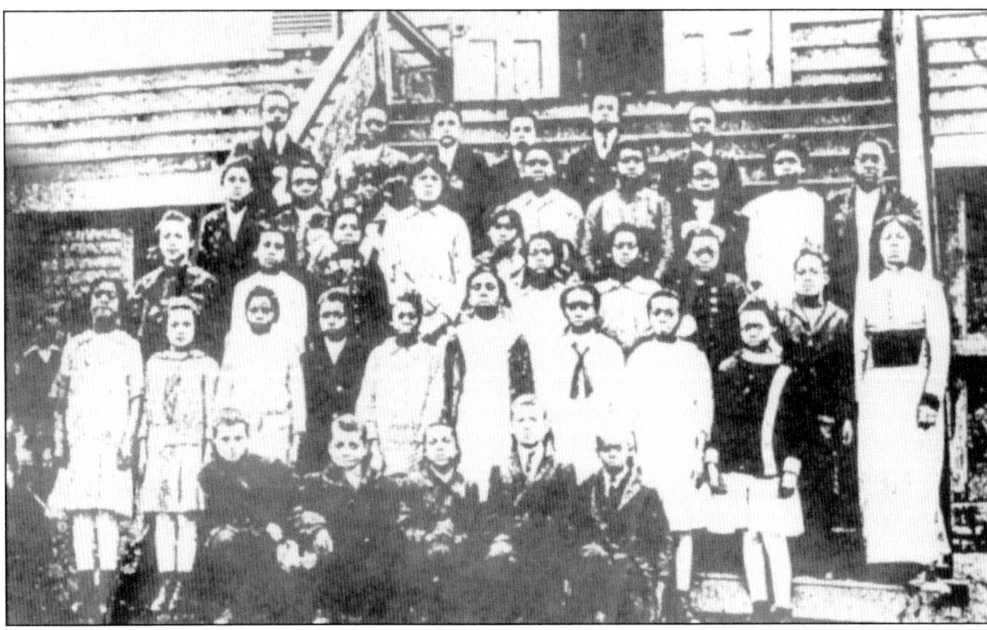

[Howard School, Fifth Grade, 1915.] Howard School was built in 1867 on the corner of Lincoln and Hampton Streets under the sponsorship of the Freedmen's Bureau and the New York Society. It was named for Gen. O.D. Howard, commissioner of the Freedmen's Bureau. In 1900, Howard was the only black school in Columbia, and it had 14 teachers and 1,272 students; later it had 25 teachers and 1,650 students. After Booker T. Washington High School was built, students north of Gervais Street went to the Howard School.

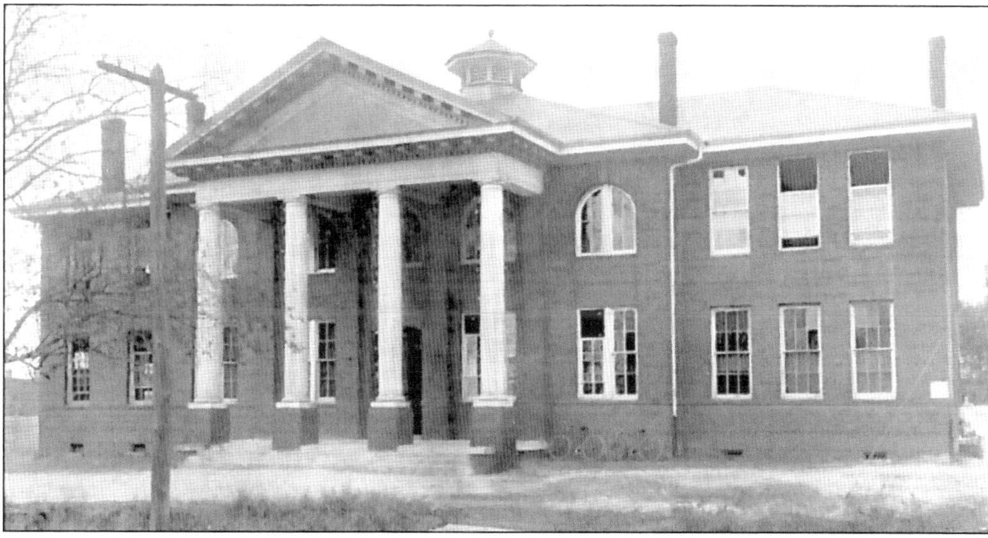

[WAVERLY SCHOOL, 1912.] The Waverly School was built at Oak and Lady Streets in 1911 and served the area east of Laurens Street and the railroad tracks. The school was annexed into the city and joined the Columbia City school system in 1913 when it had 9 teachers and 674 students. Because more and more African Americans moved into the area, the school was changed to a black school in 1923. It closed at the end of the 1970–71 school year. The Waverly community is bounded by Gervais, Harden, Taylor, and Heidt Streets.

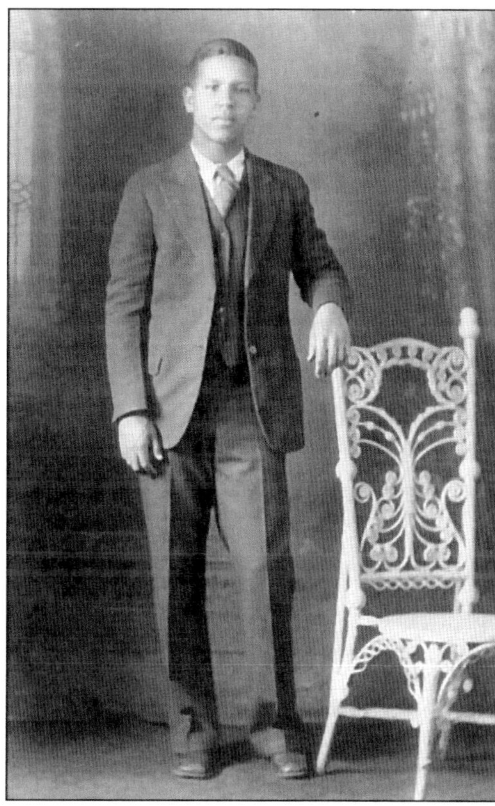

[A.P. WILLIAMS JR., 1932.] A.P. Williams (1914–1992) attended local schools before graduating from Booker T. Washington High School and the Eckels College for Embalming and Sanitary Science in 1933. He then founded funeral homes in Columbia and Lexington. Williams was a member and trustee of Zion Baptist Church in Columbia. As an active member of the Democratic Party and NAACP leader, he served as both vice president and president of the Richland County and Columbia NAACP branches, and was a leader in desegregation and civil rights activities. This portrait was taken by Richard S. Roberts, a noted Columbia photographer who documented the African-American community with photographs of the people, places, and activities for several decades.

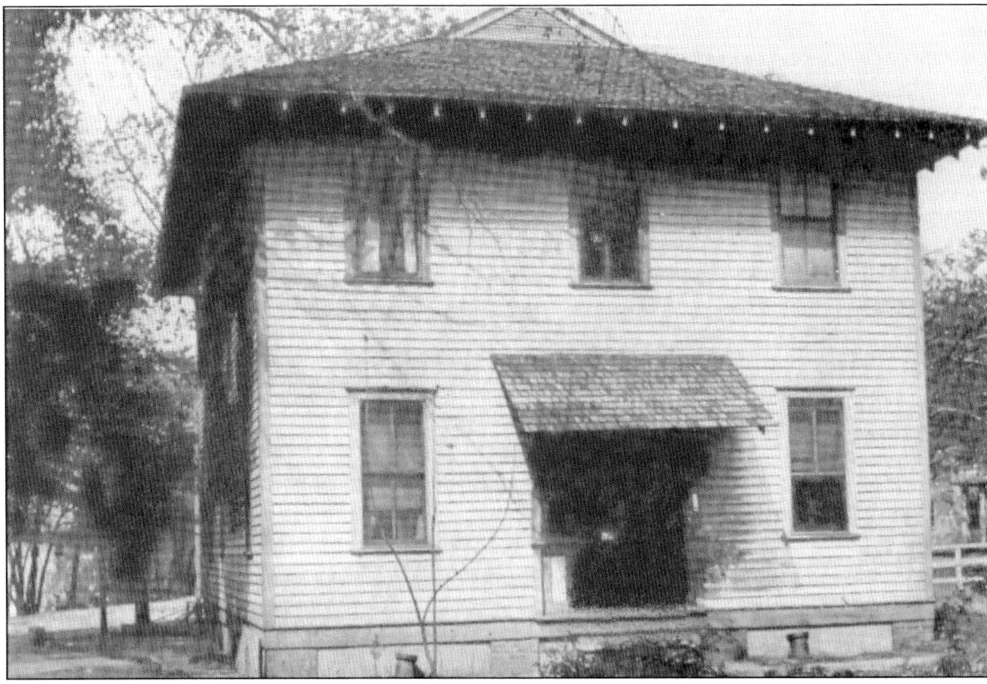

[Hospital, Benedict College, 1917.] Benedict Hospital was a two-story frame structure erected in 1914 for the care of the African-American students who were ill. The first floor had a reception room, a kitchen, a men's ward with bath, and the superintendent's apartment, while the second floor had the sterilizing and operating rooms and the women's ward with bath. It closed in 1926.

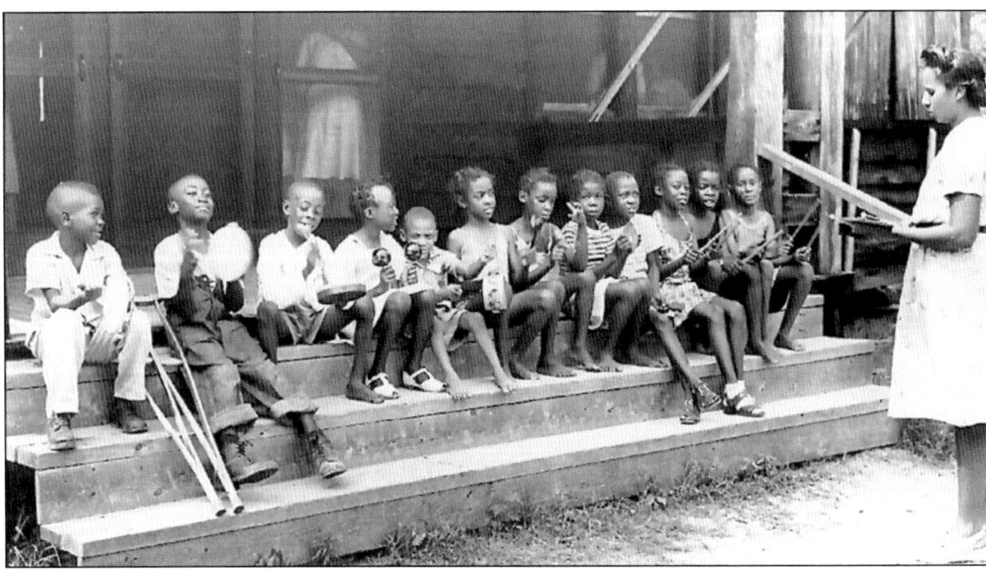

[Fairwold Camp, *c.* 1920.] This African-American campsite was located in the Fairwold area of Richland County, which was north of the 1910 city limits and near the 2000 junction of Fontaine Road and I-277. This rural site was a thinly populated agricultural area. In this picture, a teacher seems to be leading the children in a musical lesson.

[**Nursing School, Benedict College, 1917.**] Benedict's school was a three-year program covering theoretical and practical training in the hospital. One of their outstanding students, L.N. Crawford, who attended elementary, high school, and college, graduated from Benedict's nursing program to begin an exceptional nursing career in several states. Later, she was asked to be South Carolina's State Director of Practical Nurse Training among African Americans.

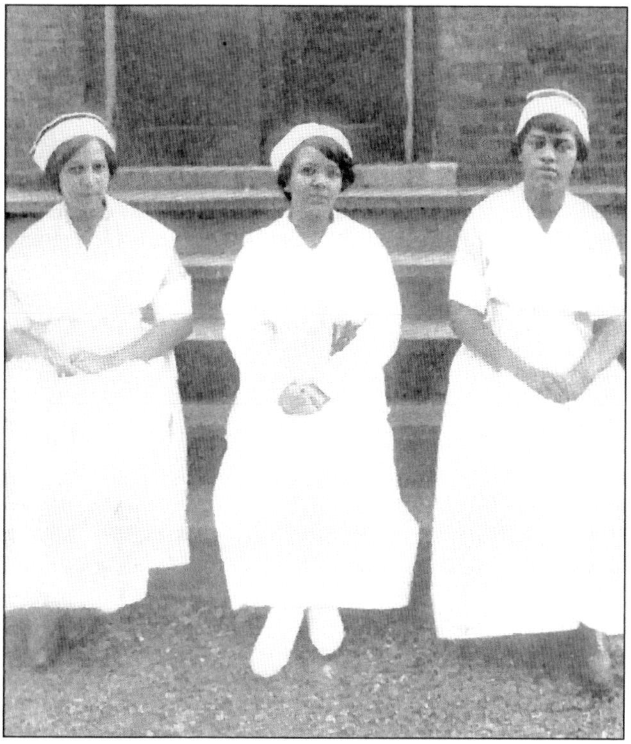

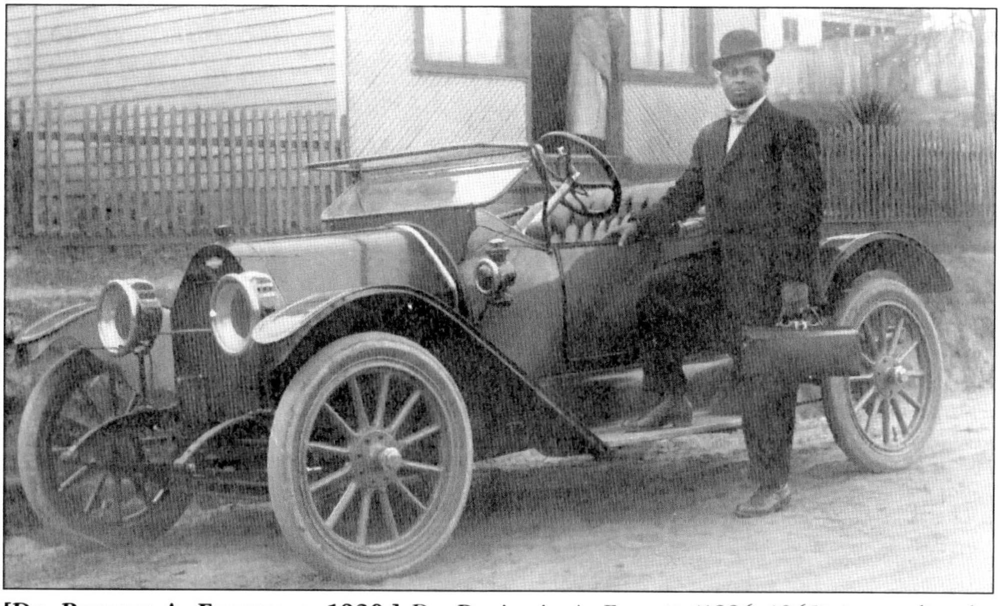

[**Dr. Benjamin A. Everett, *c.* 1920.**] Dr. Benjamin A. Everett (1886–1965) is standing by his car in front of his office on the corner of Pine and Senate Streets. A native of Texas, he finished his medical training at Meharry Medical College in Nashville, Tennessee in 1912. Everett moved to Columbia in 1913 and became one of six African-American doctors in Columbia. He married Eliza Victoria Champion, and they had a family of seven children. He was a member of both the Congaree and the Palmetto medical societies.

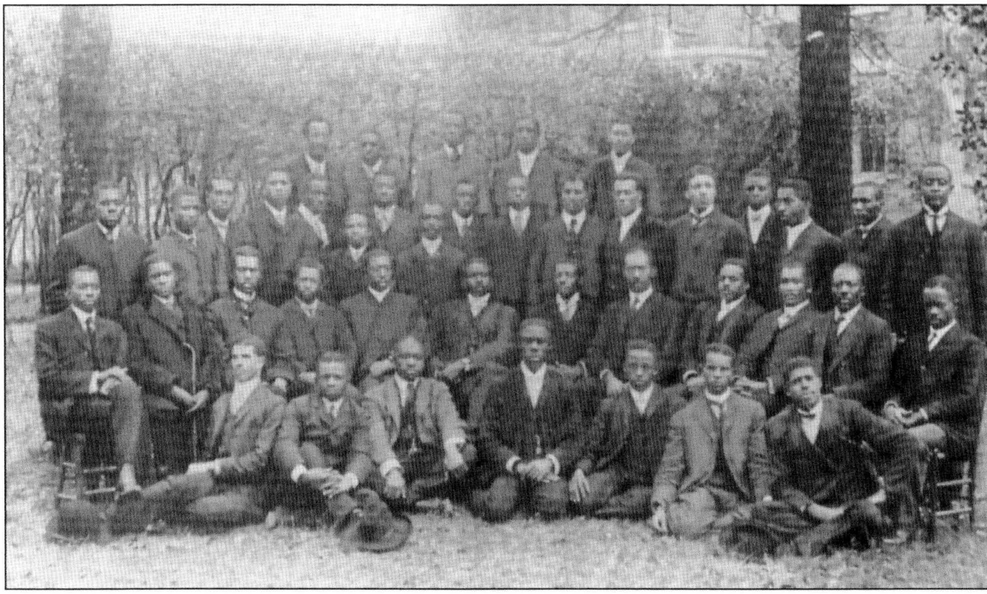

[MINISTERIAL CLASS, BENEDICT COLLEGE, 1906.] Benedict College was founded in 1870 by the American Baptist Home Mission Society through the interest of Mrs. Bathsheba A. Benedict, who bought an 80-acre plantation for a college campus site that would train African-American students to be teachers and preachers in their communities. In 1894, it was incorporated as Benedict College. Benedict's 1906 ministerial class is pictured above. In 1908, Benedict had 21 teachers, 300 residents, and 405 other students.

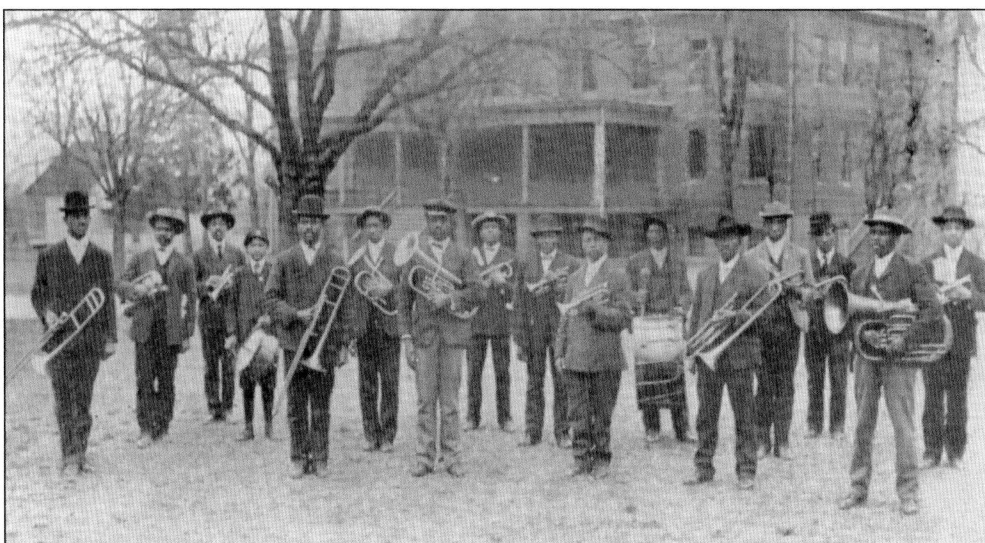

[BAND, BENEDICT COLLEGE, 1906.] Benedict's band was a 16-instrument marching group under the direction of Alonzo Hardy. It was a part of the music program that includes vocal and piano training over six grades and a four-year organ course. Their band played at various academic, athletic, and social venues.

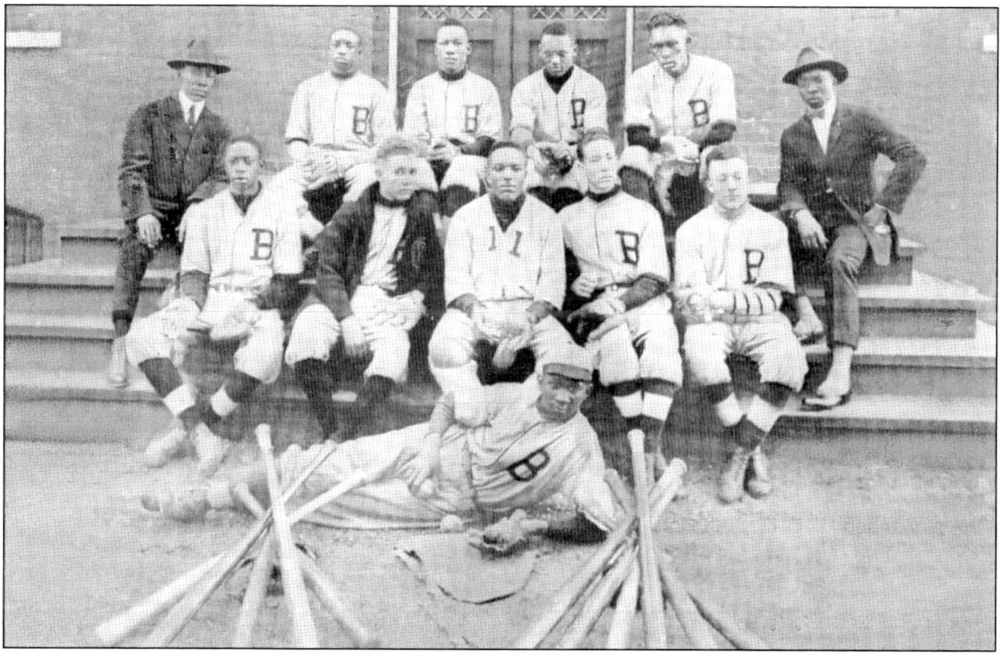

[BASEBALL TEAM, BENEDICT COLLEGE, 1917.] Benedict College's baseball team needed to use high school and college students in order to field a team; some members even played seven or eight years. James H. Walker was the manager and Glasgow Humphries was the captain of the 1917 "Tiger" team.

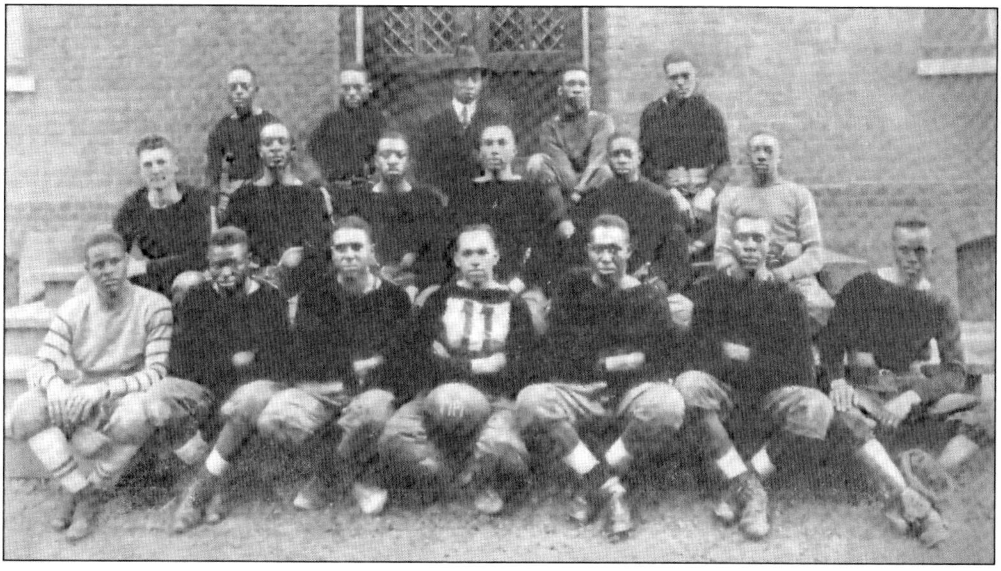

[FOOTBALL TEAM, BENEDICT COLLEGE, 1917.] The Tiger champion football team put Benedict College on the front pages of African-American football publications. Like the other Benedict teams it also used high school and college students. W.P. Williams was the manager and J. Blaine Rowe was the team captain of the 1917 team. The Tiger team played in the Georgia-Carolina League of black colleges in the three states with the Tigers winning five successive championships in the mid-1920s.

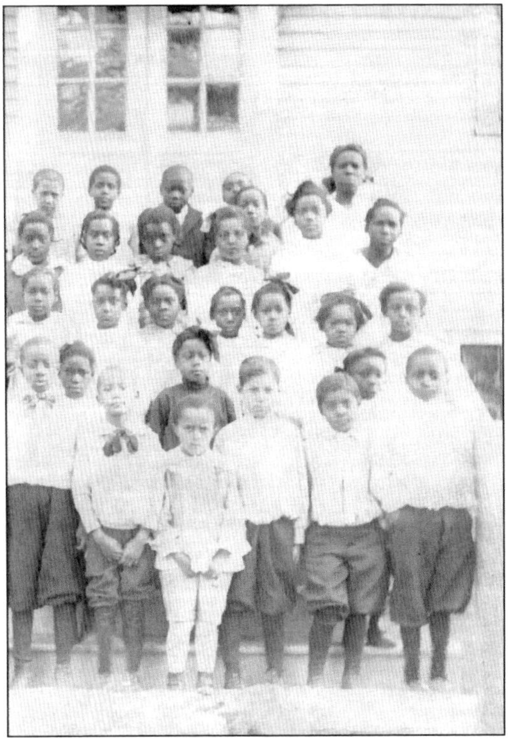

[Graded School, Allen University, *c.* 1910.] One of Allen's contributions to the Waverly community was to offer elementary classes to the African-American children living in that area. In 1908, Allen had 15 teachers and 150 students. In that era, a student could start school in the first grade, graduate with a college degree, and be prepared to be a teacher or preacher.

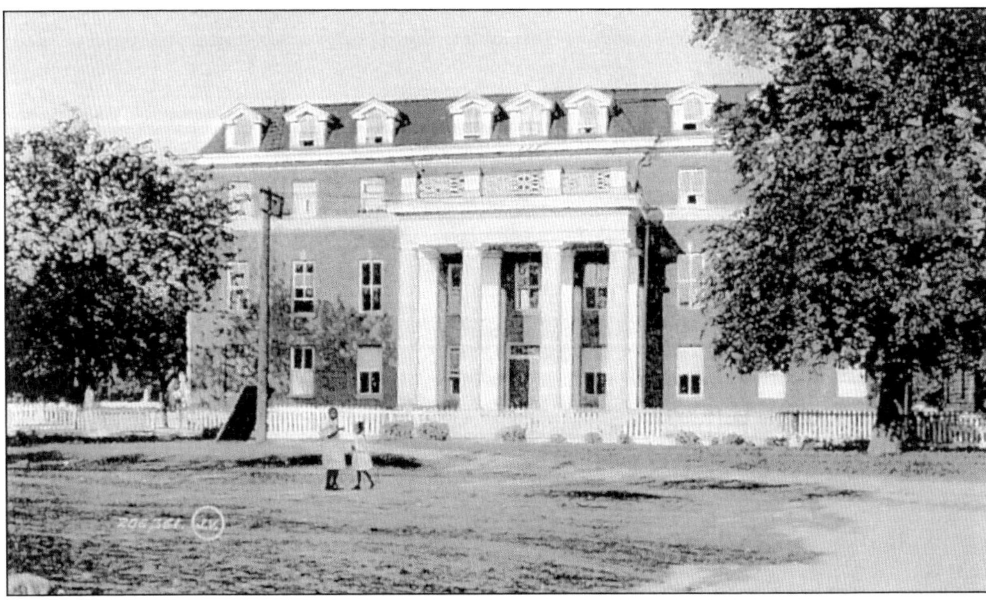

Allen University [Columbia, SC, 1907]. Allen University, initially called Payne Institute when it was established at Cokesbury in 1870, moved to Columbia in 1880 and was incorporated as Allen University. It was named after Bishop Richard Allen (1760–1831), who founded the African Methodist Episcopal Church in 1891. The Levi J. Coppin Hall, a four-story dormitory seen above, was constructed in 1906 at the corner of Harden and Hampton Streets. It was renovated in 1956.

[Ms. Walker & Penn, c. 1920s.] The portrait shows Lorinda Boulware Walker (seated) and Maggie Belle Penn (standing), two Columbia ladies who were seamstresses that made and altered clothing for African-Americans in their community. This portrait was made by J.W. Johnson, who had his photographic studio at 1109 Washington Street in Columbia

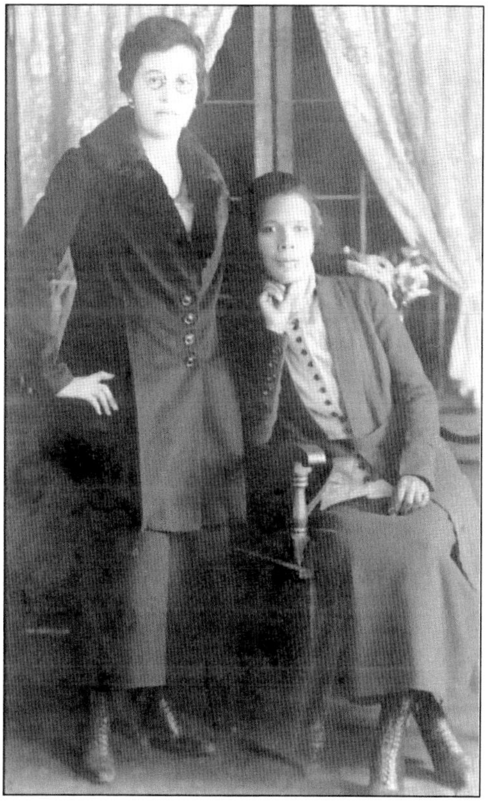

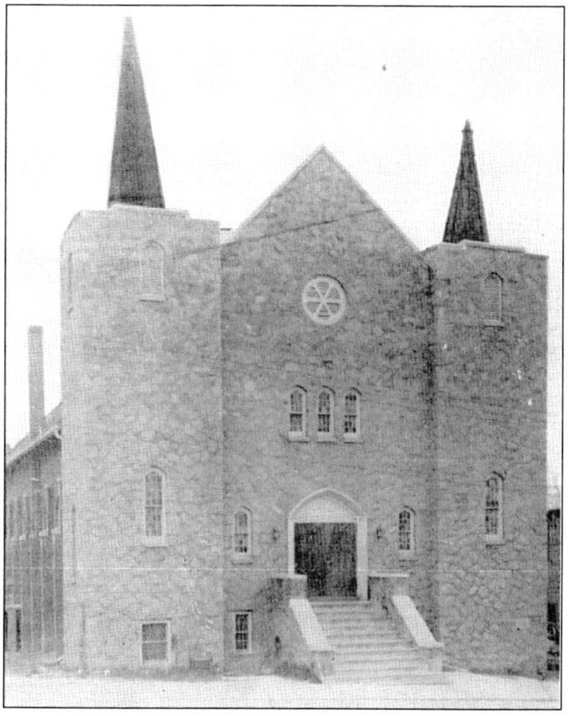

[Union Baptist Church, c. 1940s.] The African American Union Baptist Church's initial structure was dedicated on July 20, 1907 at the juncture of Assembly and Blossom Street across from the Blossom Street School (page 74). Continuing modifications occurred during the next decades when the stone edifice above was constructed. It served the black community of Ward One, which was positioned from Gervais Street to the southern railroad tracks paralleling the Rice Street extension and from the Congaree River to Wheeler Hill. The University of South Carolina bought this property for $100,000 and adjacent lots in 1966, razed all the buildings on the block, and built the Coliseum. The church's site is now beneath the arena. The congregation rebuilt their sanctuary on Germany Street.

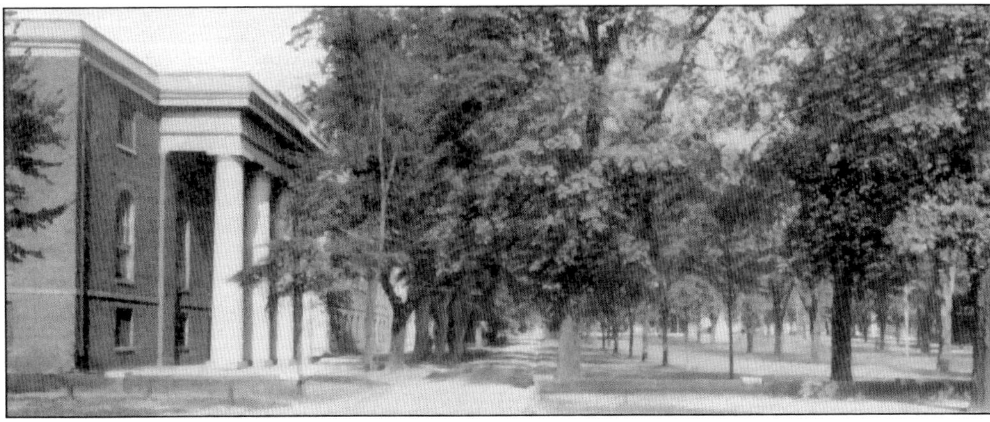

The Library and Campus, University of South Carolina, Columbia, SC [1907]. The University of South Carolina's South Caroliniana Library was completed in 1840 and possibly designed by Robert Mills. This Greek-Revival structure was the first separated college library building in the nation. The second floor reading room is a replica of the Bullfinch Reading Room at the Library of Congress. Additional east and west wings were designed by Columbia Architect J. Carroll Johnson in 1927. It contains excellent collections of historical books, papers, manuscripts, pictures, postcards, and maps of South Carolina.

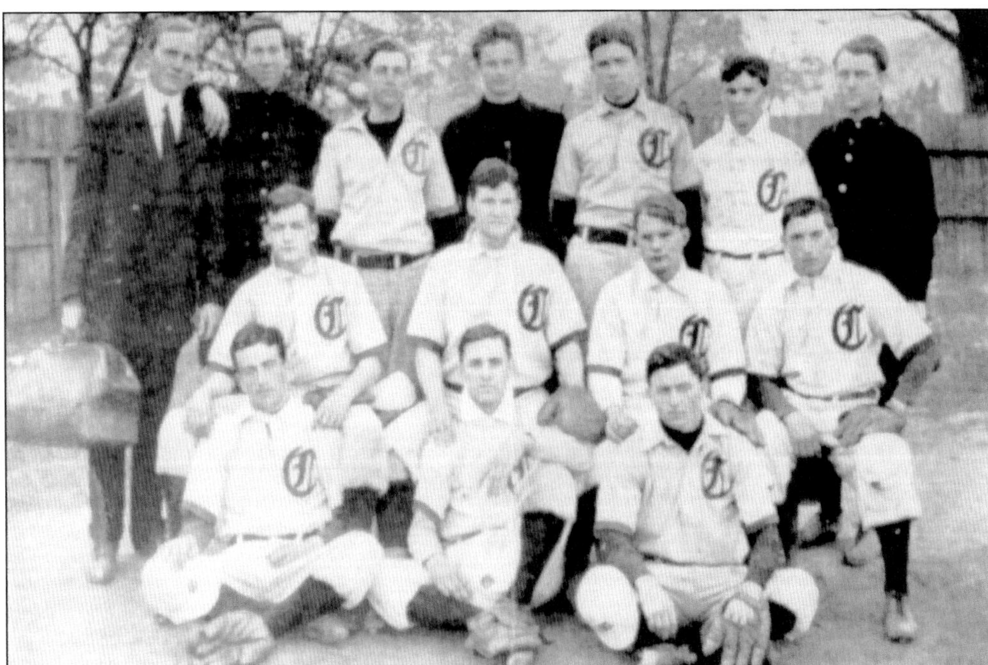

[Baseball Team, University of South Carolina, 1910.] Members of the 1910 varsity baseball team received individual postcards of their official team portrait, which was also placed in the annual. This example brags about their victory over the Citadel's team. The 1910 team, coached by "Vinegar Bill" Breitenstein, had a record of 11 wins and 7 losses. Players included Belser (C), captain; C.T. Graydon, manager; H.G. Officer, assistant manager; Foxworth (2nd); Wideman (3rd); McMillan (SS); Simpson (RF); Havird (LF); Harper, Wyche, Shaw (P); Watts (CF); Waring, and Metts (1st).

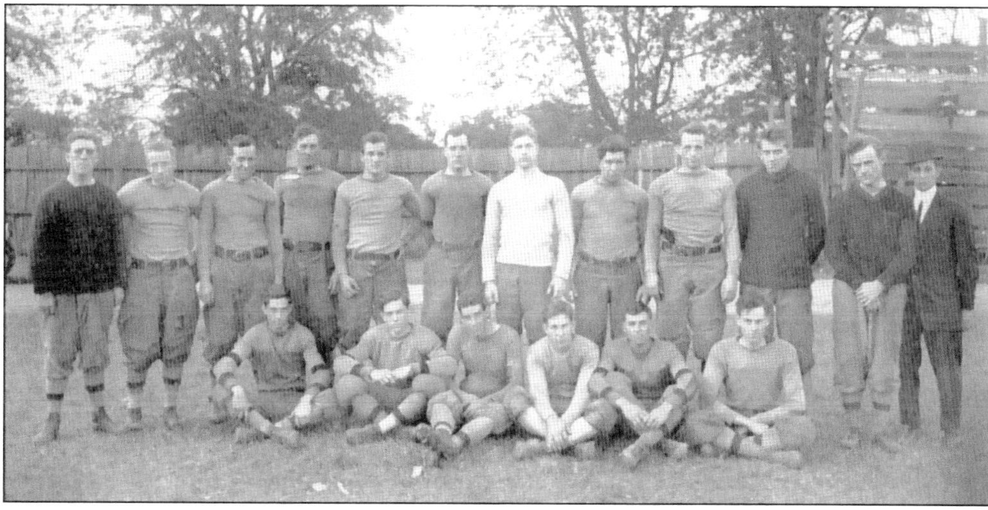

[FOOTBALL TEAM, UNIVERSITY OF SOUTH CAROLINA, 1913.] Dr. N.B. Edgerton, coach, and J.G. Driver, assistant coach, led the 1913 varsity football team to a record of five wins (Carolina 22–Clemson 7), two losses, and one tie. Their roster included C. Fitzsimons Jr., manager; B. Davenport and M.L. Hannahan, assistant manager; Alfred von Kolnitz, captain (LHB), Girardeau (C); Stoney (RG); McGourm (RT); Porter (LG); Mills (LT); Sligh (RE); Hill (LE); Langston (RHB); Heyward (QB); and Passcidaigue (FB).

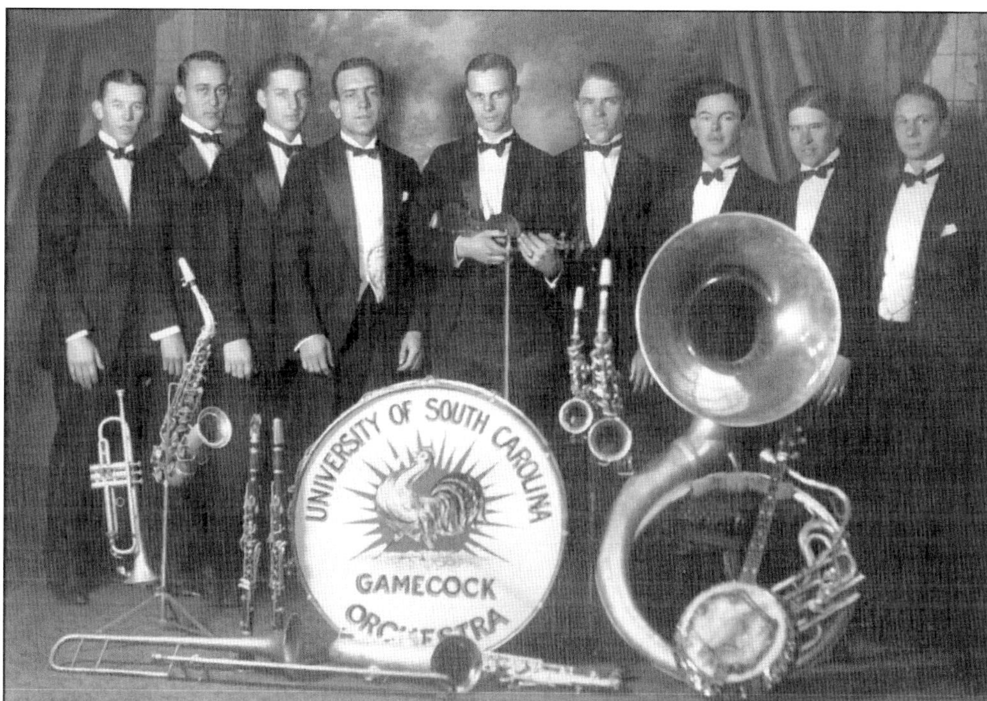

[ORCHESTRA, UNIVERSITY OF SOUTH CAROLINA, 1926.] The orchestra, from left to right, included W. Watson (piano), E. Whitehead (trumpet), L. Edwards (trombone), T. Stone (drums), N. Wimberly (director, violin), P. Lupo (sax), A. Lupo (bass), F. Lupo (sax), and C. Saunders (banjo).

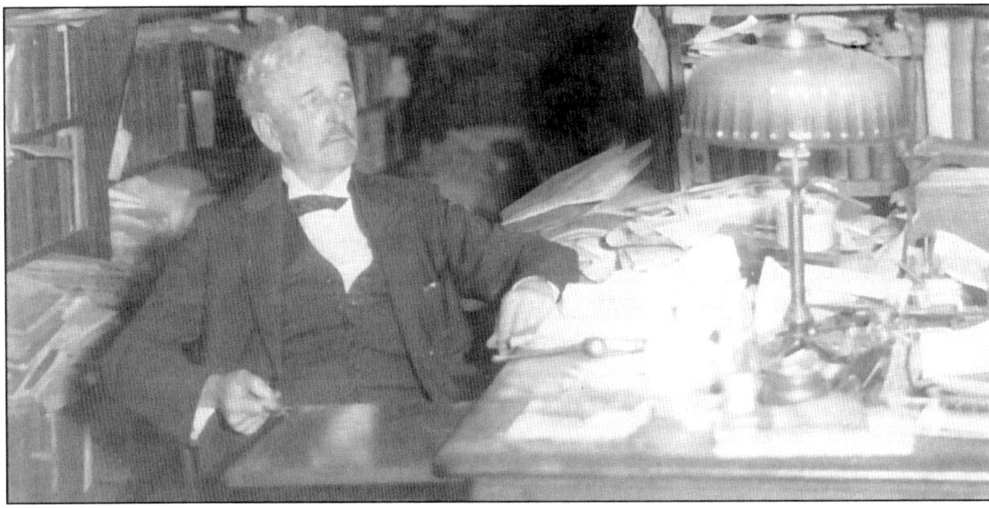

[PROFESSOR YATES SNOWDEN, 1910.] Yates Snowden (1858–1933) was a professor of history at the University of South Carolina from 1905 to 1933. He graduated from the College of Charleston in 1879 and studied at Columbia University in 1904–05. The College of Charleston gave him an honorary doctor of laws degree in 1910. Professor Snowden was a recognized authority on the history of South Carolina and its economic, political, and cultural facets. Snowden was a member of the Historical Commission of South Carolina from 1907 to 1929.

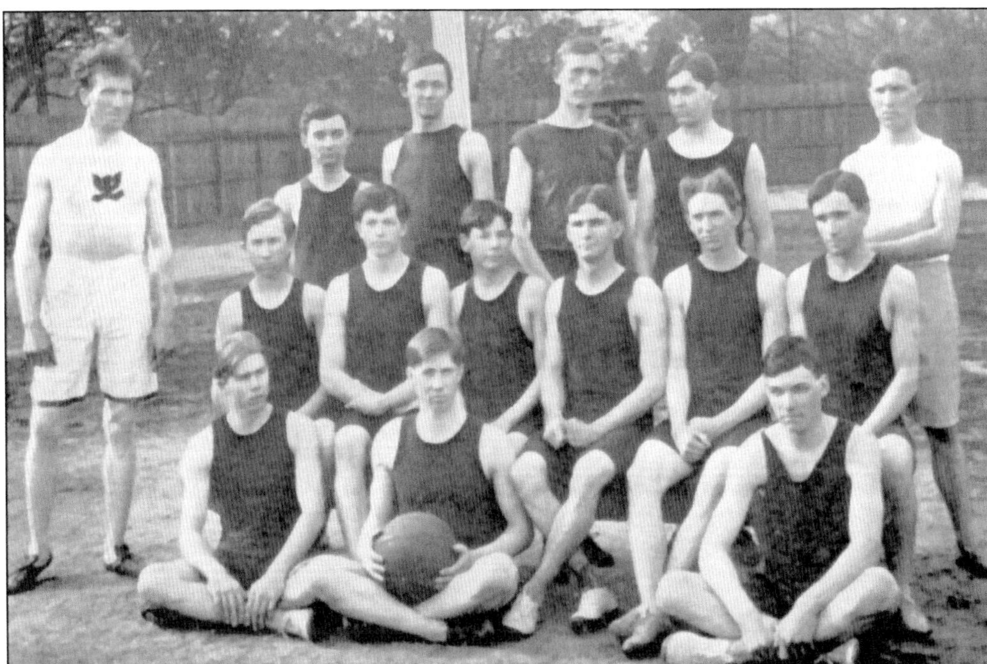

[BASKETBALL TEAM, UNIVERSITY OF SOUTH CAROLINA, 1908.] The 1907–08 varsity basketball team included C.C. Kinard, L.W. Warren, P.W. Jayroe, P.W. Ferguson, J.C. Vassy, R.M. McLeod, J.B. Jackson, A.B. Adams, V.J. Rector, L.O. Bruce, W.F. Hiers, J.O. Crout, P.W. Wright, and E.W. Bodie.

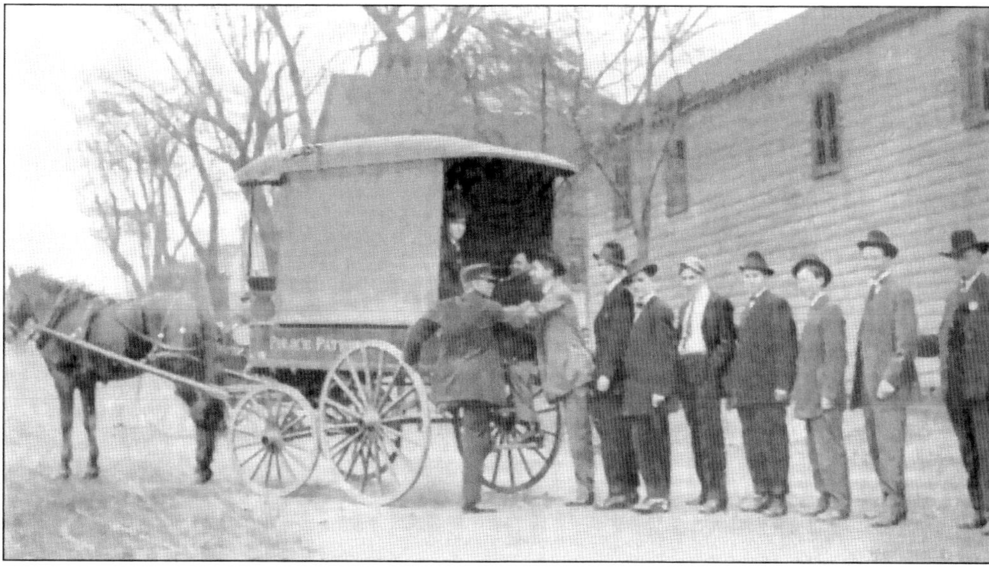

[EDGEFIELD COUNTY CLUB, 1911.] The University of South Carolina's Edgefield County Club was one example of a student social club in 1911 when fraternities were not permitted on campus. Students then formed unofficial clubs with some named after their home county. The Edgefield County Club illustrates the students' free-spirited nature by using comical slogans, titles, and staged club photographs. The officers of this club were B.T. Rainsford (1st turkey), P.L. Wright (2nd turkey), J.S. Herin (dispenser of uniforms) and M.A. Wright (pick sharpener).

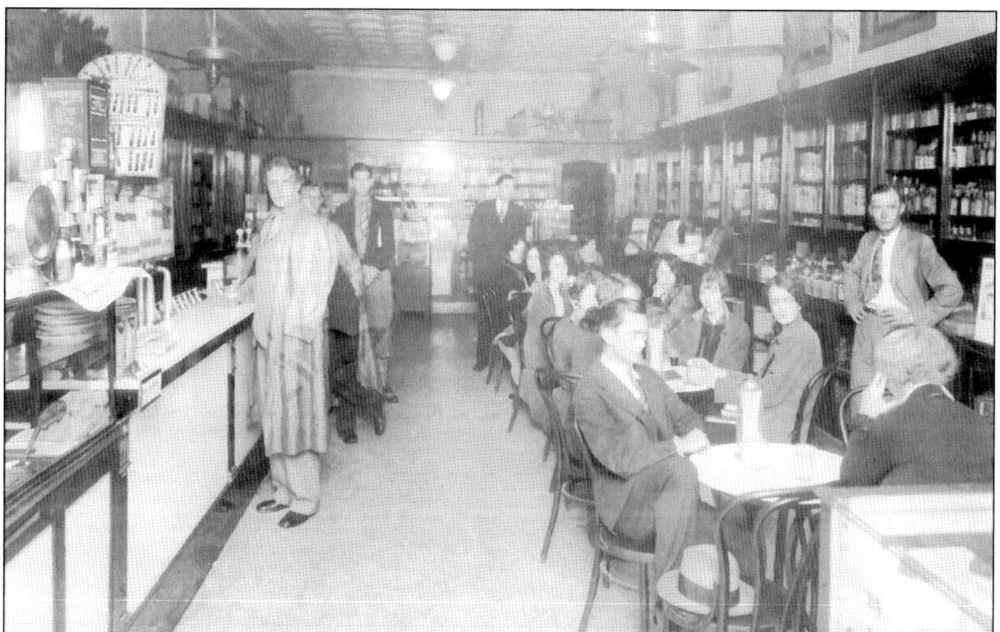

[BURNETT'S DRUG STORE, C. 1920S.] Burnett's Drug Store at 829 Main Street near the corner of Main and College Streets was a convenient meeting place for students at the University of South Carolina in the late 1920s.

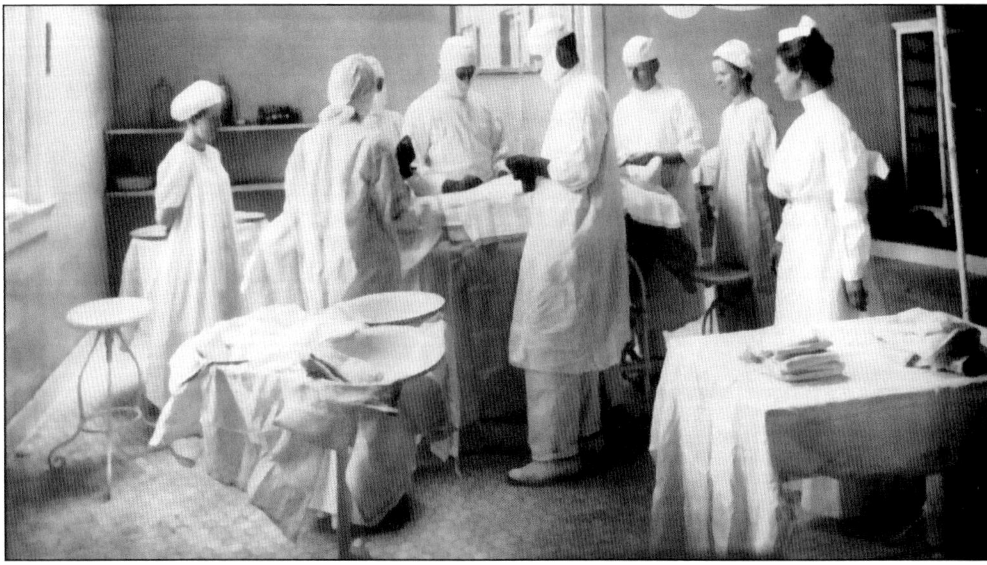

[**Surgery, Hospital Room, Columbia Hospital, 1909.**] Columbia's initial surgery was accomplished in the homes of the patients. With the expanded 70-bed facilities in 1909, surgical rooms developed controlled hygienic conditions. The hospital administration was turned over to the 26 doctors in the Columbia Medical Society who created individual departments, became organized, and were offering more scientific and professional care. The society managed the hospital until 1921 when it transferred the 3-story, 115-bed hospital to the Richland County legislative delegation.

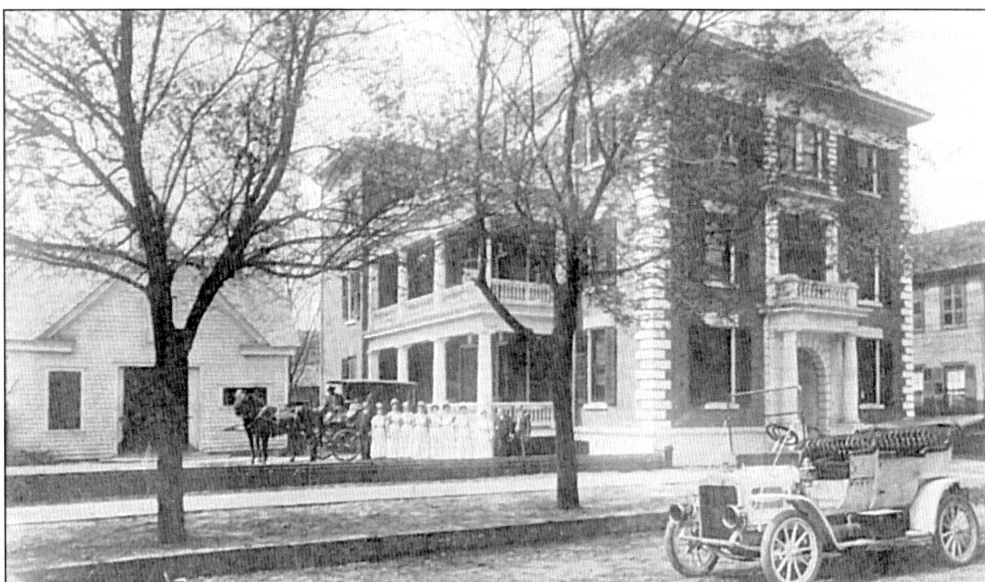

Knowlton Hospital, Columbia, SC [1908]. In the early 1900s Dr. Augustus B. Knowlton, a specialist in abdominal surgery, opened Columbia's first private general hospital at 1517 Marion Street. Under the name of the Knowlton Infirmary, it operated 70 beds until 1914 when it was purchased by the South Carolina Baptist State Convention and became the South Carolina Baptist Hospital.

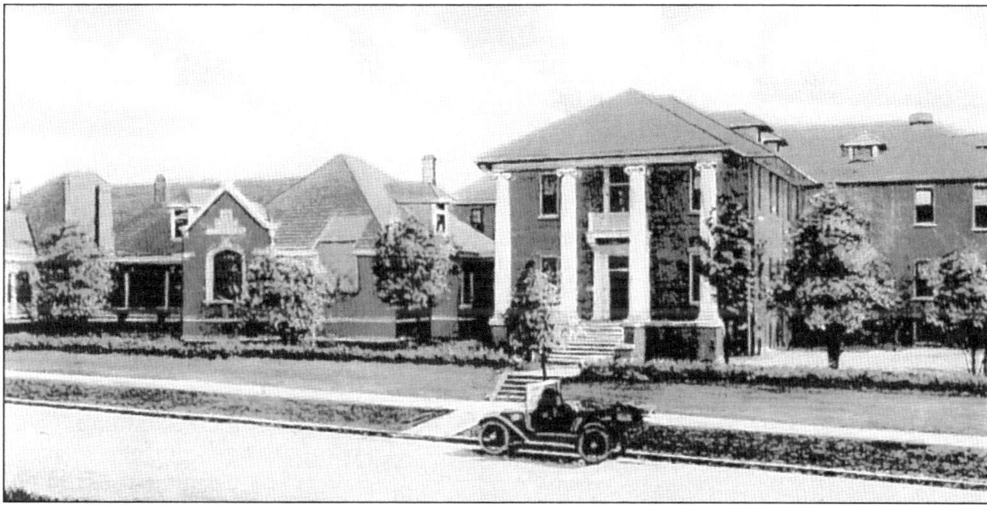

Columbia Hospital, Columbia, SC [1910]. The Columbia Hospital Association, formed by the United King's Daughters, was formed in 1892 with a 20-bed, two-story brick hospital, erected in 1893 at 2000 Hampton Street. Additions were made in 1904 and in 1906. In 1910, two wings were added to the main brick building, which expanded the bed total to 115. Rates of $10.00–$15.00 a week were charged for private rooms and $5.00–$7.00 for wards.

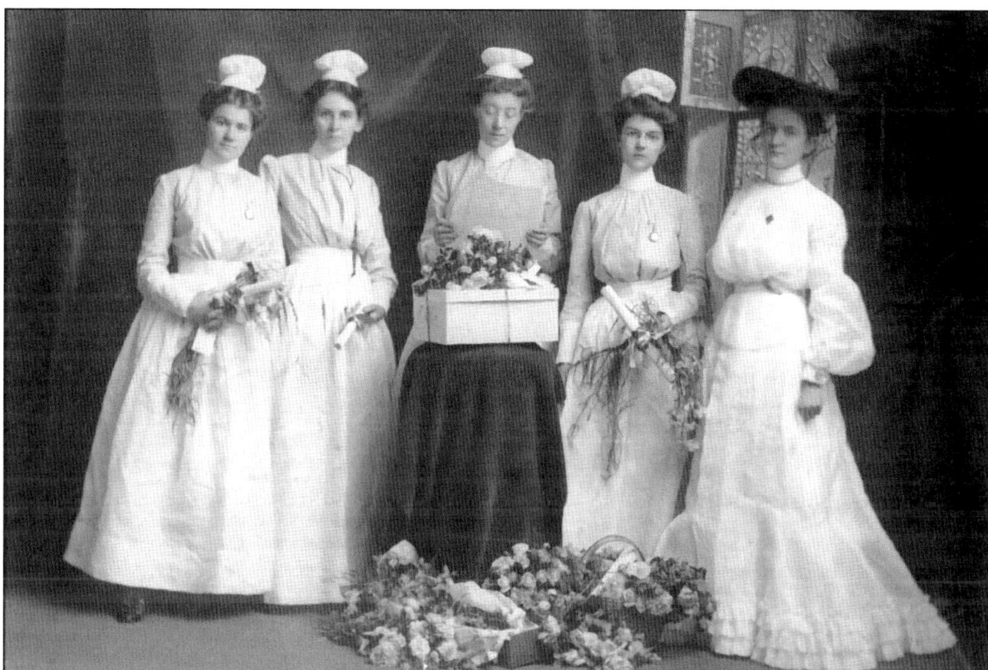

[Nurses, Columbia Hospital, 1910.] The Columbia Hospital Training School for Nurses began in 1897. Their extensive duties covered medical care and cooking for the patients, along with making out bills and ordering supplies for the hospital. The nurses' uniform included a blue gingham dress, linen collar, white apron, and a linen cap. The Walter Taylor home for nurses (1907) stands in the center of the grounds that cover four acres.

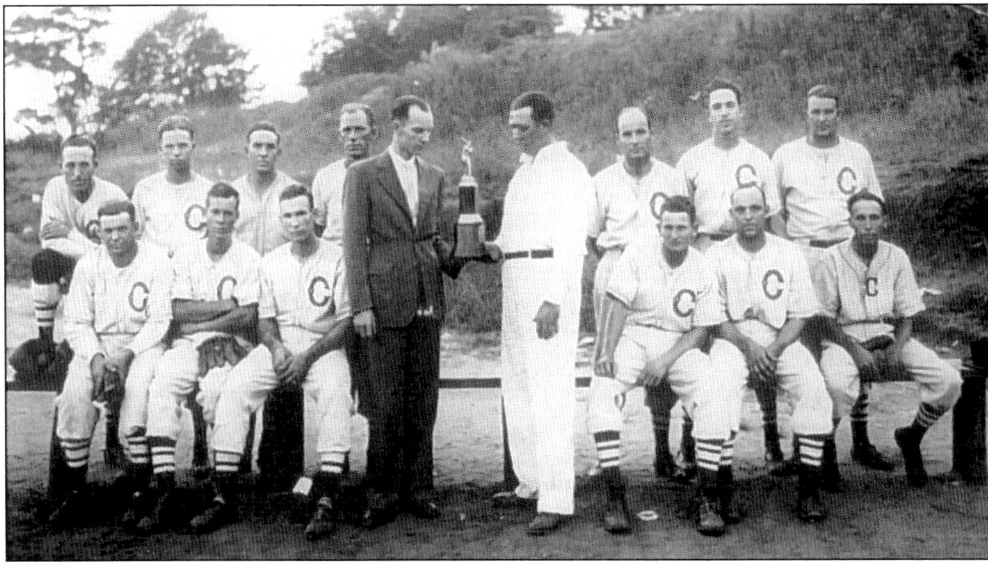

[Columbia Baseball Team, 1920s.] Baseball was the favorite pastime during this era. The employees of various city departments created amateur baseball teams during the first decades of the 20th century; their games were played at the fairgrounds' baseball field. The image above has the championship trophy being given to the winning city team.

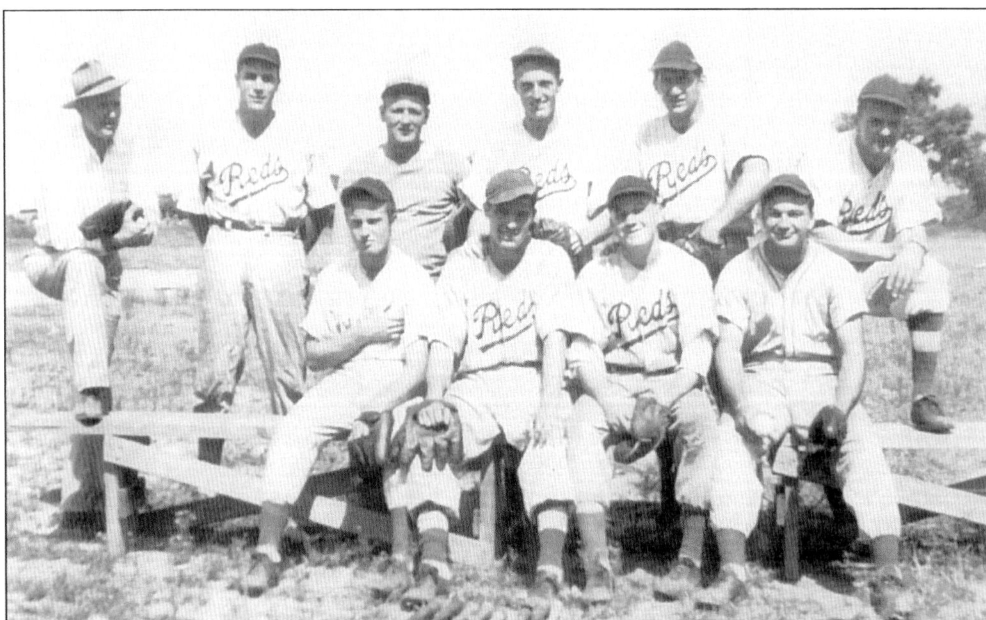

[Reds Baseball Team, 1930s.] During the 1930s, Columbia had a minor league team affiliated with the Cincinnati Reds of National League. The Columbia team also used the name "Reds" and played in the South Atlantic (Sally) League. The picture above includes William Howard Henry (1909–1986) from Swansea standing in the back row, extreme right. They played their games at the Assembly Street baseball field, which is still being used in 2000.

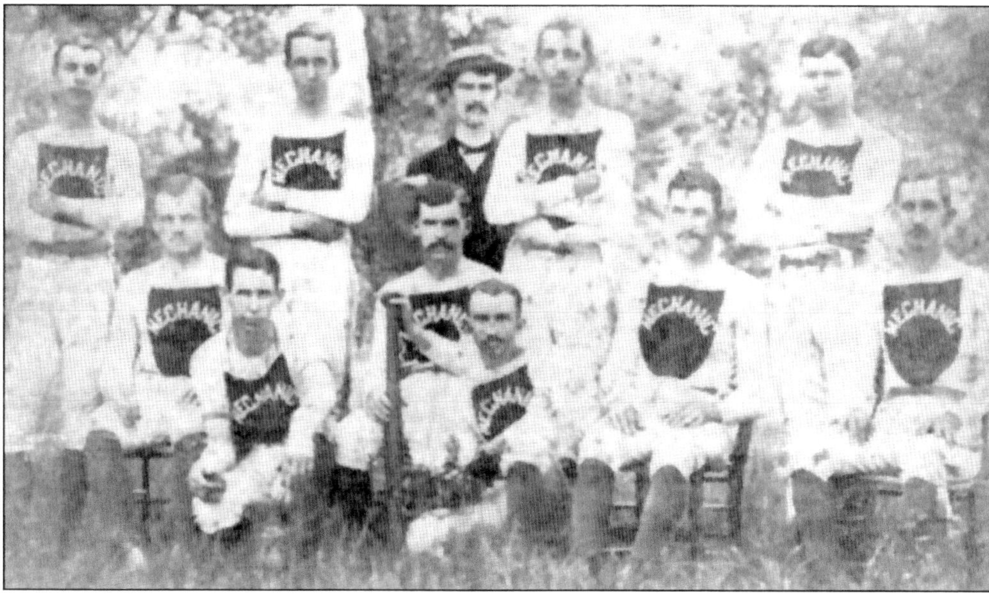

[Mechanics Baseball Team, 1910s.] Each community during the first third of the 1900s sponsored and enthusiastically supported amateur baseball teams. The passion crossed all groups, young and old, white or black, poor or rich. Sponsors like retail stores, mills, churches, or clubs would field teams with some hiring ringers (illegal substitutes) who excelled in pitching or hitting. The picture above of the Mechanics Baseball Team consisted of railroad workers. These teams played in loosely organized leagues in the city.

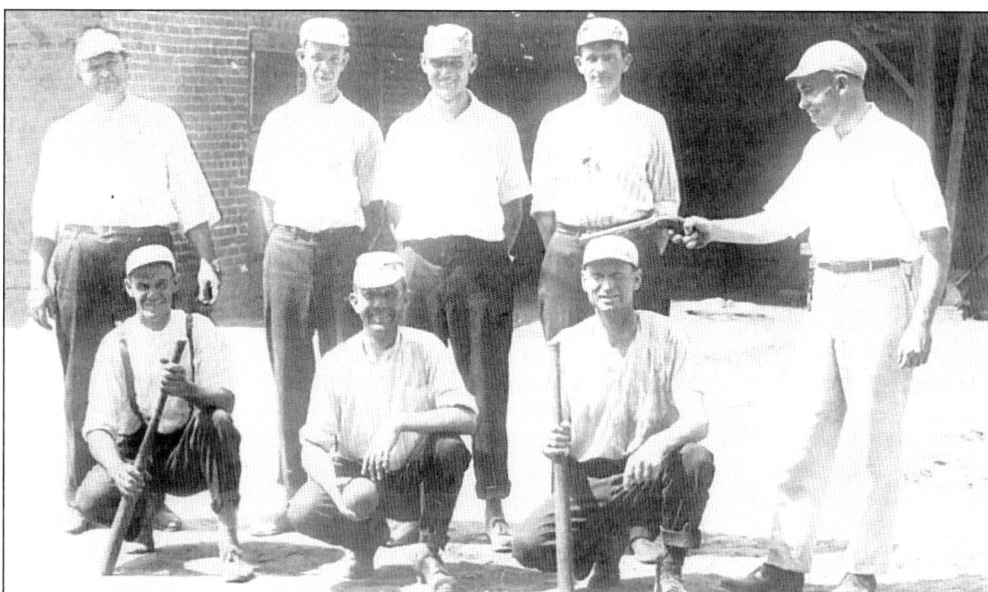

[Baseball Team, Fire Department 1903.] The Fire Department's baseball team, photographed by T.C. Zobel, is just one of many teams made up of workers of various groups, who played games on weekends. Various sponsors supported boy scouts' and girl scouts' teams, as well as other youth teams.

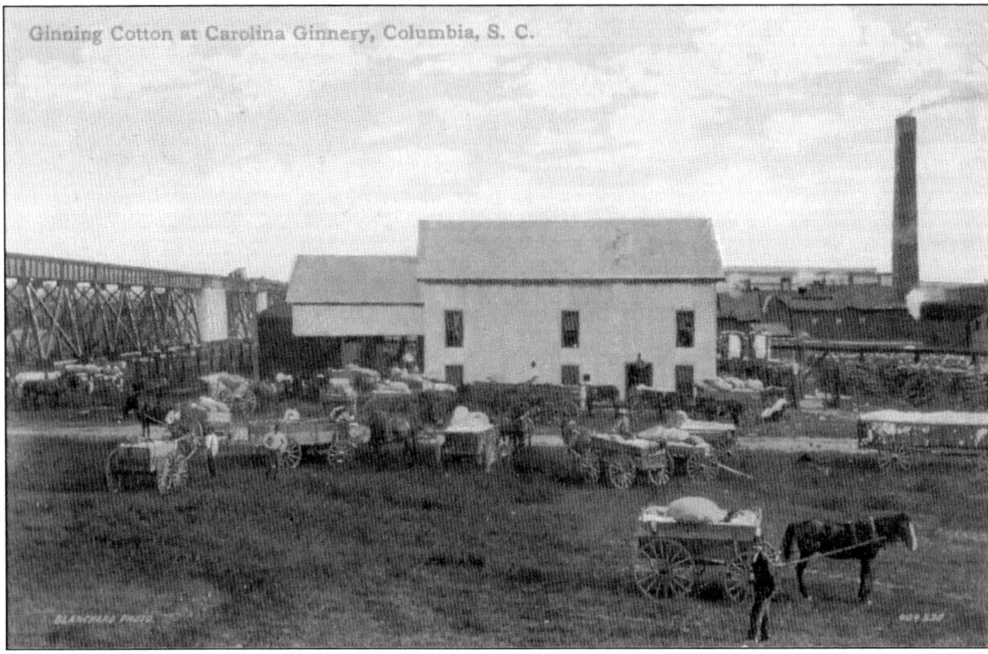

GINNING COTTON AT CAROLINA GINNERY, COLUMBIA, SC [1908]. The cotton gin was a part of every town in the cotton belt. This view of a cotton gin has the Seaboard Air Line railroad trestle, built in 1900, along the right-of-way on Lincoln Street from Pendleton Street to Olympia in the background, along with a smoke stack in the distance.

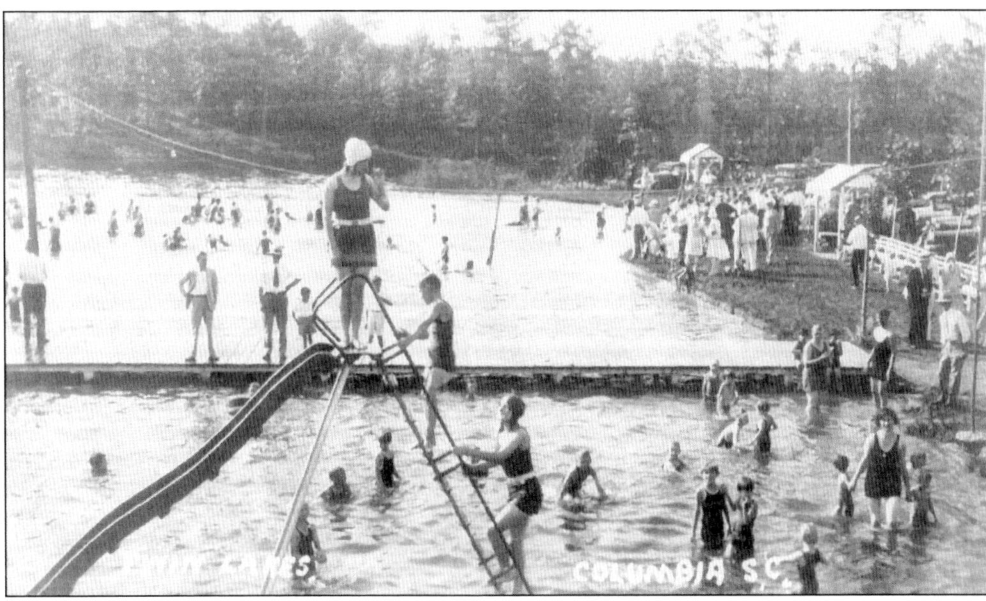

TWIN LAKES [*c.* 1930s]. Public swimming pools and air conditioners did not exist in the Columbia of this era. To escape the heat, those who were able to travel did go to one of the lakes in the area. Twin Lakes was the most popular public swimming site because of its easy access, the convenient pavilions with dressing areas, and the snack bars. During World War II, Fort Jackson took it over for a recreation area.

Four

VIEWS OF CAMP JACKSON

In January 1917, an inspection tour of the land between Garners Ferry Road and Old Camden Road was given to several army officers. In May 1917, Maj. D. MacArthur said it was official that Columbia would be a site for one of the camps. Hardaway Construction Company from Columbus, Georgia., received the contract to build quarters for 30,000 men within 90 days. In June, Maj. W. Couper, director of project, arrived in Columbia; by mid-summer, 10,000 men were constructing the camp, called a "Field Artillery Replacement Depot." Major Couper turned the camp over to the U.S. Army on January 19, 1918. An initial $8,897,430 had been spent to construct the camp that could house 40,647 men and 12,247 animals. The camp then consisted of 1,554 buildings on 2,737 camp acres in a 12,804-acre reservation of sand hills previously thought to be worthless for farming. The total cost of Camp Jackson was $12 million. On July 12, 1917, the Columbia's units, Company F (105 men), Company G (94 men), and Company H (122 men) of the South Carolina National Guard arrived at the site to begin organizing the camp. The first recruits, many from South Carolina, arrived on September 1, 1917. The camp's population peaked at 44,242 in July 1918. Seventy thousand soldiers were demobilized in 1919.

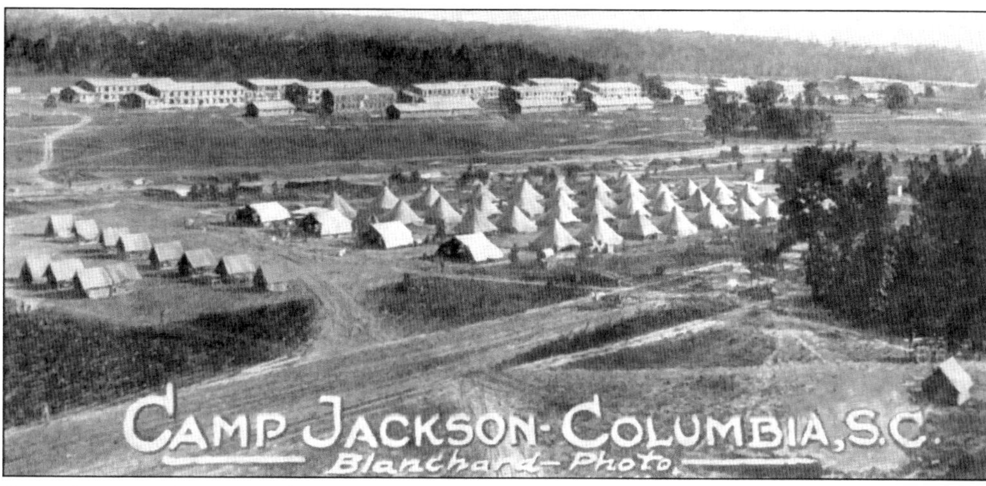

CAMP JACKSON, COLUMBIA, SC [JUNE 1918]. The Act of May 1917 created the 316th Field Artillery Regiment of the U.S. Army at Camp Jackson, which formed the heavy artillery unit of the 156th Field Artillery Brigade, 8th Division. By August 28, 1917, the camp had 10,585 men. The 81st "Wildcat" Division, commanded by Gen. Charles J. Bailey, was organized and began training on August 25, 1917. The infantry regiment of the 81st left for Camp Sevier on May 18, 1918, and later left for France, where it saw action in the Lorraine and Meuse-Argonne campaigns. The artillery unit of the 81st Division remained at Camp Jackson before leaving for France in August 1918. The 30th ("Old Hickory") Division trained from August 1917 to May 1918. The 5th moved in after May 18, 1918.

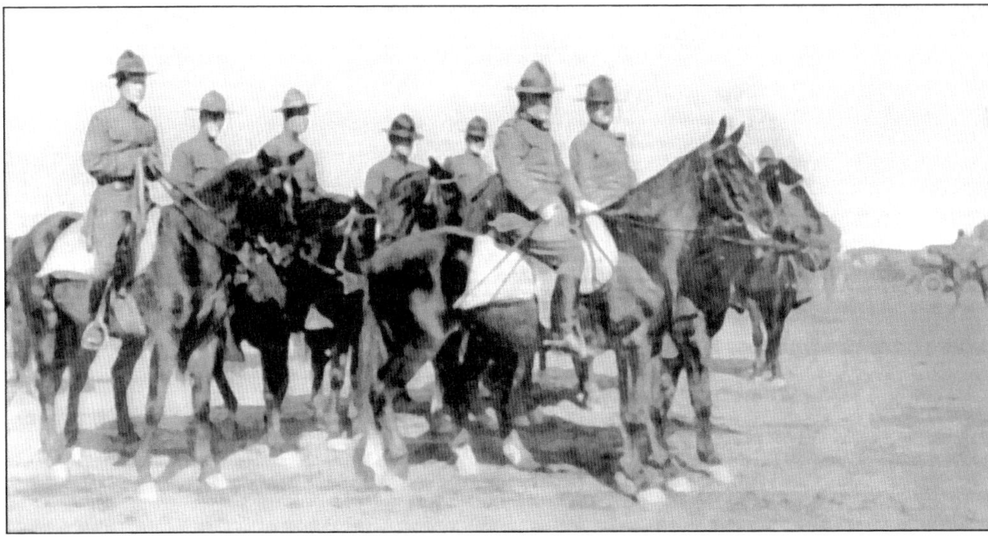

Major General Bailey and Staff, Camp Jackson, Columbia, SC [*c.* 1918]. The generals directing the training at Camp Jackson were Brig. Gen. C.H. Barth, August 26,1917; Maj. Gen C.J. Bailey, October 15, 1917; Brig. Gen. R.M. Danford, September 4, 1918; and Brig. Gen. T.H. Rees, December 18, 1918. The generals directing demobilization were Brig. Gen. W.E. Cole, January 7, 1919 and Brig. Gen. S.L. Faison, April 4, 1919. Camp Jackson was abandoned on April 25, 1921. The wrecking of Camp Jackson was in process in 1925 when it was reopened as a training base for South Carolina National Guard units that summer. It continued in that capacity until 1939.

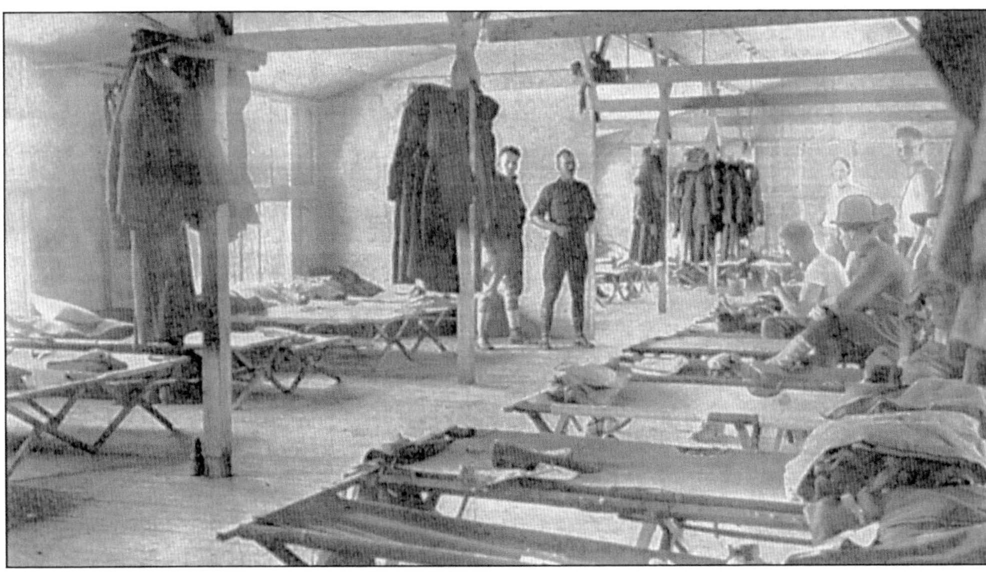

Dormitory in the Cantonment Barracks, U.S. National Army, Camp Jackson, Columbia, SC [*c.* 1918]. The 1,554 buildings in Camp Jackson included an administration building, officers' quarters, barracks, bath houses, canteens, mess halls, kitchens, a post office, a hospitality house, telephone and telegraph exchanges, hospitals, a library, a YMCA hut, a fire station, a theatre, a Knights of Columbus Hall, Christian Science Welfare buildings, and stables.

Souvenir, First Wild Cat Reunion, Columbia, SC [Sept. 20–22, 1920]. Over 4,000 veterans came from across the nation to visit old comrades at the first 81st Wild Cat Division reunion in Columbia. W.C. McGowan of Columbia, president of the Wild Cat Veterans Association, and supporting staff organized a full schedule of events. Brig. Gen. A. Moses and Gen. C.J. Bailey attended the reunion, along with veterans from the 120th, 156th, 316th, 317th, 318th, 321st, 324th, and the 371st units.

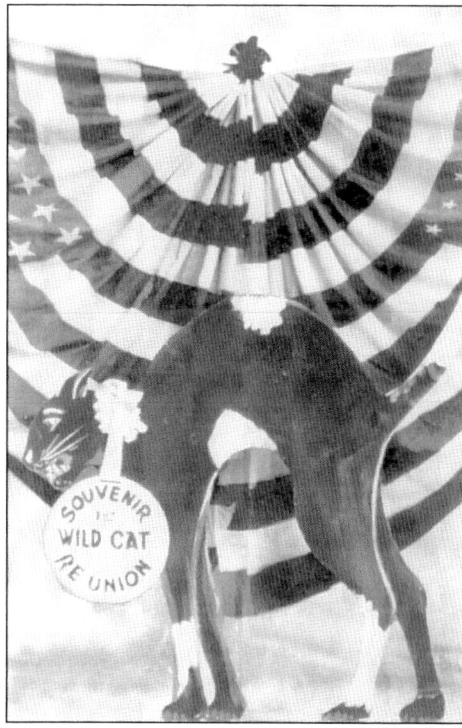

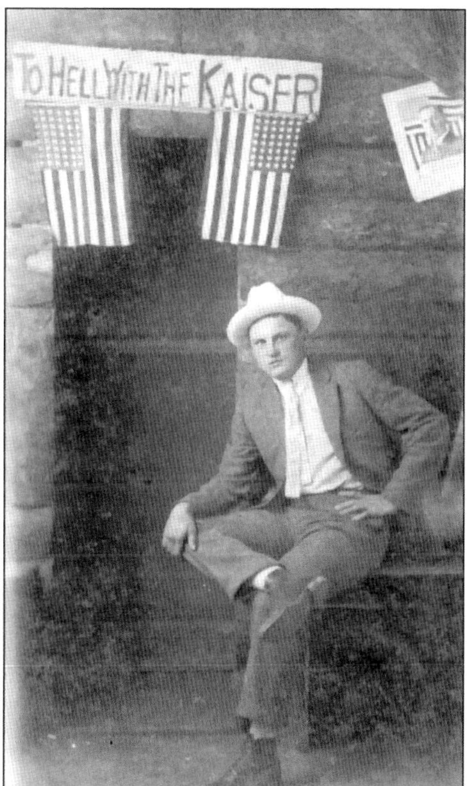

[To Hell with the Kaiser, 1918.] A military uniform tradition was established at Camp Jackson by the 81st Division who trained on the southeast corner of the reservation near Wildcat Creek. Corp. Dan Silverman of Company I, 321st Infantry Regiment designed crude cloth emblems of wildcat heads, which were worn on the sleeves of the 1st & 2nd Brigade, 120th Infantry Division. The custom found wide popularity and was adopted throughout the Army. In 1918 the patriotic exuberance of the young men of Columbia and South Carolina inspired them to have their pictures made in front of backgrounds with signs and flags. Verdgree (Victor) Jowers (1903–1967) of Columbia, pictured left, was such a man. Later he worked in the construction tool business. He married Minnie Derrick and had one son, Dr. Lawrence Victor Jowers (1921-1995), who Married Lula Mae Sutton. They lived in Columbia.

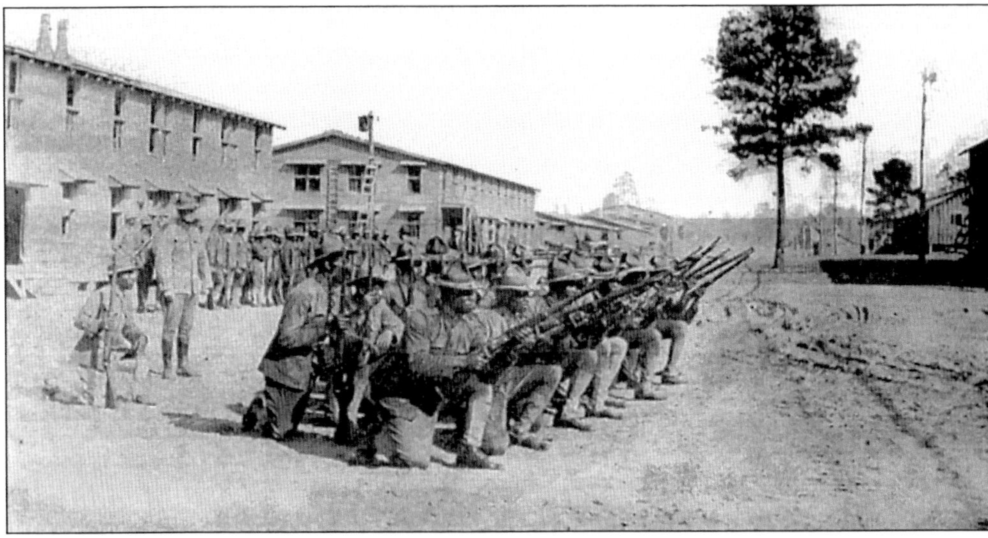

COLORED RECRUITS DRILLING AT CAMP JACKSON, COLUMBIA, SC [1918]. In October 1917, the first black draftees arrived at Camp Jackson. By July 1918, there were 6,704 African-American enlisted men in basic training at Camp Jackson. They joined the First Provisional Colored Division of the 371st Infantry Regiment. Trainee, Corporal Freddie Stowers of Anderson County shipped out in Company "C" of the 371st and was placed in the 93rd Infantry Division. Stowers was a squad leader during the September 28, 1918 attack on Hill #188 Champagne-Marne sector, France, and though mortally wounded, he took charge, pressed forward "displaying great courage," and "extraordinary heroism" until he died. Stowers posthumously received the Medal of Honor during ceremonies at the White House on April 24, 1991.

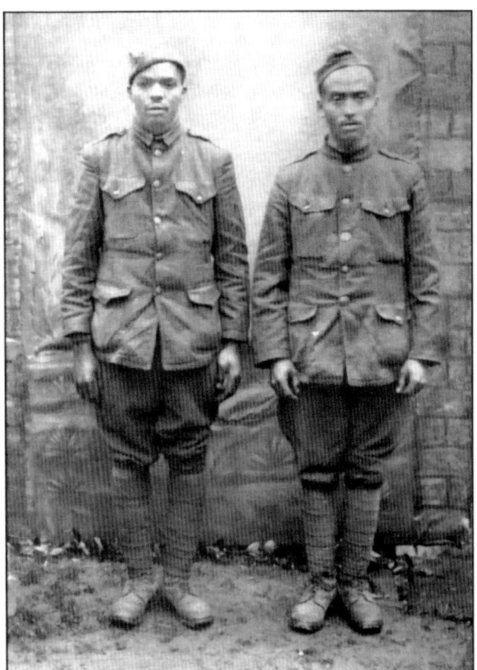

[ARMY PRIVATES, 1918.] This portrait of Priv. Thomas Carter of Summerville and a friend was probably taken while they were in basic training at Camp Jackson and before they shipped out in August 1918 to Europe as members of the First Provisional Colored troops of the 371st Infantry Regiment in the American Expeditionary Forces under the command of Gen. J.J. Pershing. The Armistice was signed on November 11, 1918, and the regiment returned in February 1919.

Five

VIEWS OF LOWER RICHLAND

Lower Richland's landscape is an east-west section of coastal plain extending from the Congaree Swamp north to the fall line zone at the sand hills. This area—the best farmland in the county—was where the early settlers built their homes. Its isolation was partially relieved by railroad service from 1842 to 1871. A dozen depots were placed along the routes of the Southern and Atlantic Coast Lines, and small communities developed around them. During the Civil War, many small farmers were conscripted and few returned. Their wives and children farmed as best they could but often lost their land to taxes that they could not pay. Large planters that had their wealth in land, slaves, mansions, and confederate bonds also suffered great losses. Lower Richland was devastated as Sherman's troops destroyed buildings, homes, the railroad system, and trestles.

The evolving rural public school system of 1900 was the major force to uplift the Lower Richland area. In 1910, Richland County had 16 segregated school districts with 108 schools (53 white and 55 black) and 10,894 students (4,584 white and 6,310 black) for a total departmental expense of $139,125. Each district occasionally published statistics that listed the total number of schools, teachers, students, etc. Unfortunately, the county neither recorded nor published individual records of the one-room or two-room frame schools in isolated areas. A 1915 school district map showed the location of some schools. The earliest Richland County Superintendent of Education's annual report found was one from 1950 that listed some of these rural schools as active, closed, or sold.

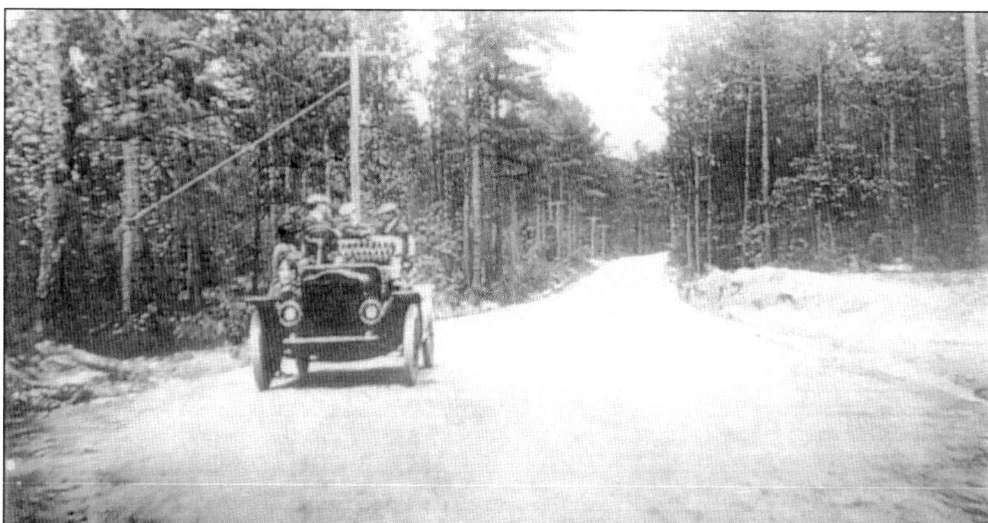

TWO NOTCH ROAD, COLUMBIA TO CAMDEN, SC [*c.* 1910.] Richland County had 400 miles of county roads which were maintained by county chain gangs who worked to bring roads up to a high grade of utility.

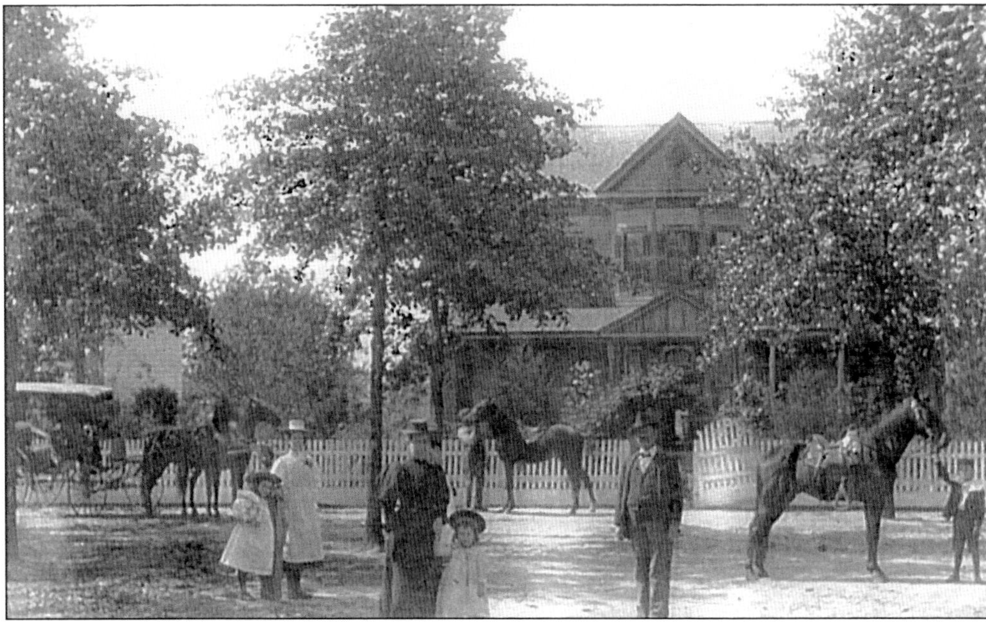

["Mecca," *c.* 1900.] Mecca, the family home of James Walton and Mecca McCants Burnside, still stands by US 378, two miles beyond the Veterans Hospital. Their son, James Allen Burnside, continued to run the family farm after the death of his father.

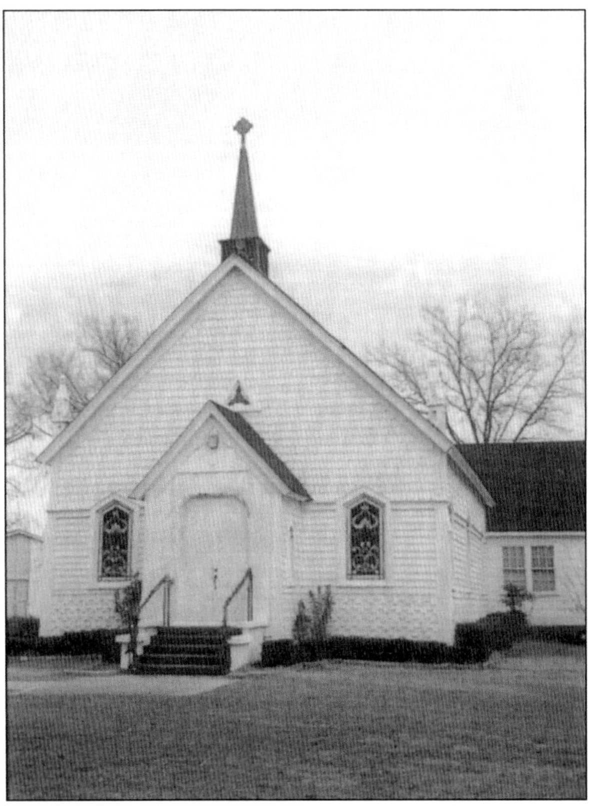

[Mill Creek Methodist Church *c.* 1930s.] Mill Creek Methodist Church was organized and this church was built in 1800 on land given by Mrs. William Goodwyn. Mill Creek, named for the many grist and saw mills using its waters, was the initial name for this historical community in the late 1700s. However, the name was changes to Lykesland when the Atlantic Coast Line placed that name on their depot. Successive schools were also built adjacent to this site.

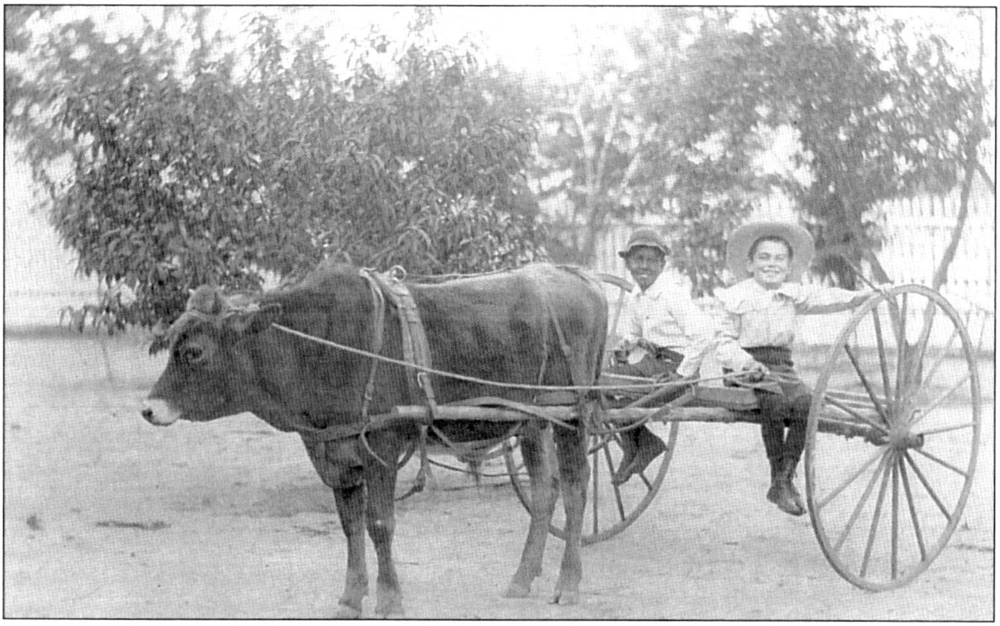

[James Allen Burnside, *c.* 1895.] James Allen Burnside, right, (1888–1969) son of J.W. Burnside, is shown above with Dick Williams, left, on the family farm at Mecca. J.W. Burnside died when James was 14, so he dropped out of school and ran the family farm and dairy. Later, James married Margaret Kathleen Neeley, daughter of the Reverend John William Neeley, a Methodist circuit preacher who lived in the Columbia College area.

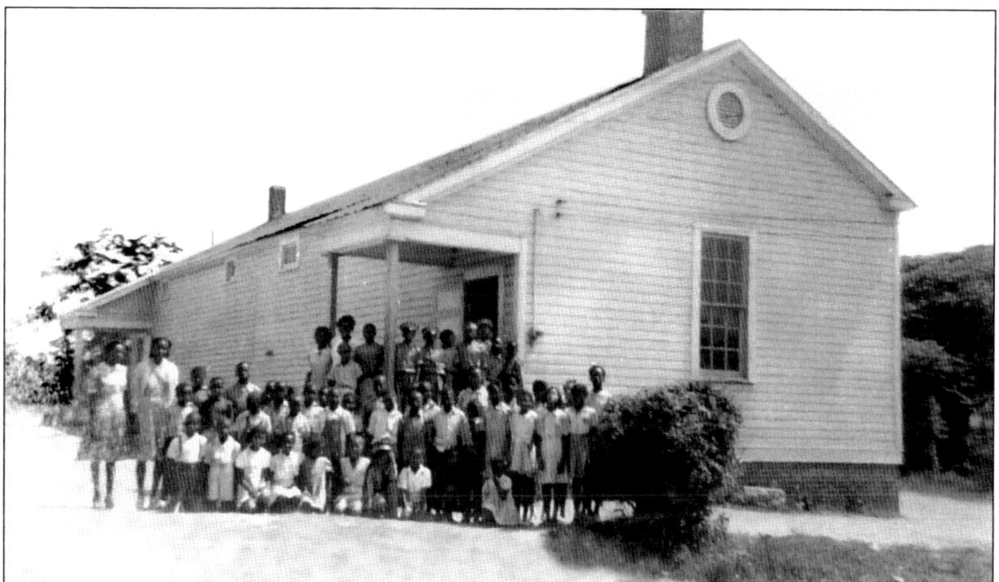

[Blackville School; 1930s.] The Blackville African-American school was a part of Olympia School District #4, which included the rural county area outside the city boundaries on the south and eastern sides. Unfortunately, many of the one-room and two-room school houses are not listed site by site across the lightly populated county areas. This two-room frame school is in that category.

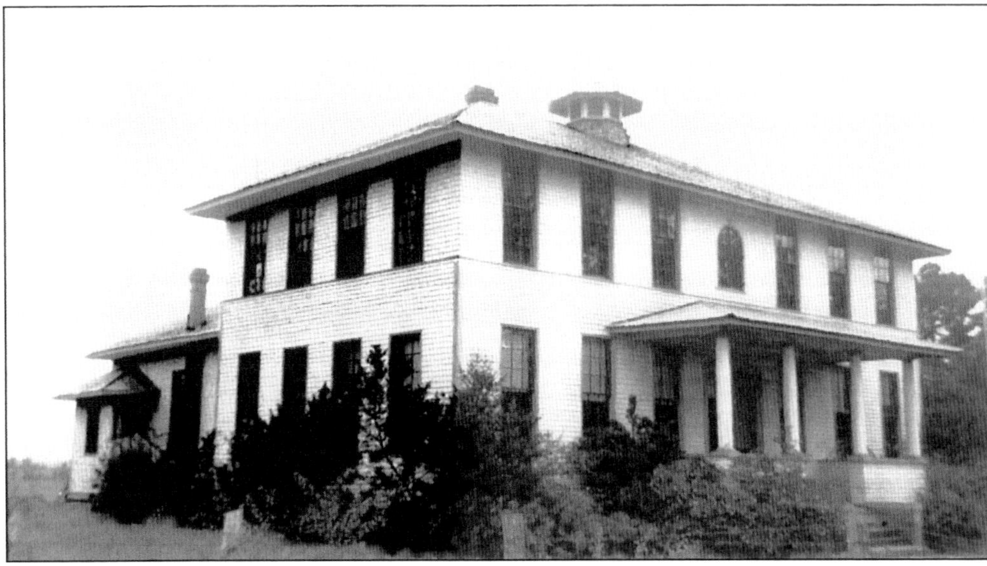

[**Hopkins School, *c.* 1930s.**] The town of Hopkins was established in 1891 by W.H. Lyles and Col. J.T. Sloan. In 1901, the Hopkins School District #6 had 4 white schools with 6 teachers, instructing 109 students in a 34-week term, and 5 black schools with 5 teachers, instructing 628 students in a 21-week term. The two-story high school shown above was near Cabin Creek and Horrell Hill Road. In 1910, it had 1 full-time and 2 part-time teachers; in 1913, it had 4 teachers and 64 students.

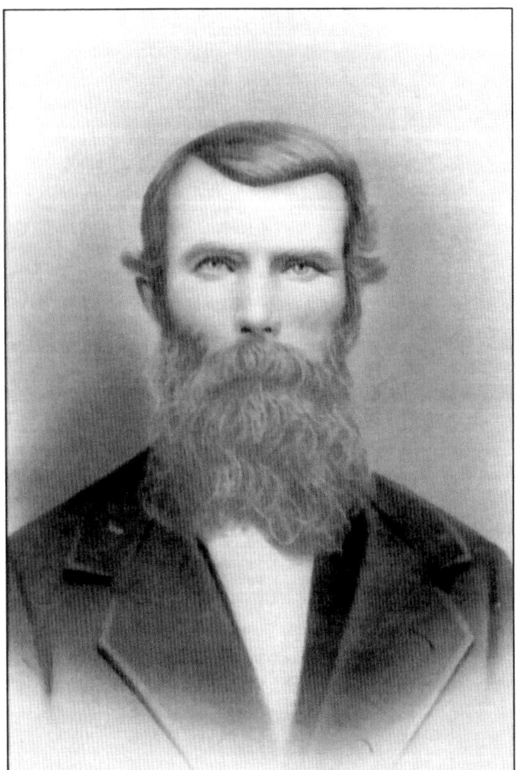

[**Nathan Daniels, *c.* 1880.**] Nathan Daniels (1836–1916) married Lavinia Smith and was a member of Company A, 4th South Carolina State Troops. They lived near the State Capitol and their home and possessions were lost in the 1865 fire that destroyed Columbia. After the Civil War, he obtained land from the Wade Hampton estate off Wildcat Road and became a farmer. The image above was reprinted at a later date. They are both buried in Beulah Baptist Church Cemetery.

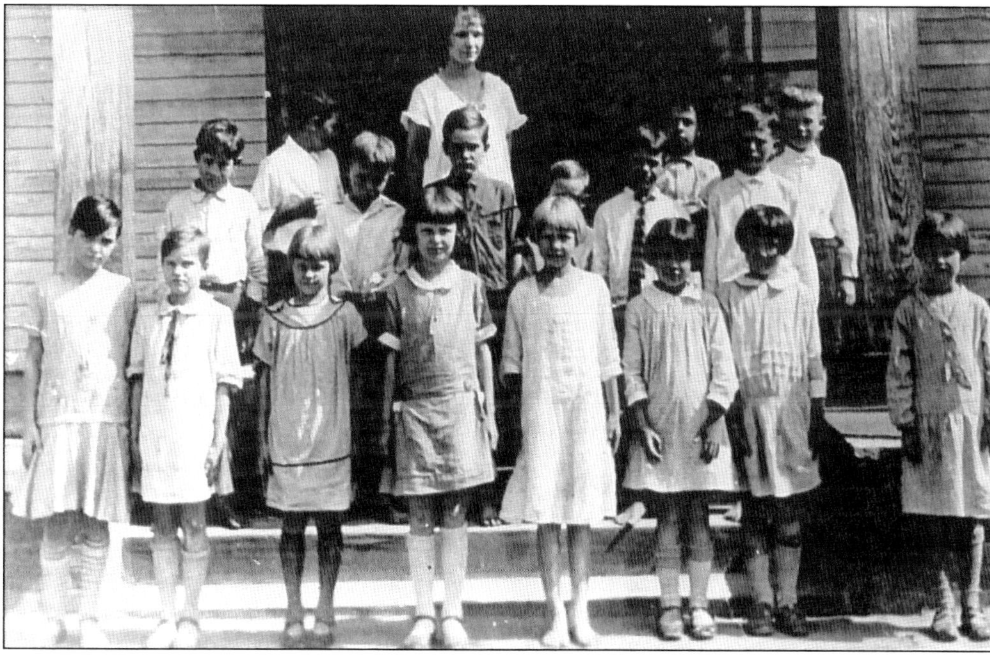

[SCHOOL CLASS, LYKESLAND SCHOOL, 1927.] This 1927 school class picture shows children living in the rural community around Lykes depot. Miss. Annabel Neeley was their teacher. In 1910, Richland County had 16 districts, 104 schools, and 4,584 white students. In 1915, the school had 5 teachers and 68 students, which increased to 73 in 1922.

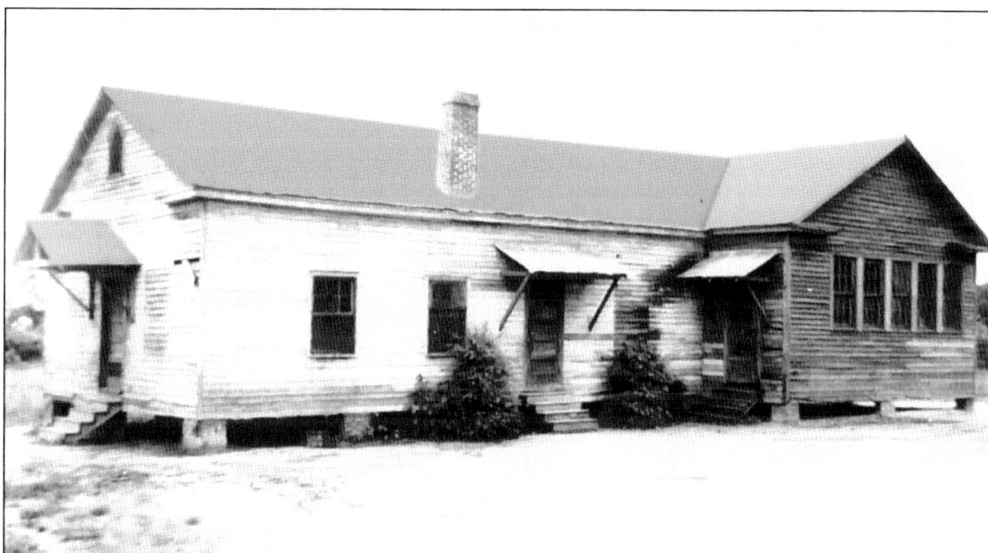

[ARTHUR SCHOOL, c. 1920s.] Arthur School served the African-American community in the Giles Creek area, which was divided by Bluff Road near Atlas Road in the Lykesland School District #5. In 1913, this one-teacher school had 95 students. Arthur, Reeder Point, and Mill Creek Schools were consolidated into Atlas Road School about 1950. That building has been altered but still stands.

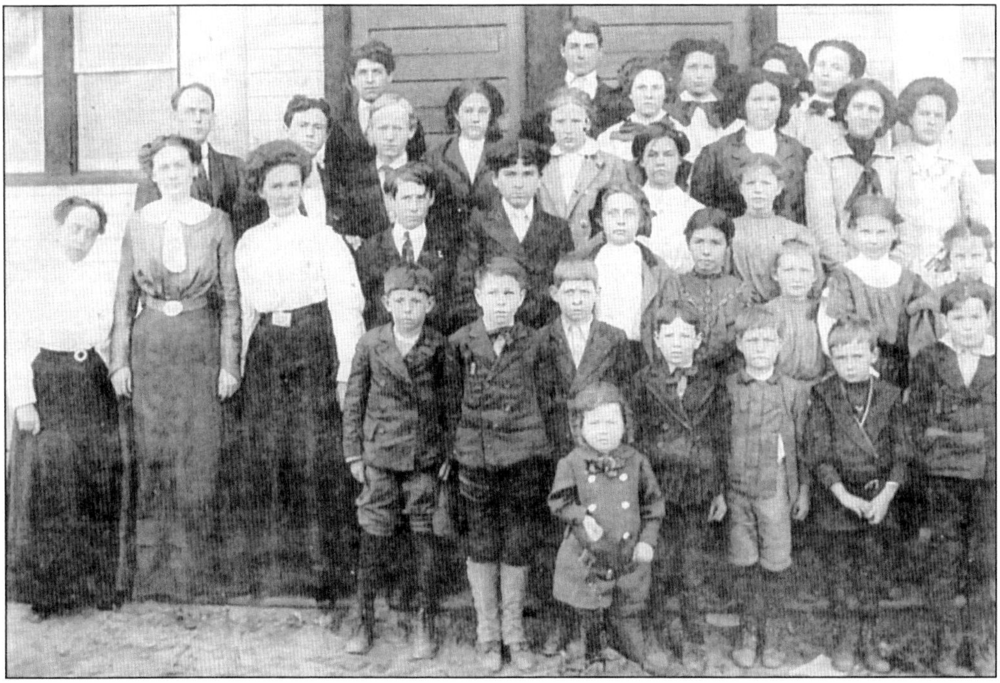

[STUDENTS OF HORRELL SCHOOL, **1909.**] In 1901, the Horrell Hill School District #7 had 3 white schools with 7 teachers and 84 students. Its 2 black schools had 2 teachers and 110 students. The class picture above shows the 32 students of the 1909–10 Horrell Hill School along with Kay Williams, principal. The school included grades 1 through 10. In 1922, the school staffed G.K. Williams as principal and 6 teachers who taught 86 students.

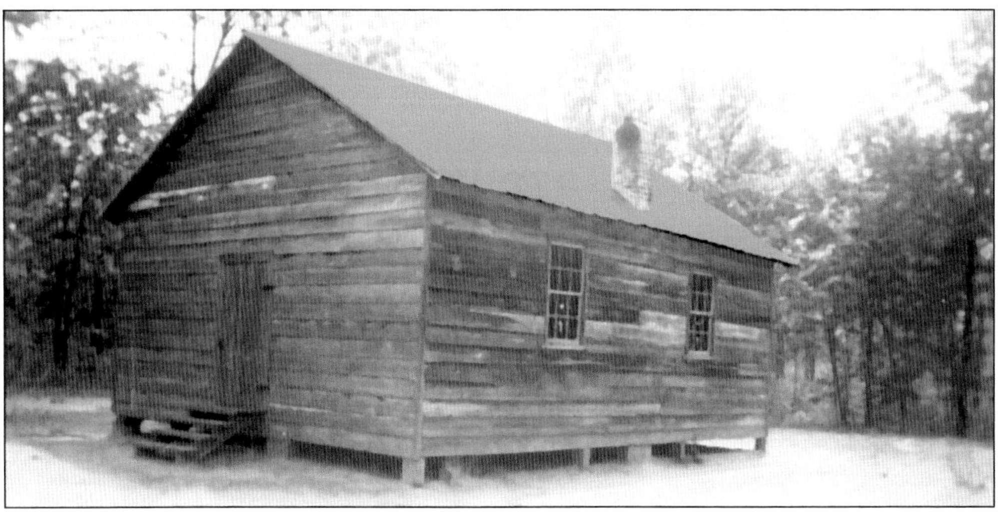

[PINEWOOD, *c.* **1910.**] Pinewood School taught the African-American children living near the junctions of Cabin Creek Road and Martin Luther King Boulevard in Hopkins School District #6. In 1913, 1 teacher taught 130 students. In 1922, State Superintendent of Colored Schools J.B. Felton described rural black schoolhouses by saying "Many of them are not only filthy and germ-breeding places but are so small that the children can hardly be packed in them and can neither be kept warm in the winter nor cool in the summer."

[Horrell Hill School, c. 1920.] In 1895, Howell Morrell became the teacher of the one-room Horrell Hill school. The community was so impressed with his instruction that they erected this two-story structure, which was by far the best in Lower Richland. It stood near the junction of Garners Ferry and Horrell Hill Road and had 44 students and 4 teachers in 1913. On April 30, 1924, a tornado destroyed the school and killed four little boys. The storm killed a total of 23 people in Richland County.

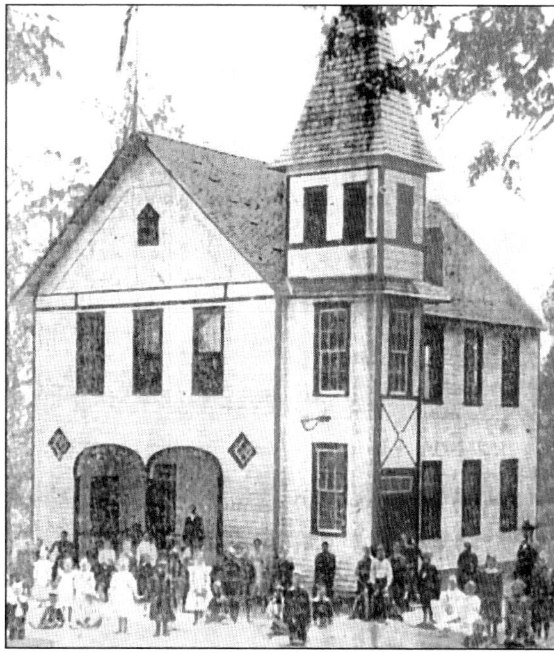

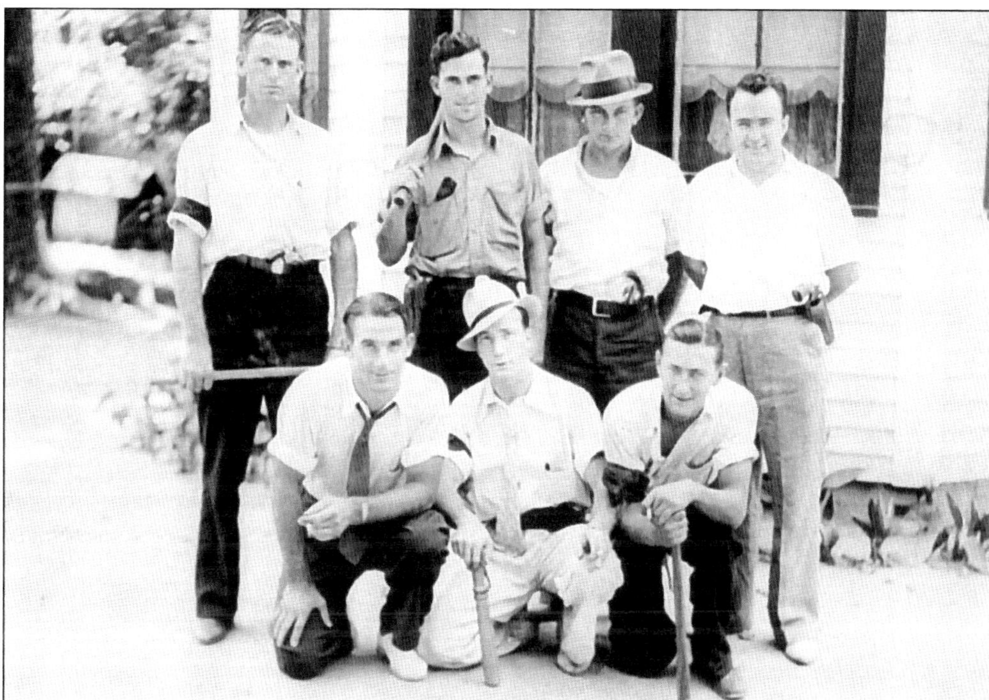

["The Flying Squadron," 1933.] Governor Blackwood commissioned this group, "the Flying Squadron," to go to the Graniteville cotton mills in the Horse Creek Valley near Aiken to break up union strikes and keep the mills running in the 1933–1935 era. The volunteers earned $40 a week plus transportation, room, and board. In this picture, John A. Harmon and Laurence [Burts] Harmon from Horrell Hill are standing in the back row, to the left.

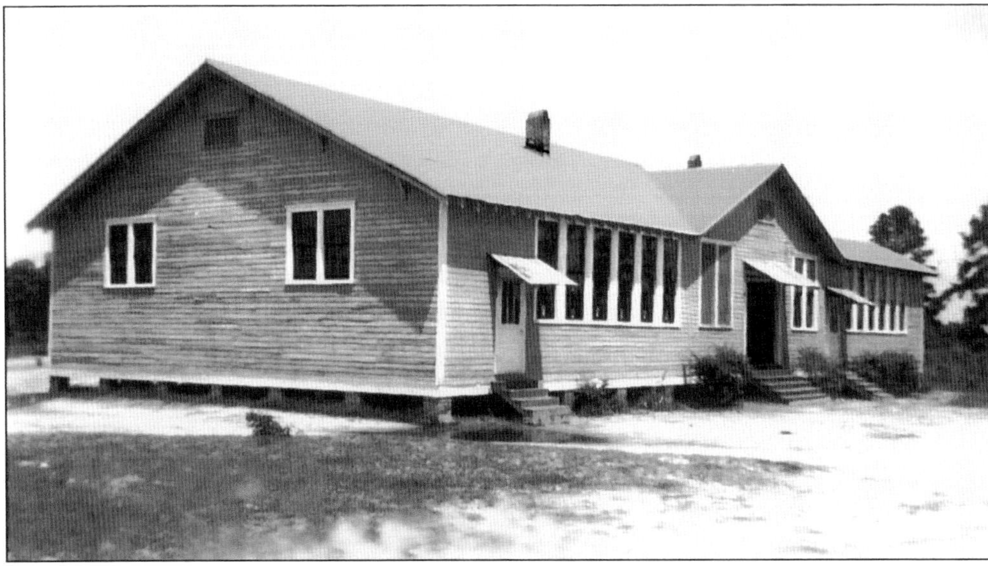

[GADSDEN SCHOOL, 1930s.] Gadsden was named for Pres. James Gadsden of the Louisville, Cincinnati & Charleston Railroad, which built a train station in that area in 1840. Passengers going to Columbia had to finish the trip by stage coach. In 1880, Gadsden had 3 general stores, a harness shop, and a population of 50. The Bellewood School District #8 had three white schools and seven black schools. The three-room Gadsden School served the African-American community near the junction of Congaree Road and Zeigler Road.

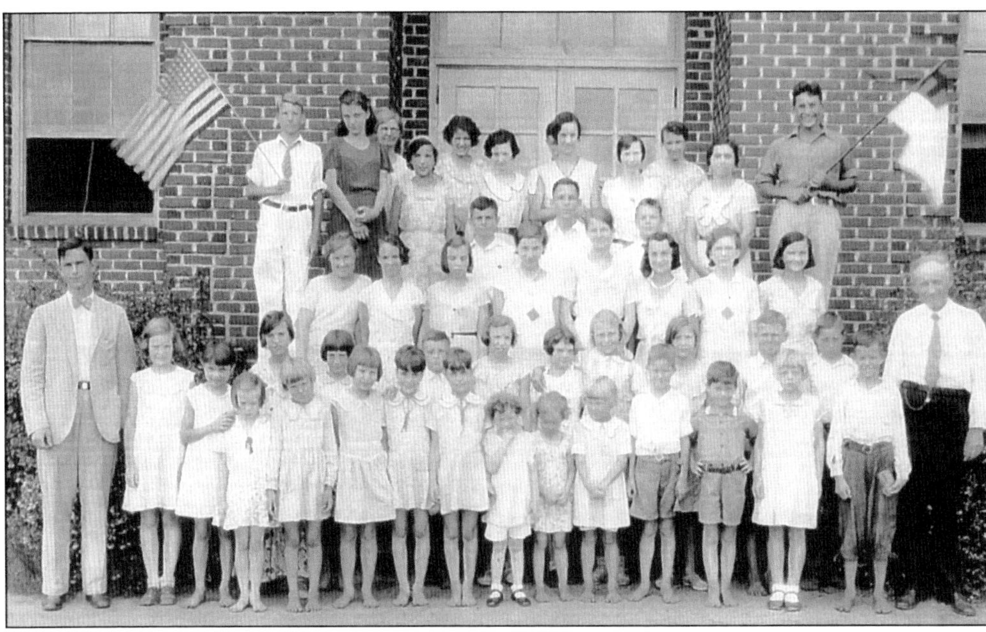

[VACATION BIBLE SCHOOL, 1932.] The 1932 Beulah Baptist Church's Summer Vacation Bible School is photographed in front of the Horrell Hill Grammar School on the west side of US 378. Mott Gelzer Baldwin, principal at the Lower Richland High School, was a teacher in the bible school and was standing in the first row, far left. Dr. John Knox Hair, minister of Beulah Baptist Church, is standing on the first row, far right.

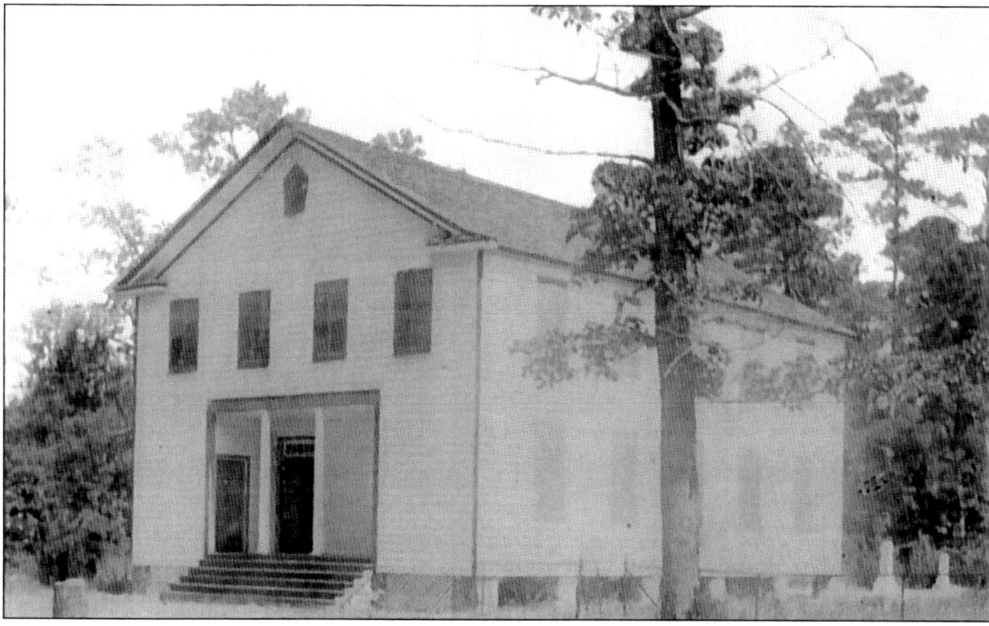

[Beulah Baptist Church, *c.* **1925.**] Beulah Baptist Church evolved from the initial Congaree Baptist congregation and then moved to the Horrell Hill area near Cedar Creek. The sanctuary shown above stood from 1828 to 1934. An 1865 racial conflict caused the blacks to build their church across the road from this one. On February 18, 1934, at the end of the service, a defective flue caused a fire on the roof and the sanctuary burned to the ground. It was replaced by a new brick one in 1936.

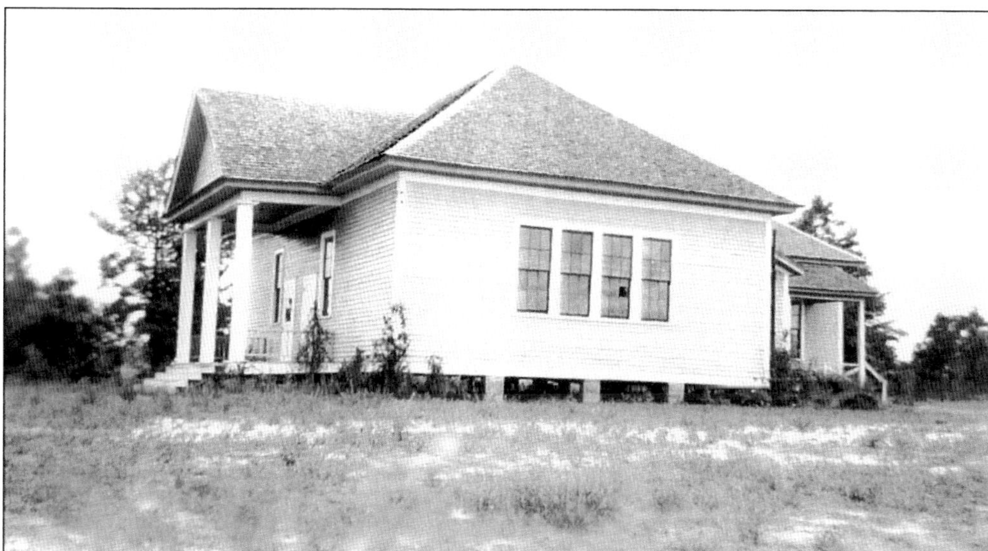

[Weston School, *c.* **1930s.**] Weston School (Bellewood District #8) was located north of the Southern Railroad and east of Cedar Creek and Clarkson Pond near Weston Road. Initially a two-teacher school for white children, it was given to the African-American community when a new four-room school was built for whites in Gadsden. In 1913, the one-teacher school had 103 students.

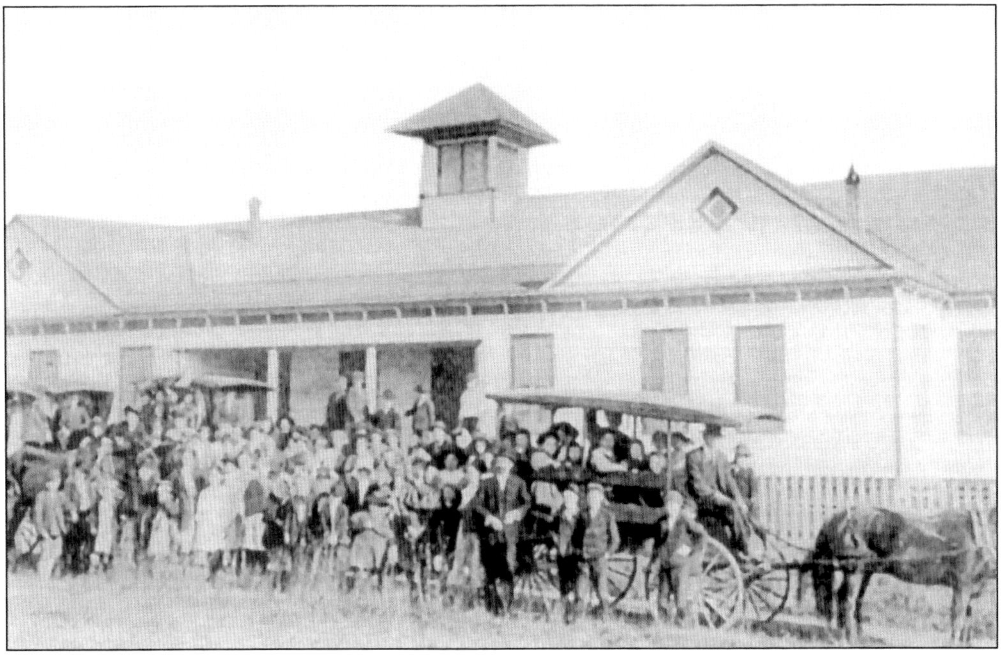

[**Eastover Consolidated School, *c.* 1912.**] Eastover, 27 miles southeast of Columbia, developed around the Seaboard Railroad depot. In 1901, Eastover School District #10 had 5 white schools, 5 teachers, and 99 students. In 1911, a dozen one-room schools with 104 students were consolidated into one school in Eastover with 5 teachers.

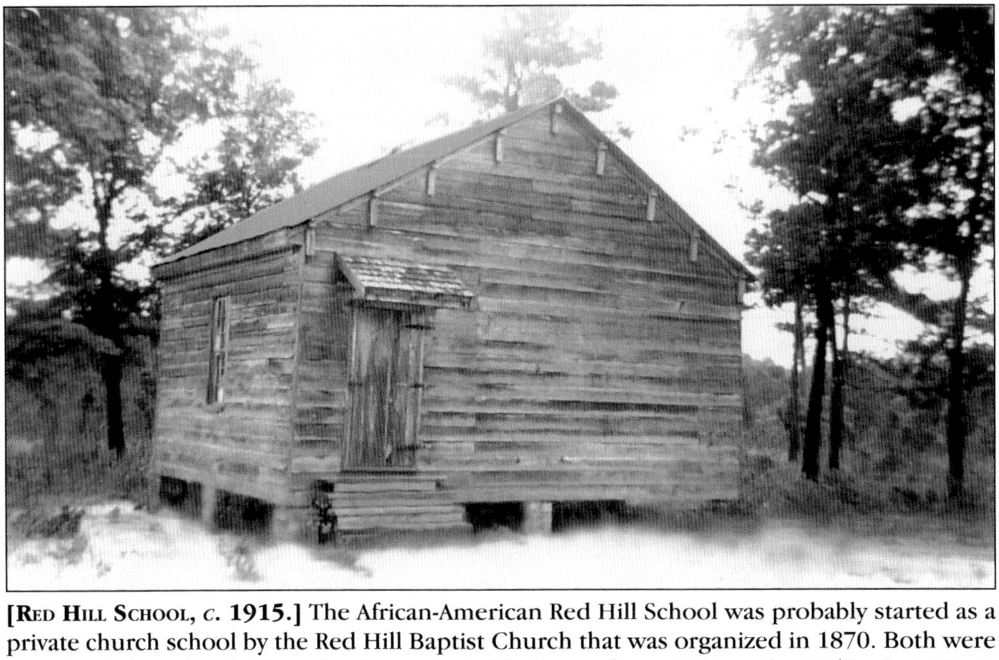

[**Red Hill School, *c.* 1915.**] The African-American Red Hill School was probably started as a private church school by the Red Hill Baptist Church that was organized in 1870. Both were on Whistle Top Road. The school was probably in use from 1890 to the 1940s. In 1913, it had 140 students. Tom Gregory taught at Red Hill, took the train to Gadsden, and walked to the one-room schoolhouse. It was on the 1915 Richland County School District map.

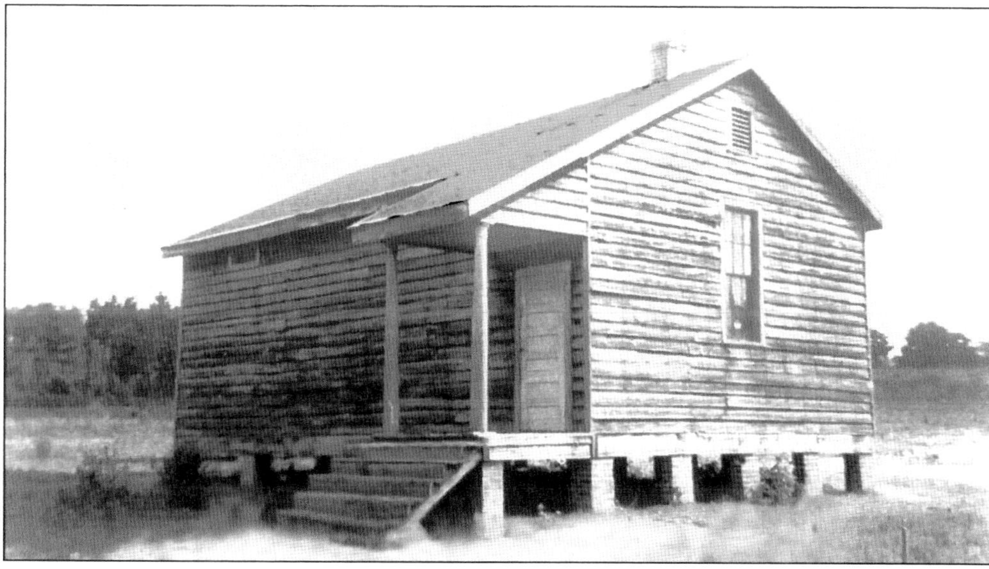

[COOL SPRINGS SCHOOL, *c.* **1915.]** Cool Springs School was located in the old Union School District #14 near the southern boundary of Camp Jackson and north of Caponia Church, near Harmon and Old Leesburg Roads. State supervisors of education of that era decried rural one-room school education, stating that most teachers were without college training and many changed positions year to year, and that they must teach all grades together, without teaching materials, in a 22-week term.

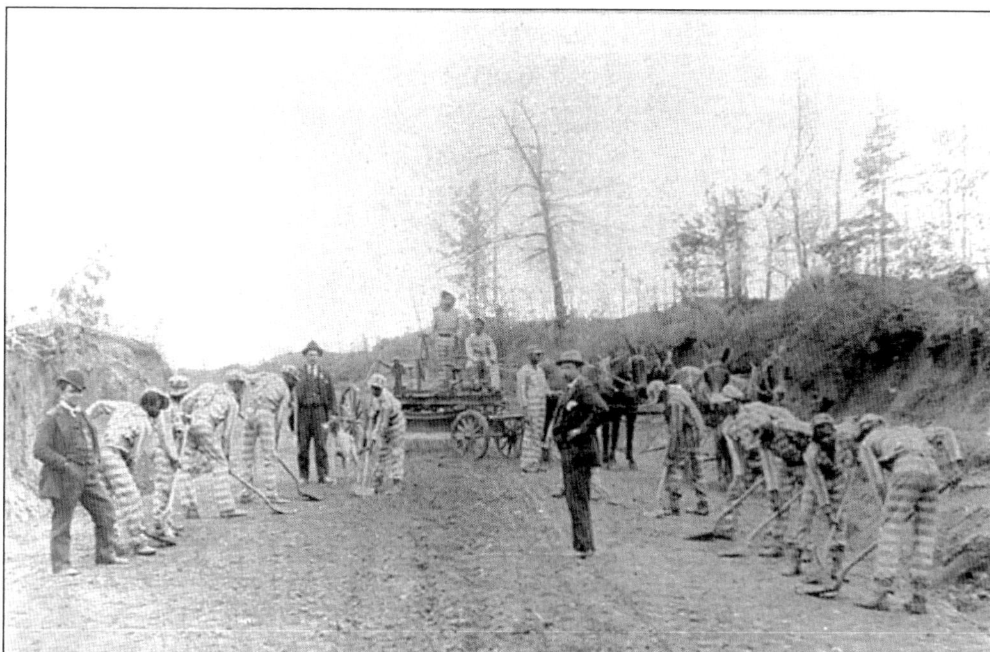

[RICHLAND COUNTY SHERIFF'S CHAIN GANG, CAMP **#1,** *c.* **1910.]** Chain Gang #1 was located northwest of Eastover between Chain Gang and House Roads. Their main function was to keep the dirt roads in a usable condition.

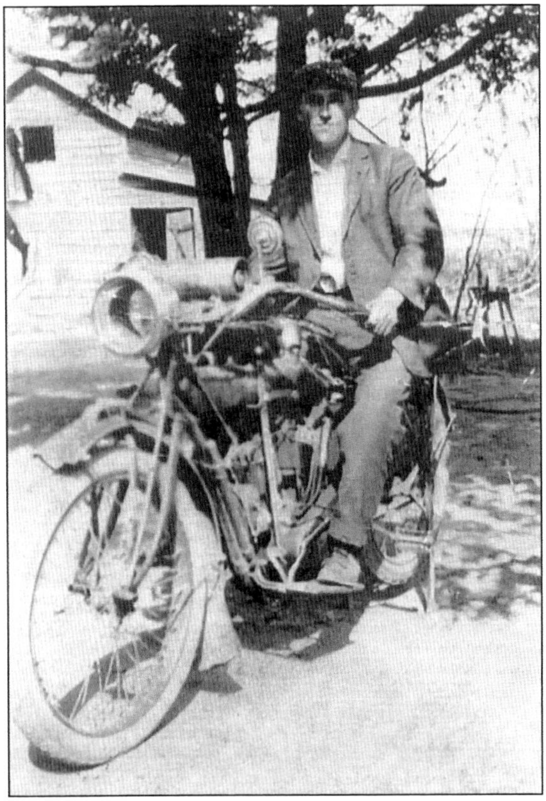

[Drayton K. Brooks Sr.] Drayton K. Brooks (1890–1967) of Horrell Hill worked for South Carolina Electric and Gas in the street car division at the barn (page 24) on Gervais Street. As a young man, he enjoyed his motorcycle as a convenient means of transportation from his farm to other rural sites in Lower Richland County.

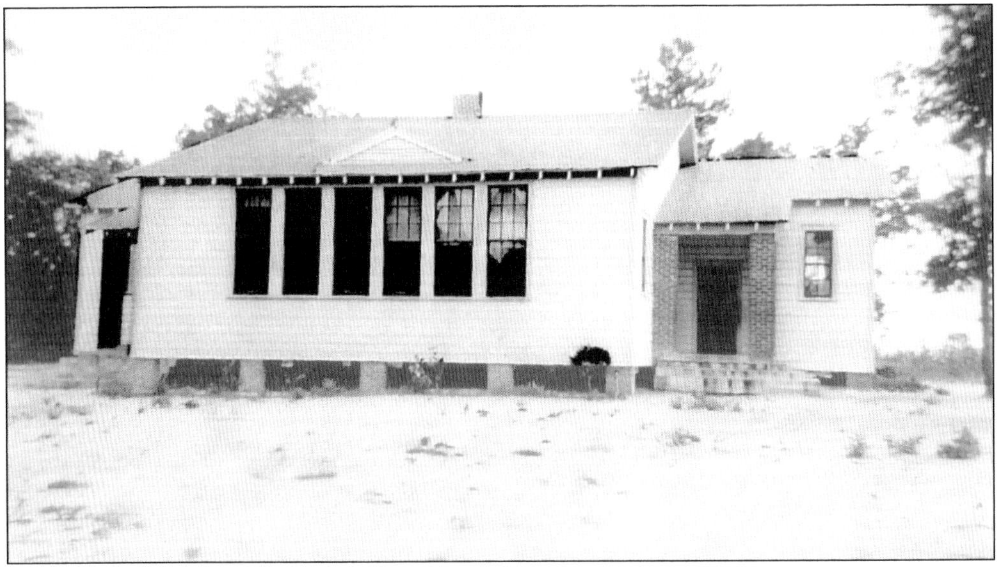

[Cross Roads School, *c.* 1930s.] This area had a small Episcopal mission in 1844. Cross Roads School was located in this community at a site on the north side of Garners Ferry Road and east of McCords Ferry Road. It may have been started as a private church school. This school had as its principal the Reverend I.B. Butler and became one of the best black schools in this county.

Six

Views of Upper Richland

The west side of the Broad River was originally the northeastern border of Lexington County. The 1913 map on page 8 shows the new boundary between Lexington and Richland County, and the new one involving Fairfield County. The eastern tip of the Dutch Fork area, between the Saluda and Broad Rivers, and a 710-square-mile strip bordering the Broad River were annexed on February 9, 1912. A second annexation of a 770-square-mile area occurred on March 11, 1922, and is not shown on this map. The Broad River sections included the White Rock, Ballentine, Piedmont, and Summerville communities. They were annexed because the people of this area felt that the Lexington County politicians neglected service obligations, such as road upkeep and school maintenance. A third annexation on February 19, 1913, added 760 square miles from Fairfield County and altered Richland's northern boundary. These new areas included Cedar Creek, Camp Ground, and Blythewood and expanded the county's piedmont section, traditionally a region of small farms.

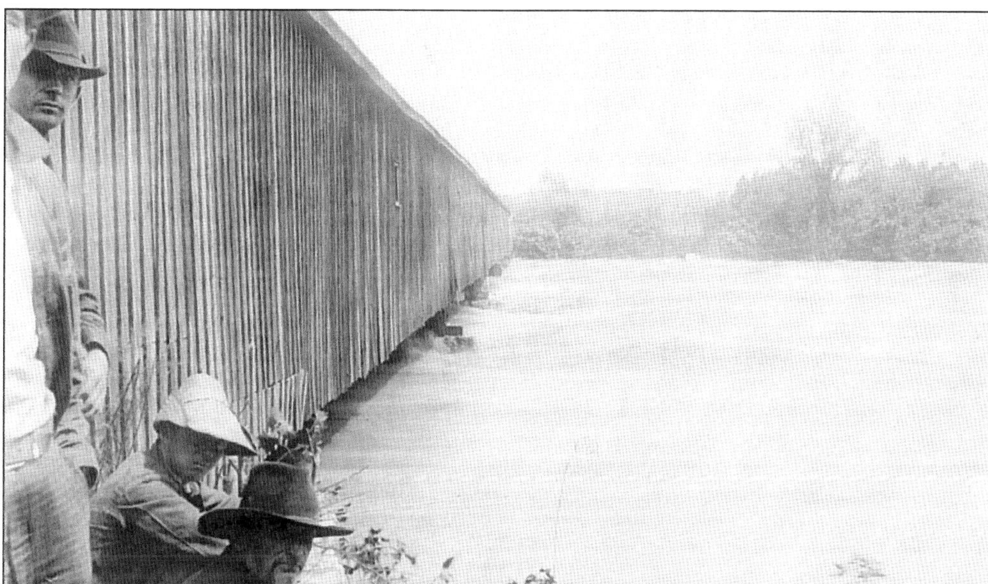

[Wooden Covered Bridge on the Broad River, 1908.] The Broad River Road bridge (old Columbia Bridge), designed by Messrs. Yates and Grey, opened on August 14, 1829. The bridge was weatherboarded and covered with shingles with a center partition running end to end and only a few windows on each side. This bridge, which crossed the Broad River near the confluence of the Broad and Saluda Rivers, was on the Newberry to Columbia Road that entered Columbia on upper Main Street. It burned in February 1865 and rebuilt later, only to be consumed by fire in 1920.

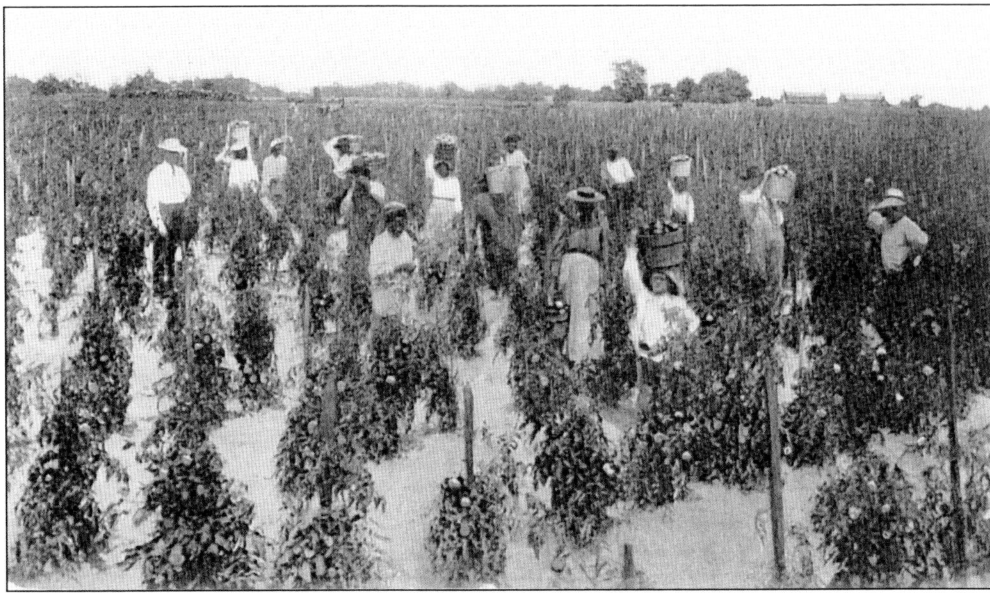

[Tomato Pickers in Dutch Fork, c. 1908.] This rather isolated rural area was made up of small family farms where cotton and produce were planted. It was a sun-up to sun-down laborious lifestyle. The Broad River almost acted like a barrier between these farms and the city on the river's north side. Their produce was taken by the only bridge to the Assembly Street market.

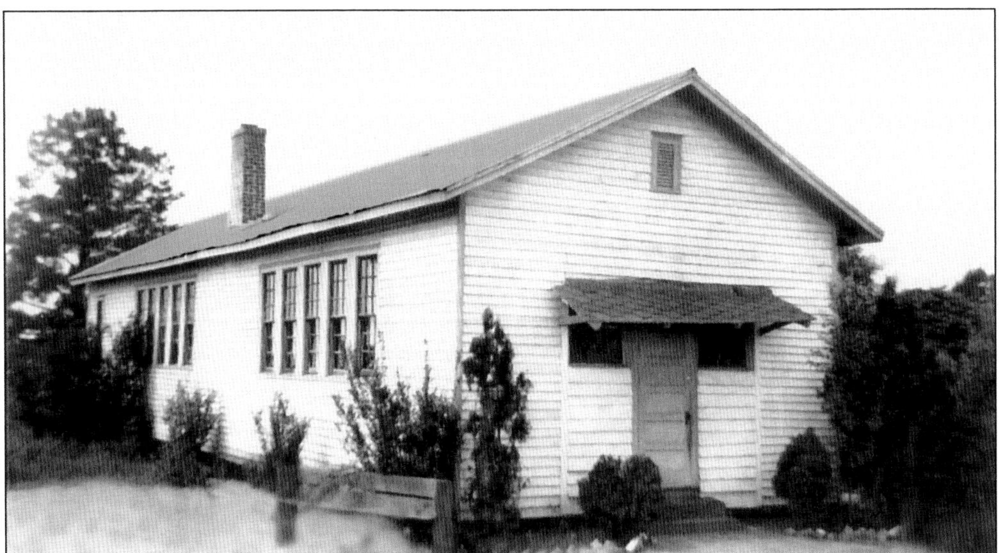

[Younginer School, c. 1925.] This two-room frame schoolhouse was built on a one-acre lot at 1334 Elm Abode Terrace near the junction of Bush River and Broad River Road. The lot was purchased in 1923 from Dr. L.M. Hook. Being almost 2 miles south of the Saint Andrews School, it served the white children living in the lower fork area between the Broad and Saluda Rivers in Saint Andrews School District #27, which had 66 students in 1920.

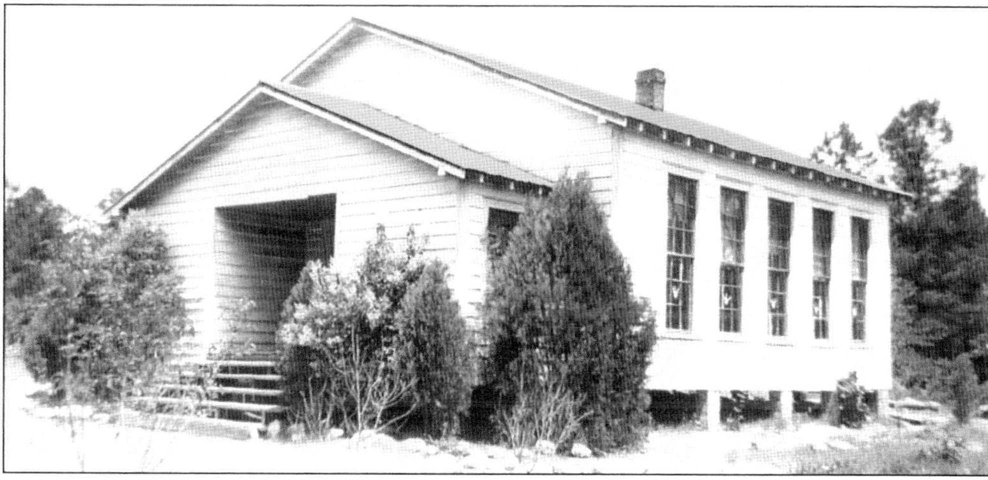

[Pine Grove School, *c.* 1930.] The Pine Grove School was located at 937 Piney Woods Road near the Pine Grove A.M.E. Church. The church probably created the initial school, which became a two-teacher school from 1923 to 1954 and was administered by the St. Andrews School District #27. The structure shown above received a Rosenwald matching grant of $700 with local support contributing $1,800. When Richland School District #1 took over the St. Andrews District #27 in 1954, the school was closed. The structure still stands in 2000 as a community center.

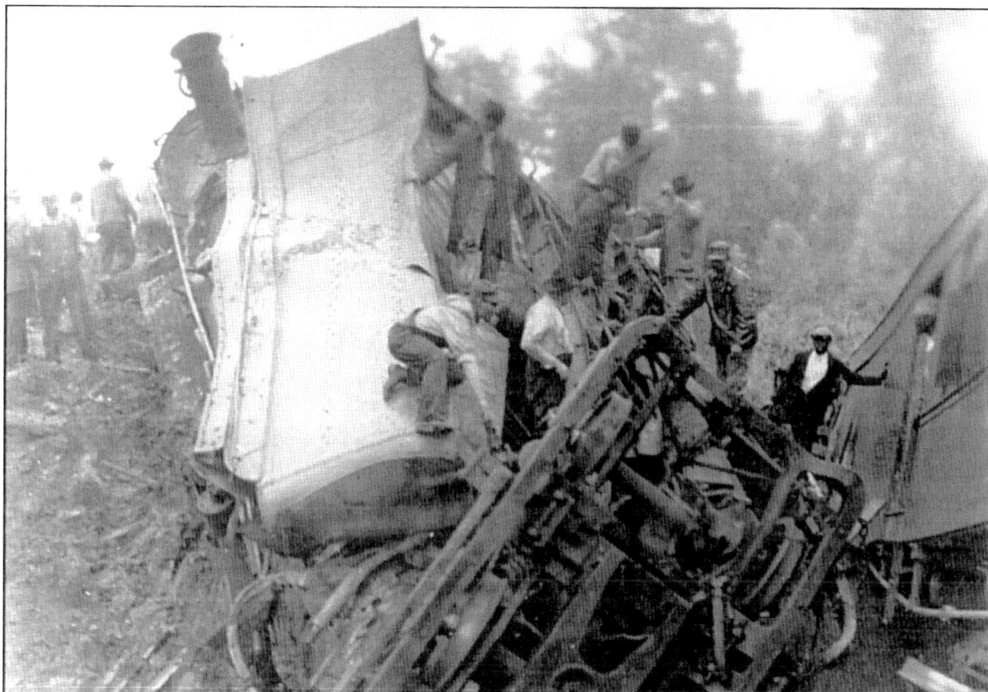

[Train Wreck, 1928.] The 1928 train wreck pictured above occurred when a deluge from a heavy rainstorm washed out the tracks of the Columbia, Newberry and Laurens Railroad near the three-mile post, which in 2000, was near the Riverbanks Zoo. The view above shows railroad workers inspecting the heavily damaged railroad rolling stock.

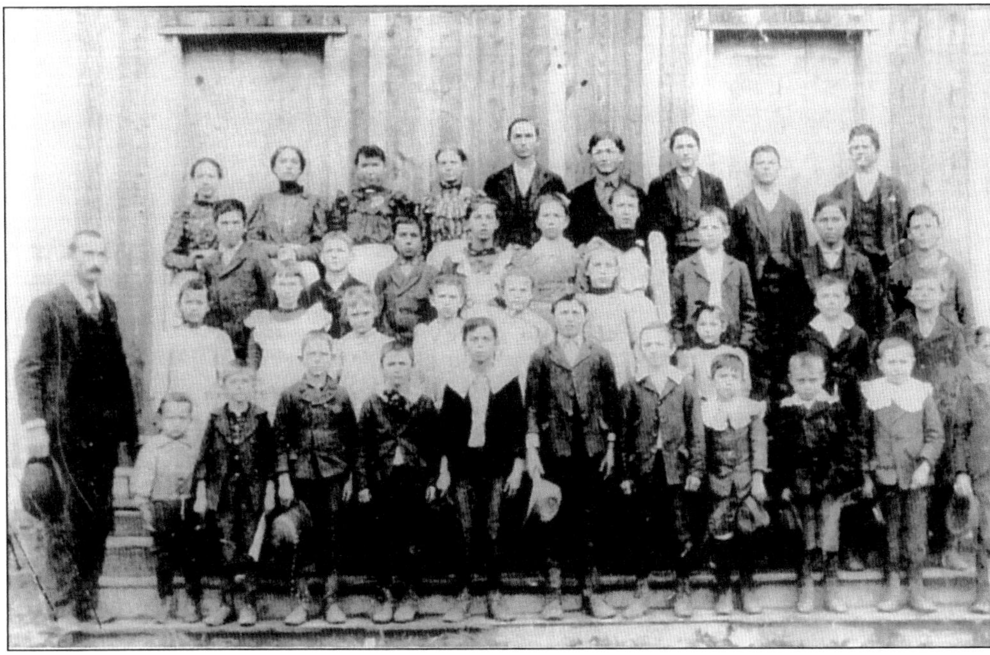

[White Rock School Students, 1902.] In 1901, the White Rock one-room school had a class of 55 students in grades one through seven. It was located in Lexington County at that time. In 1902 Jake Rauch taught 39 students. The building was located on land owned by Edward Shealy in the middle of town.

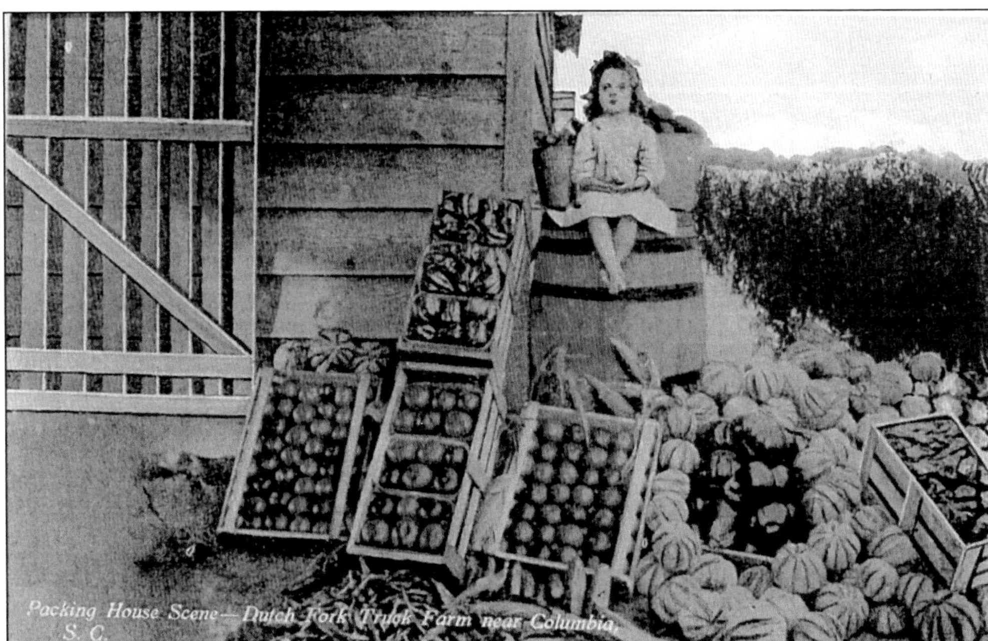

[Packing House Scene—Dutch Fork Truck Farm, near Columbia, SC [*c.* 1909]. Farmers in this area would pack crates of fresh produce to take to the farmers' market. They also kept baskets of produce to stock roadside stands.

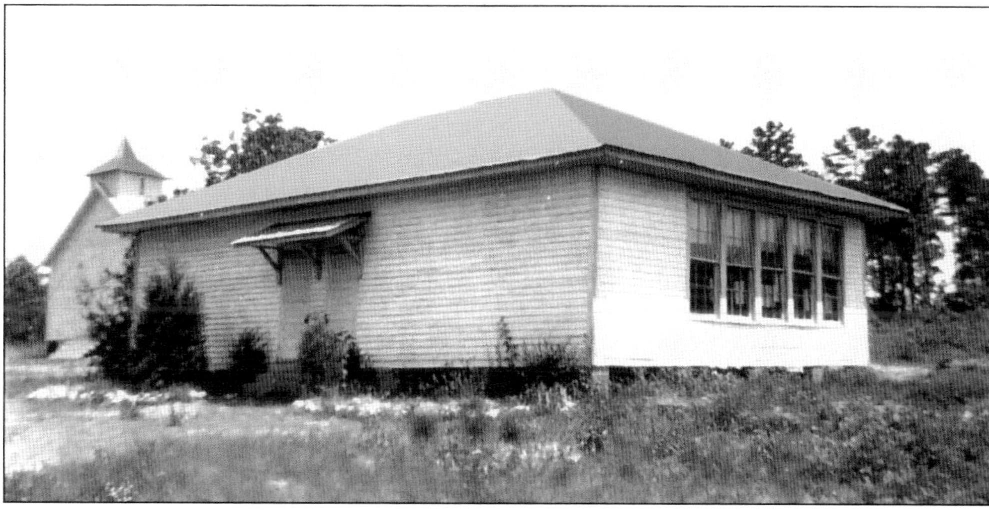

[ROSENWALD SCHOOL, c. 1920s.] The African-American St. Peters Baptist Church was organized in 1913 and most likely created the initial school next to their church property. In 1919, the congregation requested that the Piedmont School District #29 submit an application for a $700 Rosenwald grant to build a modern black schoolhouse. A two-room frame building was erected on 7900 Broad River Road beside the St. Peters church. It was used as a school from 1919 to 1953. Then, an expanded structure on this site was called the Richlex School (1953–1968). In 2000, the Dutch Fork Elementary School stands on this site.

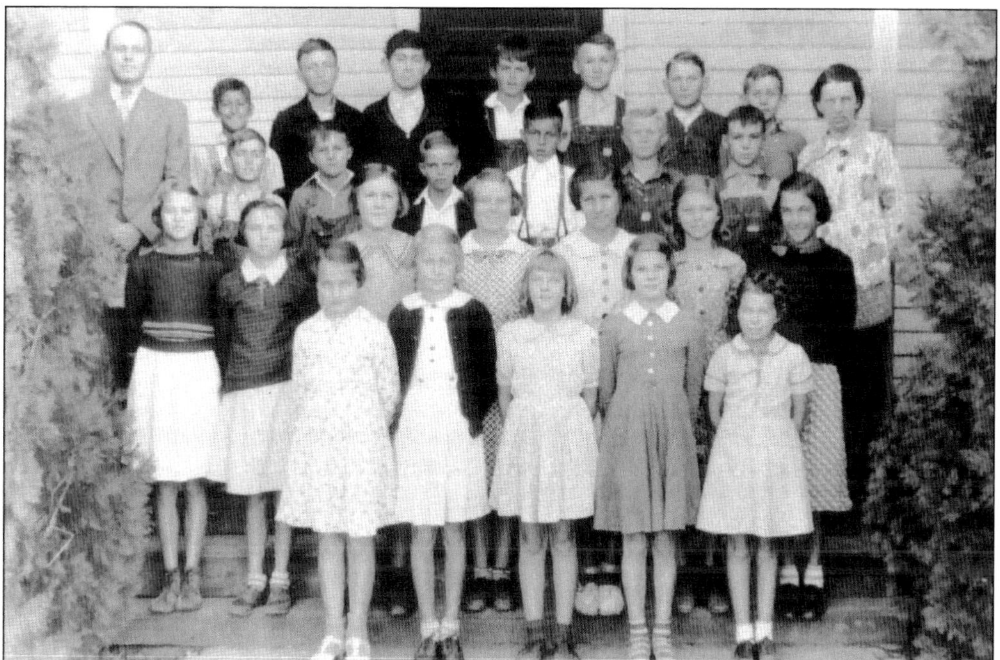

[BALLENTINE SCHOOL PICTURE, c. 1930s.] The Ballentine School, which was in Lexington County in 1900, had a one-room structure with 1 teacher and 76 students. By 1922, J.H. Kinard was the principal with 3 teachers and 40 students. The Ballentine School class picture above shows a single class in the 1930s.

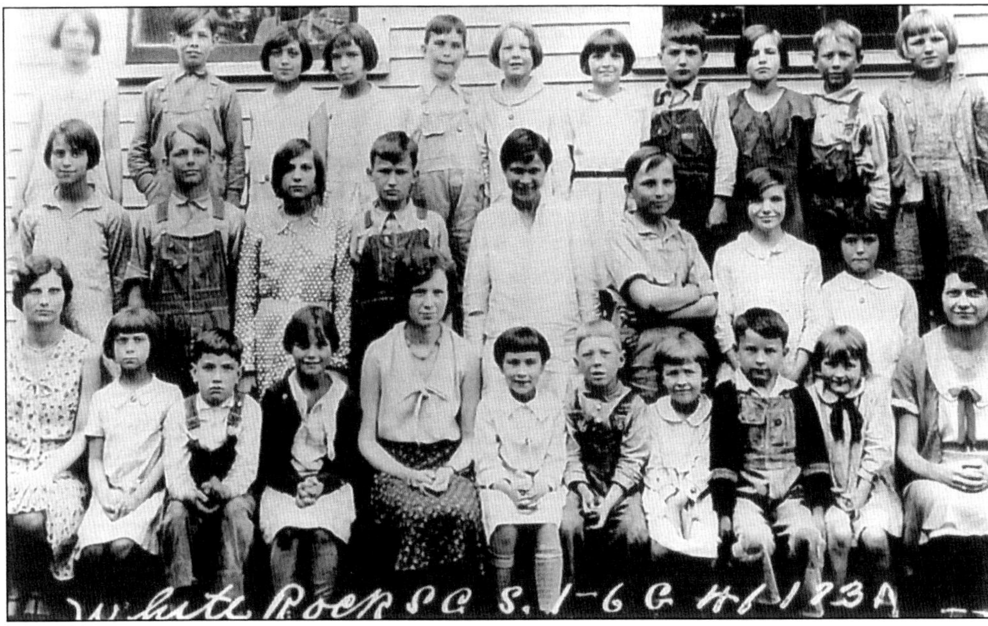

[White Rock Students 1–6 Grade, 1931.] This 1931 class portrait of the first through the sixth grades at White Rock School illustrates the size of this rural school. In 1926, Richland County was divided into 36 school districts with 118 schools (45 were "white" with a population of 10,057 and 73 were "black" with a population of 9,608 pupils). Forty-eight of the 118 schools were one-teacher schools.

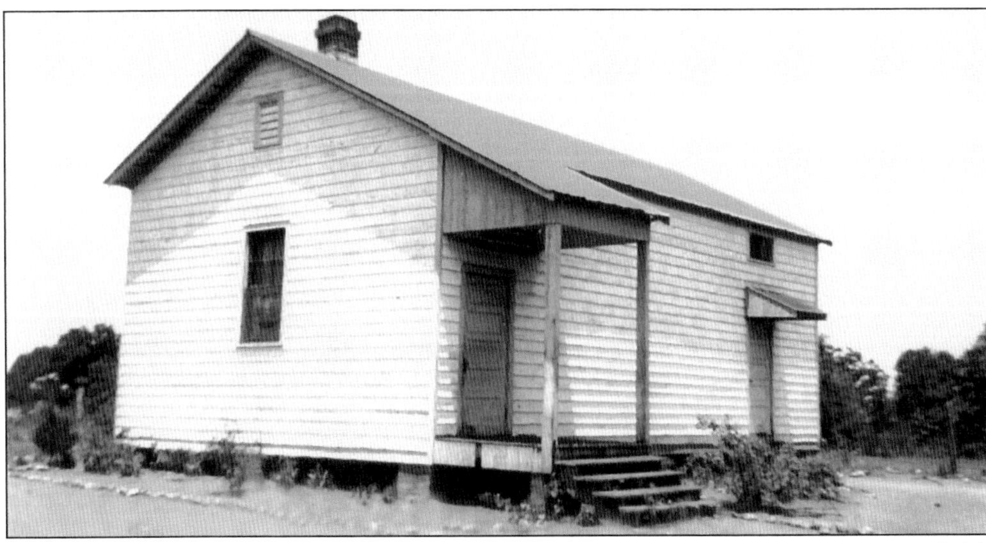

[White Rock School, *c.* 1920s.] The White Rock African-American school was probably called St. Luke and may have been a Rosenwald school. In 1925, the state built 78 new black school buildings and constructed 3 additions to existing buildings at a cost of $479,809. The divisions of the total costs were $79,326 (black donations), $19,950 (white gifts), $244,978 (district and county tax funds), $59,555 (state building funds), and $76,000 Rosenwald funds—for a total of 275 black classrooms. The 1924 ten state summer schools for black teachers had an enrollment of 1,320 teachers taught by 102 instructors costing $17,981.

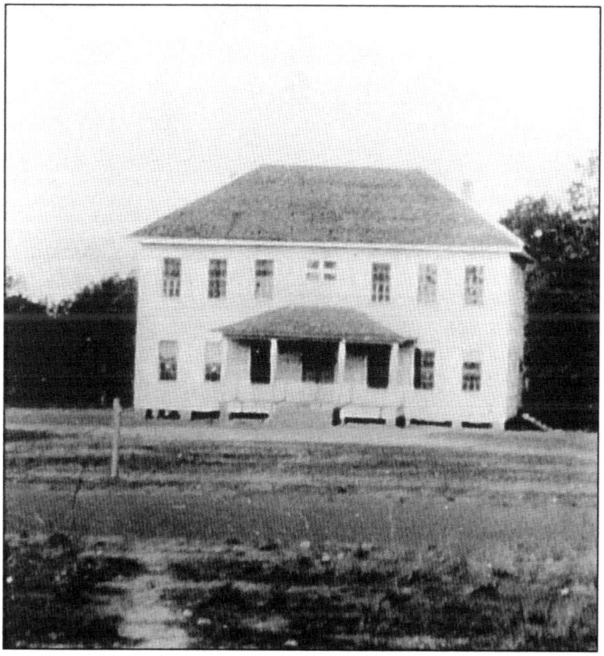

[White Rock School, c. 1920s.] The old White Rock school in White Rock School District #31 was located on what is now the Lowman Home property near the Bethel Lutheran Church. In 1922, J.M. Lowman was principal, and he and 3 other teachers taught 123 students in the schoolhouse shown on the right. The site was south of Dutch Fork Road.

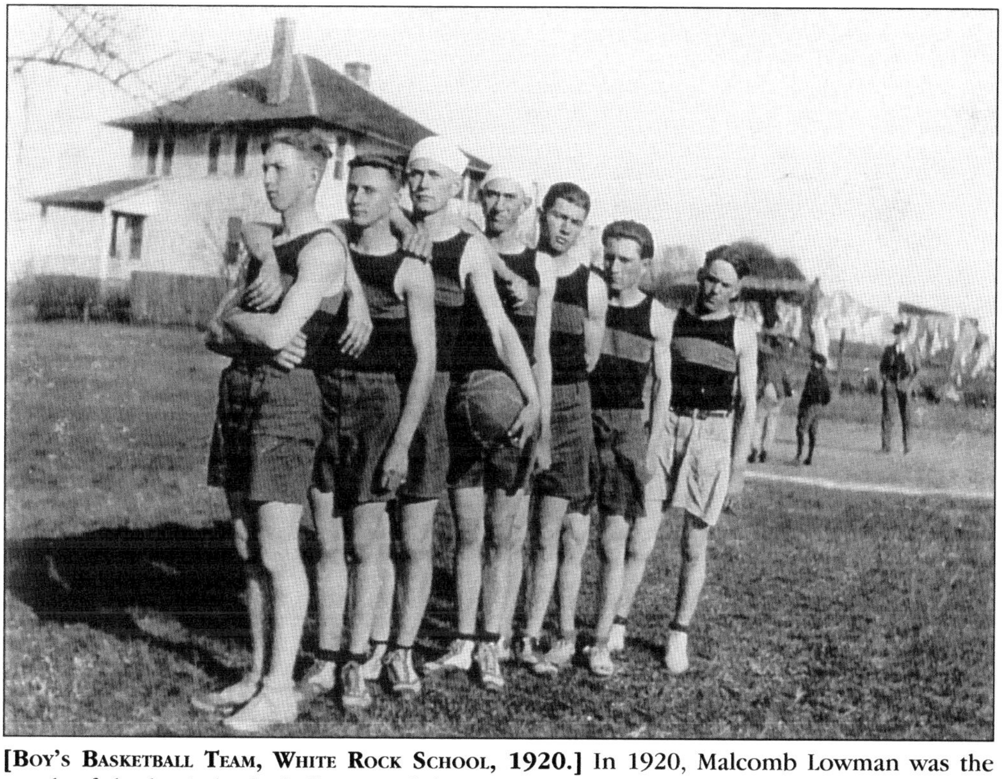

[Boy's Basketball Team, White Rock School, 1920.] In 1920, Malcomb Lowman was the coach of the boy's basketball team of the White Rock community school. The school also supported a girl's basketball team with each playing similar-sized rural schools of the neighboring Dutch Fork communities of Lexington, Richland, and Newberry Counties.

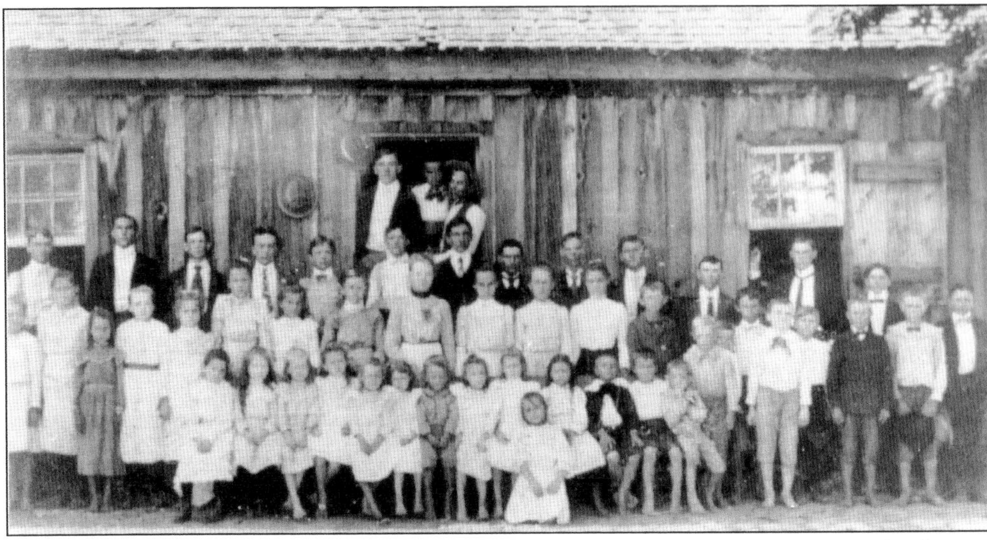

[Spring Hill School Class Picture, *c.* 1905.] Spring Hill School was located south of Broad River Road near Bookie Richardson Road in 1905. This area, then in Lexington County, included Spring Hill School, which was a one-room structure for 43 white children. The picture above includes A.P. Sites, teacher, with Dr. Henry C. Eleazer, standing in the doorway holding his son, J.M. Eleazer. In 1922, the area was annexed into Richland County and then became School District #32 with Ira B. Lever as the principal of the school, which had 3 teachers and 89 students.

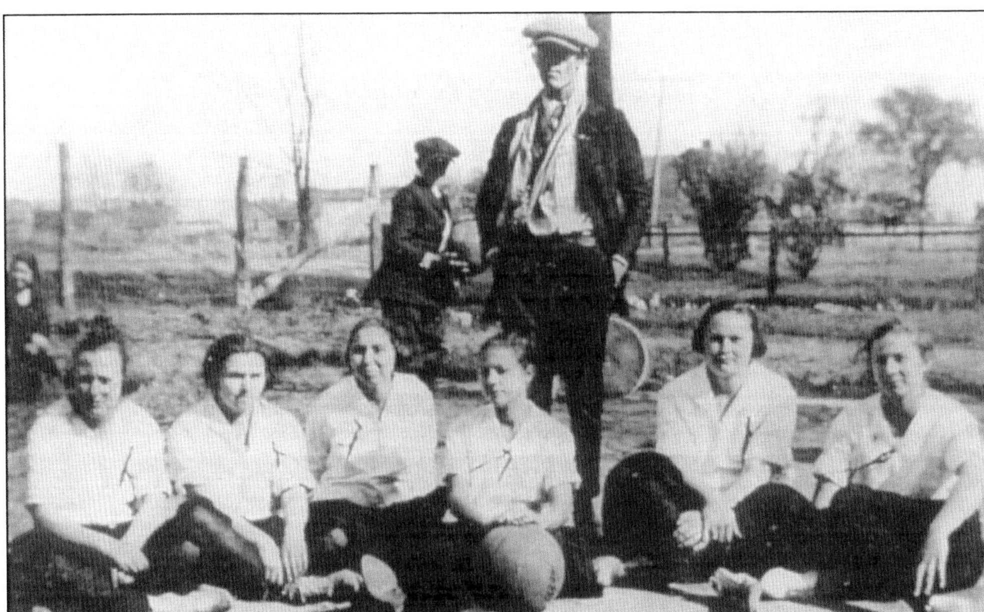

[Girls Basketball Team, 1920.] Malcomb Lowman, standing behind the girls, coached this basketball team. The White Rock school teams played DutchFork schools such as Bellentine, PIedmont, Chapin, and Spring Hill, among others.

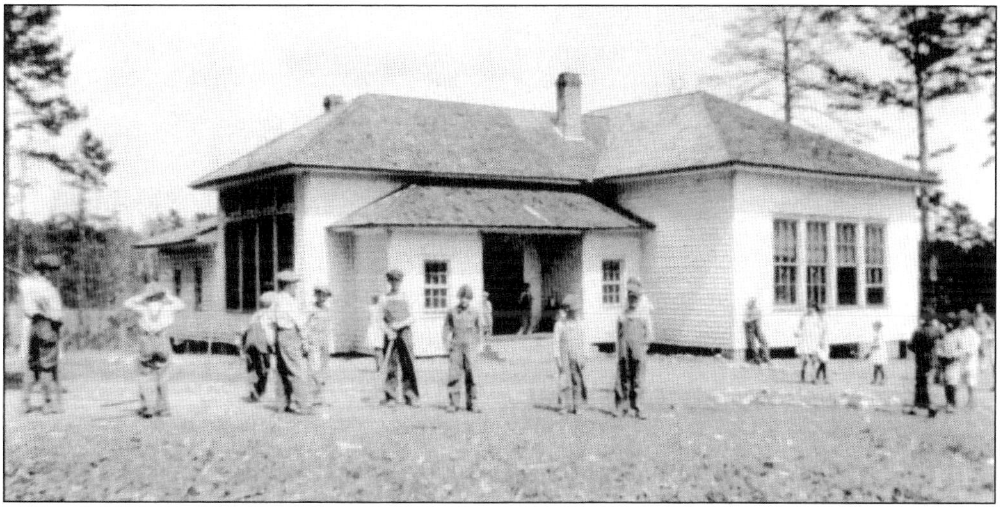

[**Folk School,** *c.* **1930.**] In 1901, the Folk School was a one-teacher school with 20 children located at the junction of Kennerly and St. Johns Roads near St. John's Lutheran Church. Folk School District #30 abutted the south side of the Broad River. By 1922, the schoolhouse above was built. P.F. Chapman was principal of a 3-teacher school with 79 students.

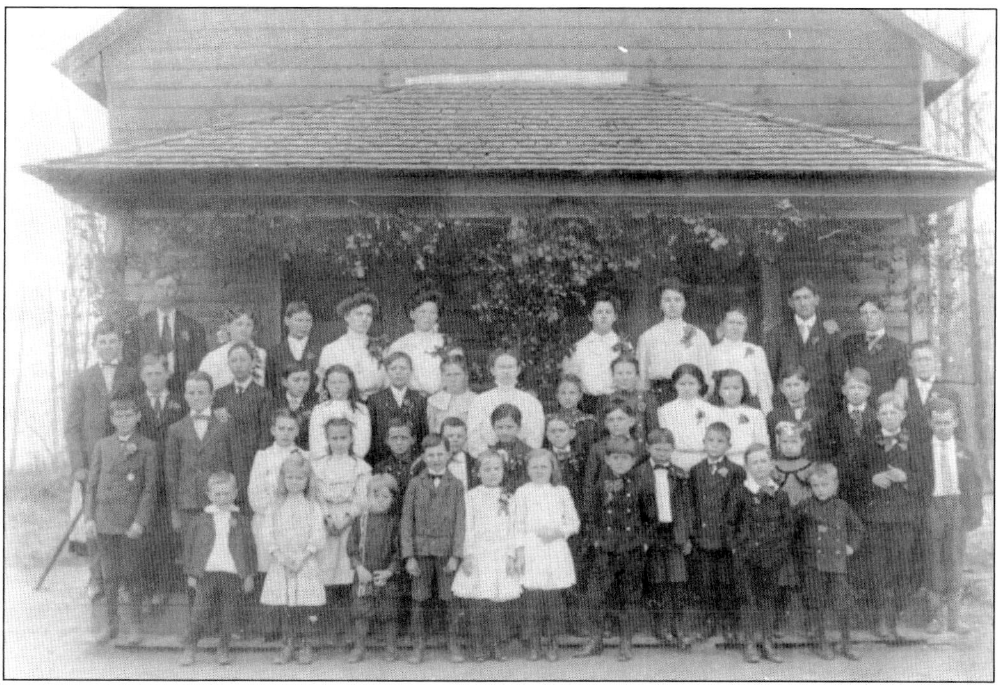

[**Summerville School Class,** *c.* **1905.**] The Summerville School, located north of the Broad River Road between Mike Stuck and Wash Lever Roads, was a one-room school with 31 students in 1901. On March 11, 1922, the 770-square-mile Summerville School District #33, which bordered both Newberry County and the Broad River, was annexed into Richland County from Lexington County. At that year, Azelia Hartman was the principal of a 3-teacher school with 88 students.

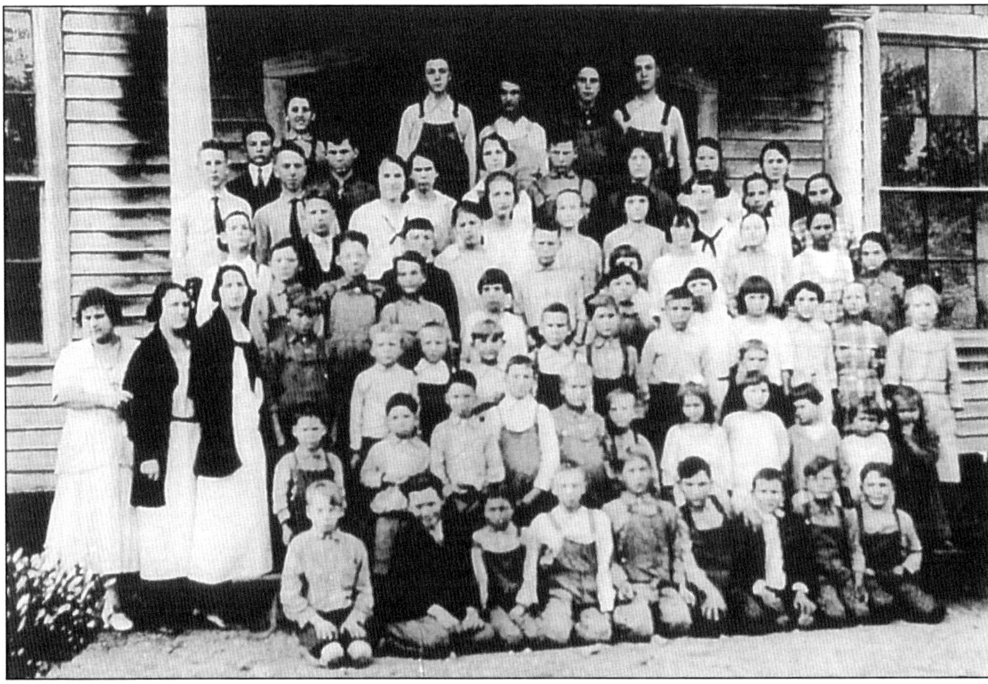

[PIEDMONT SCHOOL CLASS PICTURE, 1920.] The Piedmont School in Piedmont District #29 was located between the fork of the Broad River and Dutch Fork Roads. The first Piedmont School building burned in 1908 and it was replaced. In 1920, it had 97 students. Azelia Hartman was the principal in 1922. She and 3 other teachers taught 88 students.

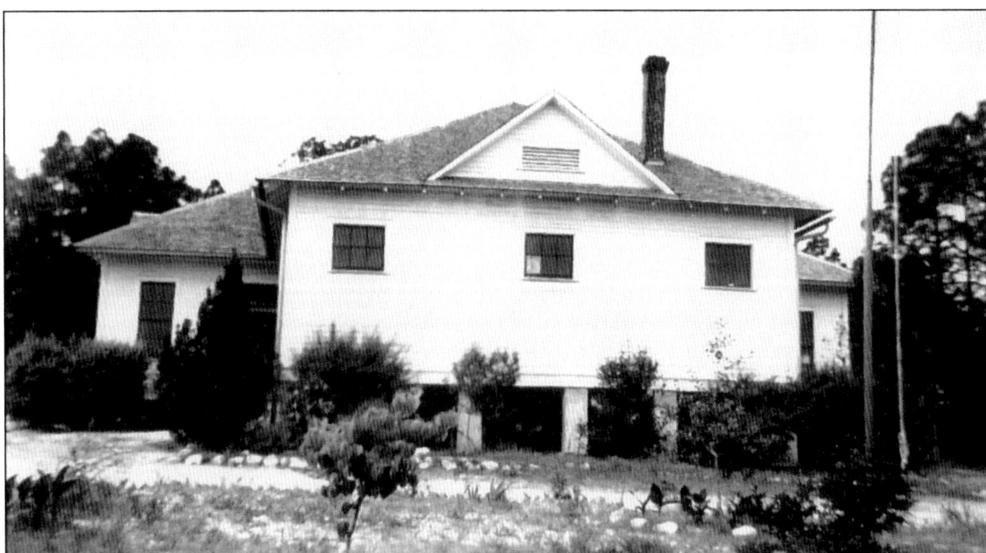

[CAMP GROUND SCHOOL, *c.* 1930.] The Camp Ground School in the upcounty section annexed from Fairfield County in 1913 was located near the junction of Camp Ground Road and Heyward Brockington Road. In 1922, M.D. Carson was the principal in this 3-teacher school housing 68 students. When the Campground School District #25 was consolidated in 1950, this school closed and the children were transferred to Hyatt Park School.

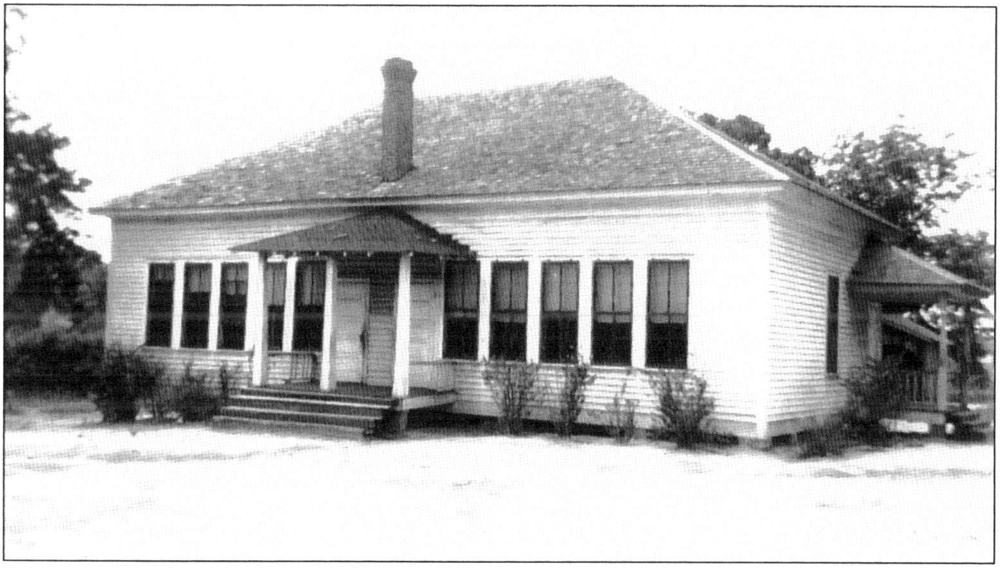

[Level School, c. 1920.] The Level School in Fairlawn District #21 was located at Wilson Boulevard and Turkey Farm Road near the junction of I-77 and US 21. In 1913, this school was a 1-room structure housing 33 children. By 1922, a new two-teacher school was built with Lettie Rawl serving as its principal and an expanded enrollment of 64 students. When the school closed, the remaining children were transferred to Crane Creek School.

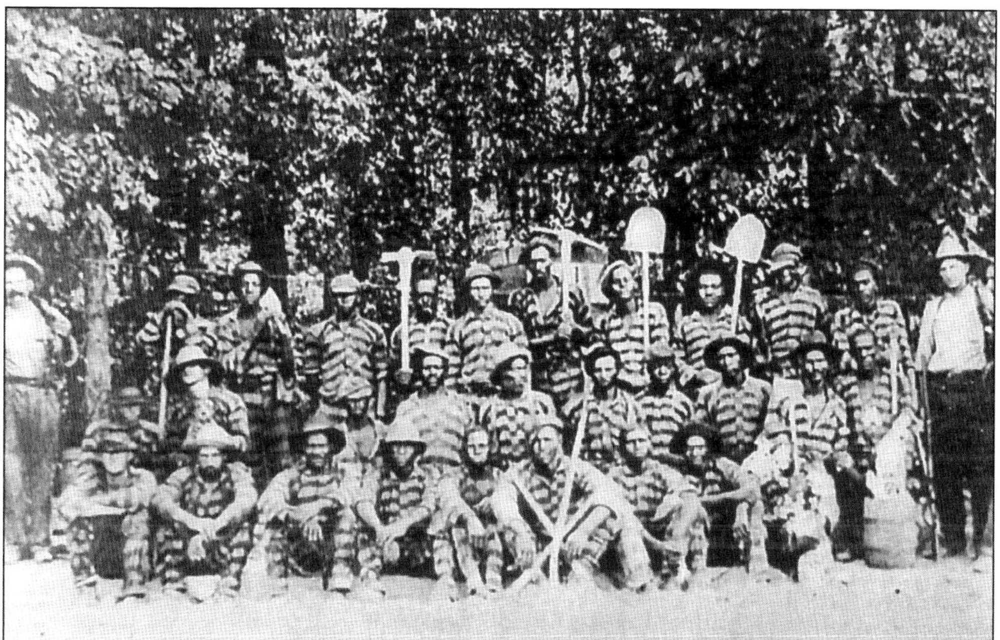

[Chain Gang Camp #3, c.1910.] Richland County's Chain Gang Camp #3 was located east of US# 321 and south of Evergreen Park near Wessinger Road. The Richland County Sheriff's Department used convict labor to maintain and repair the dirt county roads that could be washed out after each freshet during this era.

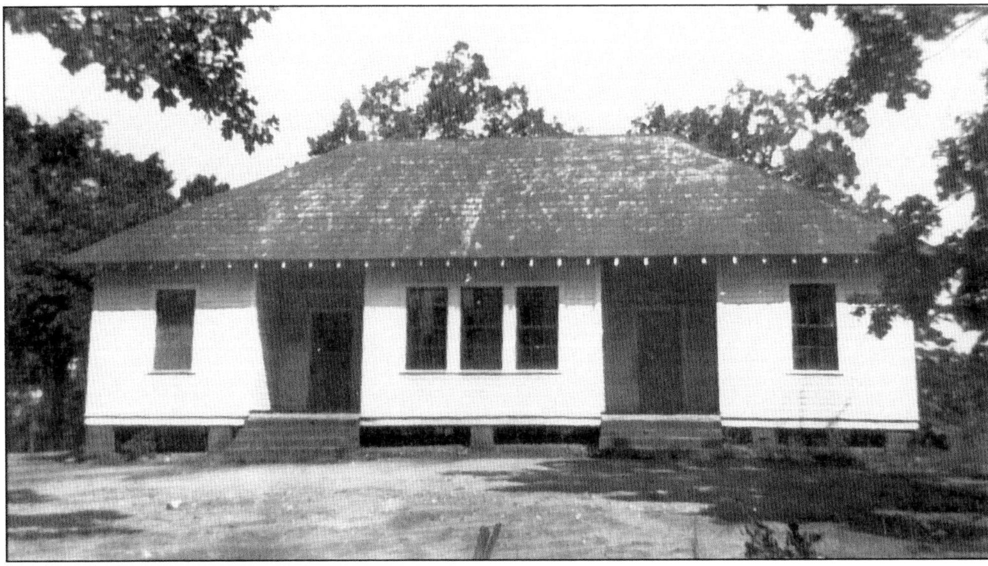

[Wayside School, c. 1920.] Wayside School was another piedmont upcounty school in the Cedar Creek area that initially was in Fairfield County. In 1913, it was 2-room school with 33 children. It had expanded to 157 students by 1922 when L.D. Golson was the principal and 1 of the 2 teachers. The site was located north of Hinnants Store Road and Cedar Creek Road.

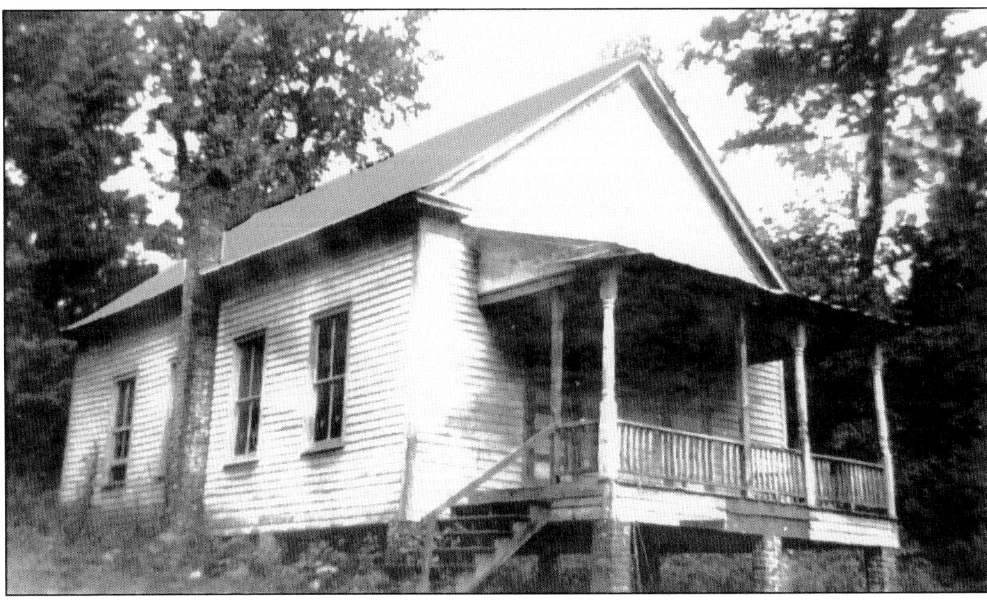

[Temple Lion School, c. 1920s.] This African-American Temple Lion School was located off Monticello Road and Heyward Brockington Road near Burgess Creek and was one of four black schools in the Camp Ground School District # 25. From 1920 to 1922, 89 black schoolhouses were erected in the state at a cost of $424,874. South Carolina's 1922 black school statistics indicated that 51.4% of the population was black, including 243,774 students taught by 3,755 teachers in 2,493 schools. The state was next to the bottom in illiteracy.

[Electrical Company Trucks with Tower, c. 1920.] The Columbia Electric Street Railway, Light and Power Company was formed in 1891 and took over several small rival companies during the next three decades. In 1924, the name was changed to the Broad River Power Company, which became the South Carolina Electric and Gas Company. in March 1937 The truck above was used during the installation and repair of the electrical lines strung throughout the county.

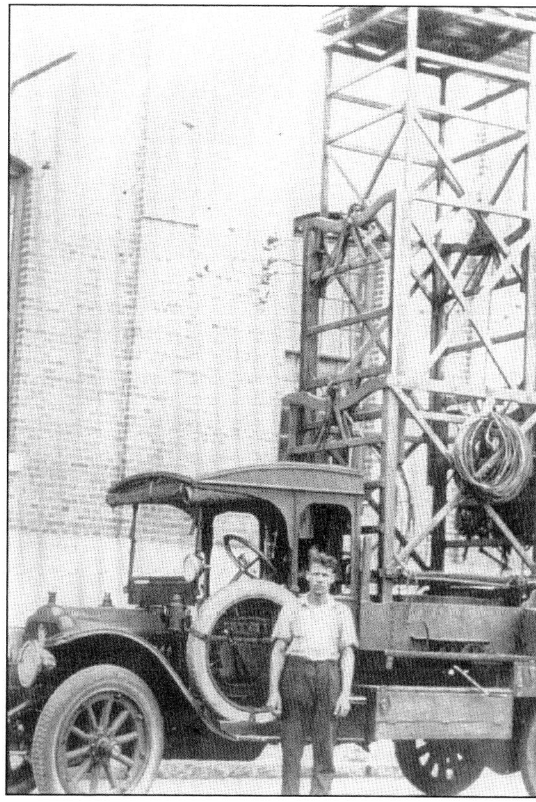

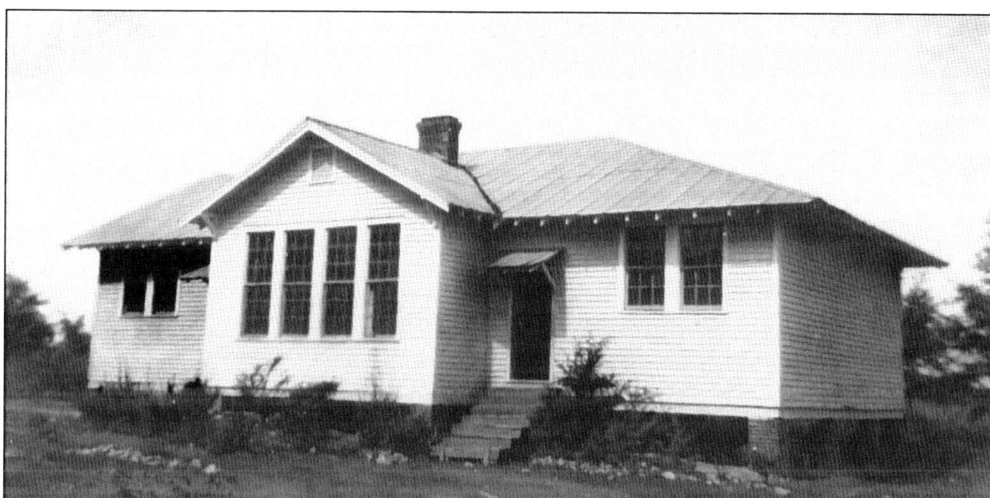

Cedar Creek School, c. 1925.] The Cedar Creek School for African-American children was located near Monticello Road and Bookman Loop. In 1913, it was a 1-room school for 70 students in the Wayside School District #26. When the school closed, the children transferred to Crane Creek School. In 1915, the state had 2,505 black schools with 198 in towns while 2,307 were rural schools. The schools consisted of 2,324 1-teacher units, 105 with 2 teachers, 24 with 3 teachers, and 52 with more than 3. Ninety-two percent of the 1-teacher country schools met for 63 days.

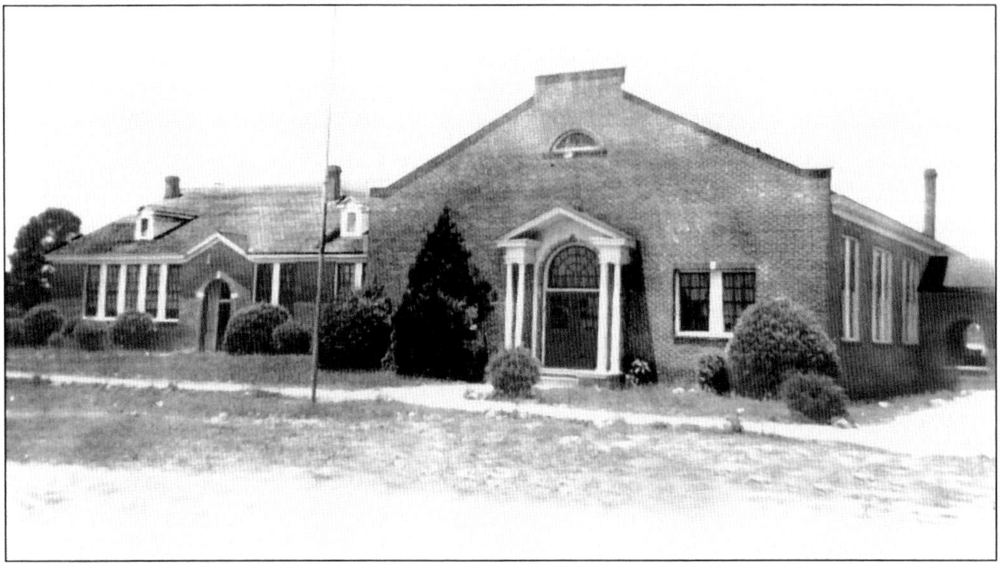

[**Blythewood High School, *c.* 1930s.**] Blythewood School was a part of Fairfield County until 1913 when the residents voted to join Richland County. In 1922, W.P. Coker was principal of a five-teacher school with 192 students. A brick elementary school, an auditorium and a high school were constructed in the 1920s and 1930s. In 1920, Richland County had 30 school districts with 121 schools housing 17,135 students (8,067 white and 9,068 black) and a budget of $358,628.

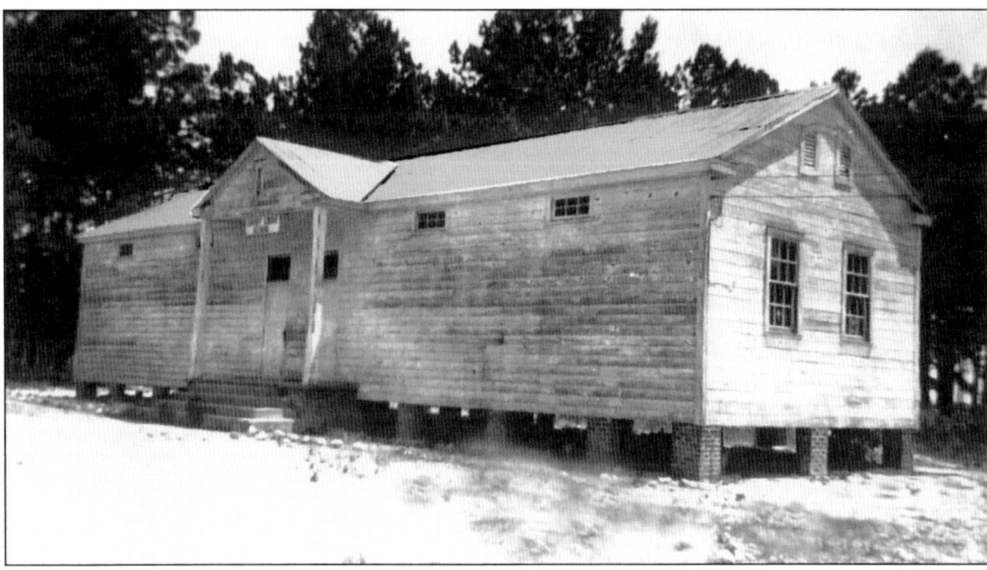

[**Shady Grove School, *c.* 1920s.**] The Shady Grove African-American School in the Blythewood School District #23 was located near Round Top Branch between Rimer Pond Road and Wade Kelley Road. In 1909, Richland County's black public school system added five new-frame public black schools to their previous total of 34, which, along with the 18 private schools, taught 2,743 boys and 3,533 girls. The average salary for black teachers that year was $196 for men and $143 for women in an annual 22-week session.

INDEX

Actors: 60, 62
Advertisement Cards: 19, 26, 58, 60–61
Artists: 63
African-Americans: 62, 70–71, 78–87, 100, 103, 105–106,108 –112, 114–115, 117–118,124–126
Allen University: 86
Army: 18, 97–100
Bands: 44, 84, 89
Banks: 22
Baptist Churches: 53, 58, 70, 87, 108–109
Baseball: 23, 70, 85, 88, 94–95
Basketball: 45, 55, 90, 119, 120
Benedict College: 82–85
Bird's-eye Views: 10, 17–18, 29, 97
Blythewood: 126
Boy Scouts: 17, 61
Bridges: 4, 45, 113
Camp Jackson: 18, 97–100
Catholic Church: 54
Chain Gangs: 111, 123
Churches: 51–58, 64, 102, 108–109
Circus: 21
City Hall: 29, 60
Colleges: 58–59, 68–69
Columbia: 1–97
Columbia Canal: 41–43
Columbia College: 68–69
Commercial Buildings: 20–21, 35
Confederate: 12–15
Cotton: 3, 71, 96
Country Clubs: 72
County Courthouses: 38–39
Depots: 34
Disasters: 69
Doctors: 83, 92
Drug Stores: 27, 91
Dutch Fork: 113–122
Eastover: 110–111
Eau Claire: 66–72
Episcopal Church: 51, 64–65
Fair: 32–33
Farming: 30–32, 114, 116
Federal Buildings: 23
Fire: 17, 36–38, 61, 69
Flood: 45, 113
Football: 79, 85, 89
Funeral Home: 81
Gadsden: 108
Generic Cards: 61
Gonzales: 16
Governor's Mansion: 28
Hampton, Wade: 12–13
Hopkins: 104
Horrell Hill:106–109, 112
Hospitals: 73, 82, 92–93
Hotels: 20, 26
Hyatt Park: 67
Interiors: 20, 26–27, 31, 44, 49, 54,90–91, 98
Jail: 39, 40
Jewish Synagogue: 56–57
Lower Richland:101–112
Lutheran Churches: 52, 66
Lykesland: 102, 105
Map: 8
Market: 30–31
Methodist Churches: 33, 56–57, 64, 102
Military: 11–12, 15, 18, 97–100
Mills, Cotton: 42–44, 46
Mills, Cotton, Activities: 44–45, 47–50
Mills, Cotton, Workers: 44, 49
Ministerial Students: 84
Monuments: 11–12, 14–16, 48
Multi–views: 2, 20
Music: 44, 49, 52, 61, 63, 82
Night Scenes: 27
Novelty Cards: 2, 99
Nurses: 73, 83, 92–93

Olympia: 44–50
Opera House: 60–62
Parades: 17–18, 21, 30, 61
Penitentiary: 40, 43
Photographers:
Police: 38–39
Political: 10–11, 16, 18, 33
Portraits:
School Portraits: 50, 53, 67, 74–77, 80, 105–106, 110,116–122
African-American Portraits: 62, 78, 80–83, 105
Rural Portraits: 47, 103–104, 112
Military Portraits: 14, 99
Portraits: 11, 13, 16, 47, 60, 80, 100, 103–104, 107
Group: 13, 22, 53, 73, 87, 108
Montage Portraits: 26
Post Office: 15, 29
Presbyterian Churches: 55, 58–59, 72
Railroad: 34–35
Railroad Stations: 34
Residences: 58, 102
Retail Stores: 20, 26, 27, 91
Rural Views: 101, 103, 114, 116
Schools:
Public: 47, 65, 67, 74–76, 80, 104, 107
High School: 77
Rural: 104, 106–107, 110, 114, 116, 118–124, 126
African American: 71, 78–82, 86, 103, 106, 108–112, 115, 117–118, 124–126
Class Pictures: 118, 120–122
Private: 54, 58, 76
Colleges: 58–59, 68–69, 82
Shandon: 64–65
Sheriff: 28
Sports: 23, 45, 55, 68, 70, 85, 88–90, 94–95, 119
Spring Hill: 120
State Buildings: 9, 28, 73
State Capitol Building: 9, 10
Store: 20, 48
Street Cars: 24–25
Street Scenes, Commercial: 10, 17–19, 23, 29, 61, 69, 71
Street Scene, Main: 10, 17, 19, 21, 23, 27
Suffragettes: 69
Summerville: 121
Taft, President: 10, 33
Theatres: 60–63
Train Depots: 34
Train Wreck: 115
Transportation:
Car: 10, 21, 30, 38, 83, 101
Truck: 36, 38–40, 125
Horse: 15, 28, 47, 98
Ox Cart: 103
Pony Cart: 47
Wagon: 19, 31, 36–37, 50, 57, 91
Twin Lakes: 96
University of South Carolina: 88–91
Upper Richland: 113–126
Water Works: 42
Waverly: 81
Weather Building: 23
White Rock: 116, 118–119
Woodrow Wilson: 11